THE AMERICAN ALPINE JOURNAL

2021

[Cover] Alden Pellett on the first ascent of Between Wind and Water, Newfoundland (p.46). *Christopher Beauchamp* [This page] Fabian Buhl paragliding from the top of Cerro Torre in February 2020. *Seán Villanueva O'Driscoll*

2021   VOLUME 63 ISSUE 95

CONTENTS

RECON

A NOTE TO READERS

COVID-19 affected nearly every aspect of life on Planet Earth in 2020, and
climbing was no exception. This edition of the AAJ is unusually small, reflect-
ing the fact that fewer expeditions were possible in 2020. We anticipate a
more typical climbing year in 2021—and a return to our usual book size with
next year's edition.

[Photo] **Eivind Jacobsen climbing the southeast
face of Jiehkkevárri, the highest peak in Norway's
Lyngen Alps. He and Finn Hovem then made the
first ski descent of the face. See p.148.** *Finn Hovem*

CLIMBS & EXPEDITIONS

[Photo] Tony McLane tackles steep quartzite on the first day of
The Hammer and the Dance (750m, 5.11c) on Neptuak Mountain,
Canadian Rockies. See p.113. *Brette Harrington*

The American Alpine Club, 710 10th St. Suite 100, Golden, Colorado

E-mail: aaj@americanalpineclub.org
www.publications.americanalpineclub.org

ISBN (paperback): 978-1-7356956-2-4
ISBN (hardcover): 978-1-7356956-3-1

2020 GREAT RANGES FELLOWSHIP

[EIGER]

Margaret Bellorado
Kevin and Leanne Duncan
Jim Edwards and Michele Mass
Dan Emmett
Gerald Gallwas
Louis Kasischke

Phil Lakin Jr.
David Landman and Marian Hawley
Craig McKibben and Sarah Merner
Kathleen Morrissey
Miriam Nelson and Kinloch Earle
Patagonia.com

Mark and Teresa Richey
Carey Roberts
Steve and Paula Mae Schwartz
Cody J Smith
Steven Sorkin
Steve Whitaker

[ALPAMAYO]

Lisa Abbott
Jonah and Warren Adelman
John Berry
John Bird
Edmund and Betsy Cabot
   Foundation
Steven Caffrey

Mitch Campbell
Alpenglow Foundation and the
   John Hobby Catto Family
Dan and Ilene Cohen
Bradford Dempsey
Bruce Franks
Scot Hillman

Thomas F. Hornbein MD
Mark Kroese
Jamie Logan
Randy Luskey
Christine O'Donnell
Naoe Sakashita
Pavan Surapaneni

Greg Thomsen
Lawrence True and Linda
   Brown
Masayuki Yokota

[ROBSON]

Michael and Matthew Ashley
George Basch
Tony Bell
Gordon A. Benner MD
Pete Brownell
Will Butcher
R.J. Campbell
Ryan Casey
Jimmy Chin
Kit DesLauriers

Jennifer Dow
The Duckworth Family
Christopher El-Deiry
James Garrett and Franziska
   Garrett MD
David Goeddel
Kristoffer Hampton
Rocky Henderson
Todd Hoffman
Richard E. Hoffman MD

Mitsu Iwasaki
Syd Jones
Brendan Leonard
George Lowe III
Robert McConnell
Brad McQueen
Hari Mix
Paul Morrow
Philip Powers
Louis Reichardt

David Riggs
George Shaw
David Singer
John and Rebecca Soebbing
Spitzer Family Foundation
William and Barbara Straka
Bob and Pamela Street
Steven Swenson and Ann Dalton
Robert Weggel
Nicholas Weicht

[TEEWINOT]

Peter Ackroyd
Brian Aldrich
Nathan Allen
Jon Anderson
Mark Andreasen
Joseph Andreotti
Peter Angood
Conrad and Jenni Lowe-
   Anker
William Atkinson
Mia Axon
Adi Azulay
Seavron Banus
Aaron Bendikson
Vaclav Benes
Stuart and Marcella
   Bernstein
Richard G. Bickel
Ronald Bixby
Fred Blau
Jim Bodenhamer
Steve Bott
Ryan Bouldin
Tanya Bradby and Martin
   Slovacek
Michael Brandt
Cale Brenchley
John Brottem
Jennifer Bruursema
Deanne Buck
Thomas Burch
Mark Butler
Ward Chewning
Diana Choi
John T. Cobb
Brendan Conway
Kevin Cooney
Billy Cox
Christopher Croft
Matt and Charlotte
   Culberson

John Davidge
Joseph Davidson
Scott Davis
Laura Dawson
Brian Deitch
Stan Dempsey Sr.
Laura Deschenes
Ed Diffendal
Melvyn Douglas
Christopher Downs
Jeff Dozier
Richard and Martha
   Draves
Ken Ehrhart
Stuart Ellison
Philip Erard
Chas Fisher
Chuck and Lisa
   Fleischman Family
Keith and Liz Fleischman
Timothy Forbes
Leonardo Franchi
James Frank
Alexander Friedman
Jim Frush
Eiichi Fukushima
Marilyn Geninatti
Clark Gerhardt
David Gerstenberger
Michael Gibbons
Charles Goldman
Russell Gray
Eric Green
Vivek Gurudutt
Roger Härtl
Robert B. Hall and Sheila
   Matz
Wendy Hall
Anonymous
Jeff Hanks
Allison Hendricks

Anne Smith and Jim
   Herson
Mark Hingston
Michael Hodges
Jennifer and Marley
   Hodgson
Scott Holder
James Holmes
Robert Horton
KT Huskins
John Hutchinson
Rob Hutchinson
Alex Intermill and Lisa
   McKinney
Caia, Vivianna, Lexi, and
   Jeremiah Johnson
Lorraine Kan
Steven Kasoff
Arthur and Diane Kearns
Adam Kilgus
Mark and Samskriti King
William Krause
James Laugharn
John Lee
Douglas Leen
Paul Lego
Sebastien Levin
Michael Limm
Daniel Lochner
Dave Lonack
Anonymous
Chris Lynch
Liam Mac Sharry
Dougald MacDonald
Brent Manning
Ryan Marsters
Bridget Martin
Troy Martin
Katie Massey
Scott McCaffrey and
   Rebecca Robinson

Thomas McCarthy
John McGarry
C. Wayne McIlwraith
Roger Mellem
Andrew Mergen
Richard Merritt
Peter and Kathleen
   Metcalf
Scott Milliman
Morgan Family
   Foundation
Kelson Foundation
Halsted "Hacksaw"
   Morris
Rod Nease
Hilaree Nelson
John Nicholson
Sean O'Brien
Peter O'Neil
CJ O'Reilly
Keith T. Oldham
Bob Palais
Charles Peck
Sasha Peretti
Samuel Perlik
Jeffrey W. Phillips DDS
John and Mitzi Raaf
Keenan Pope
Eliza Porterfield
Mark Powers
John Rehmer
John Reppy
Jim Richards
Michael Riley
Barbara Roach
Joel Robinson
John Rudolph
Amanda Ryan-Fear
Vik Sahney
Lauren Sanders
Jeb Sanford

Janet Schlindwein
Raymond VJ Schrag
Theo Schuff
Ulrika and Mark
   Schumacher MD
Stephen Scofield
David Scott
Lauren Sigman
Samuel Silverstein MD
John Sirois
Daidri Smythe
James Sneeringer
Katelyn Stahley
Todd Starr
Kent Stenderup
Rob and Jennifer
   Stephenson
Matthew Stevens
Theodore "Sam" Streibert
Anonymous
Duncan Stuart
Parisa Tabriz and
   Emerson Stewart
Jack and Pat Tackle
Steve and Krista Taylor
John Tedeschi
David Thoenen
Patrick Tolley
John L. Townsend
Angelina Trujillo
Alexander Uy
Edward Vervoort
Javier Wasiak
Anonymous
Brian Weber
Chris Weidner
Ryan Whitted
Nathan Wilhelm
Doug Wilson
Timothy Wilt
Mark Woodard

FRIENDS OF THE AAJ

Peter Ackroyd
Aaron Bendikson
Gordon A. Benner M.D.
Richard G. Bickel
Henry Bizot
P. Thompson Davis
Carla Firey
James Garrett and Franziska
Garrett M.D.
Richard E. Hoffman M.D.
Michael and Julie Kennedy
Cole Nichols
Patagonia.com
Lewis Surdam
Ian Welsted

[Photo] Rob Pizem grunts up a 45-meter chimney on Italian Cowboy, a new route in Zion National Park (see p.75). *Andrew Burr*

THE AMERICAN ALPINE JOURNAL

EDITOR
Dougald MacDonald

ART DIRECTOR
David Boersma | Mojave Creative Lab

SENIOR EDITOR
Lindsay Griffin

ASSOCIATE EDITORS
Andy Anderson, Chris Kalman, Erik Rieger

CONTRIBUTING EDITORS
Whitney Clark, Damien Gildea, David
Stevenson (Books)

ILLUSTRATIONS AND MAPS
Andreas Schmidt, Marty Schnure

PROOFREADERS
Damien Gildea, Bruce Normand, Simon
Richardson, Daniel Stevenson, and the
AAC headquarters crew

TRANSLATORS
Monika Hartman, Anna Piunova

INDEXERS
Ralph Ferrara, Eve Tallman

REGIONAL CONTACTS
Steve Gruhn, Mark Westman, *Alaska*;
Drew Brayshaw, Ian Welsted, *Canada*;
Sevi Bohorquez, Nathan Heald, Sergio
Ramírez Carrascal, *Peru*; Luis Pardo,
Colombia; Damien Gildea, *Antarctica*;
Rolando Garibotti, Camilo Rada, Marcelo
Scanu, *Argentina and Chile*; Alex von Ungern,
Bolivia; Harish Kapadia, Nandini Purandare,
India; Rodolphe Popier, Richard Salisbury,
Nepal; Tamotsu Nakamura, Hiroshi Hagiwara,
Japan; Peter Jensen-Choi, Oh Young-hoon,
Korea; Elena Dmitrenko, Anna Piunova,
Russia, Tajikistan, and Kyrgyzstan; Xia
Zhongming, *China*; Ben Dare, *New Zealand*

ADVISORY BOARD
Chantel Astorga, Kelly Cordes, Brody Leven
(ski alpinism), Damien Gildea, Colin Haley,
Mark Jenkins, Simon Richardson, Graham
Zimmerman

WITH SPECIAL THANKS TO...
Christine Blackmon, Elizabeth Cromwell,
Janusz Majer, Rodolphe Popier, Priti and
Jeff Wright, members of the American
Alpine Club, and our hundreds of authors,
photographers, and donors

Protect yourself.

Climbing can be a risky pursuit, but one worth the price of admission. With the newly enhanced Emergency Rescue & Medical Expense coverage of Membership 2.0, you can tie in a little easier knowing the American Alpine Club is on belay. No matter where you are in the world, if disaster strikes, we'll rescue you from the crag, get you to the hospital, and even help pay your deductible or other direct medical expenses once you're there.

With enhanced rescue and medical expense coverage, national policy initiatives, publications such as the *American Alpine Journal*, discounts, lodging, and more, the AAC has supported climbers for over 120 years. Learn more about the Club and join at americanalpineclub.org/join.

You belong here.

MILESTONES

At the start of 2020, many of the world's top rock climbers were training for the Olympic Games, scheduled to begin in Tokyo in July. By March, COVID-19 had postponed the Olympics and forced most climbers into lockdown. With eased restrictions in the summer and fall, European climbers began to venture outdoors (though few traveled far). Their indoor training clearly paid off, with several milestones achieved at the crags. Here, we offer some highlights from 2020 (and one from 2019) to provide context for the year's longer routes, reported elsewhere in this journal.

MARCH 2019

JACOPO LARCHER (Italy, age 29 at the time) redpointed a 30m traditionally protected pitch in Cadarese, Italy, that he named Tribe. The route is poorly protected in the easier first section, with better pro for the bouldery cruxes higher up. Larcher, who has redpointed 5.15a on bolt-protected climbs, did not grade Tribe but said it felt like the hardest climb he had done. In October 2020, James Pearson (U.K.) repeated the route. Pearson, who has climbed 9a sport routes, also declined to rate Tribe but said it had the hardest series of moves he had done on either traditionally protected or bolted rock.

JULY 2020

LAURA ROGORA (19) from Italy redpointed Ali Hulk Sit Extension Total (9b/5.15b) in Rodellar, Spain, becoming the second woman to free a 9b sport climb. In November, Julia Charnourdie (24, France) became the third, redpointing Eagle 4 (9b) at Saint-Léger-du-Ventoux in her home country.

AUGUST 2020

GERMAN CLIMBER ALEX MEGOS (27) completed Bibliographie at Ceüse, France, and graded it 9c (5.15d), the second route in the world given this rating, after Adam Ondra's Silence, climbed at Flatanger, Norway, in 2017. Megos started working on the new route (originally bolted by American Ethan Pringle) in September 2017, but he put most of his effort into it during two visits in the summer of 2020, for a total of about 60 days of work on the climb.

DECEMBER 2020

ANGELA "ANGY" EITER, the first woman to redpoint 9b (5.15b), with La Planta de Shiva in Spain, in October 2017, achieved a new milestone three years later, in December 2020: a 9b first ascent by a woman. Eiter (34) redpointed Madame Ching near her home in Imst, Austria; the route had been bolted by her husband as a gift to her. Madame Ching had about 100 moves for Eiter, and she said it felt similar in style and difficulty to La Planta de Shiva.

Also in December, the International Olympic Committee announced that climbing would be part of the Olympic Games in Paris in 2024. The field of climbers will expand, and the lead-boulder-speed combined medals planned for the 2020/2021 Tokyo Games were jettisoned in favor of individual medals for speed climbing and a combined lead and bouldering competition in Paris.

[Photo] Jacopo Larcher on Tribe in Cadarese, Italy, a strong contender for the world's hardest traditional rock climb. *Paolo Sartori*

K2 IN WINTER

TEN NEPALESE CLIMBERS MAKE HISTORY

MINGMA GYALJE SHERPA

Right from the beginning, I have been saying this expedition was for the pride of the nation, for the Nepalese climbing community, and for future generations of Nepalese climbers. The Nepalese Sherpa are regarded as the backbone of climbing on 8,000ers, and Nepal is the home of eight 8,000ers. When I realized there were no Nepalese on the list of first winter ascents of the 8,000ers, I felt ashamed. K2 was the last one in the world remaining without a winter ascent, and if we didn't succeed in 2021, we might never have another chance. This is the reason that made me go to K2 with full preparation this time.

Many climbing friends were interested in my project, but nobody wanted to spend such a huge amount of money for climbing, and the reason was COVID-19, which created an economic crisis and unemployment in Nepal. We have been jobless since November 2019, and there was very little hope in 2021 as well, so it was understandable that climbers didn't want to spend their money in

Clockwise from top left: Pem Chhiri Sherpa, Mingma David Sherpa, Mingma Gyalje Sherpa (center), Gelje Sherpa, Dawa Temba Sherpa, Kilu Pemba Sherpa, Sona Sherpa, Mingma Tenzi Sherpa (front), Nirmal Purja, and Dawa Tenjin Sherpa celebrate at base camp. *Mingma Gyalje Sherpa Collection* such a difficult time. I decided to raise and spend all my own money and take three Sherpa who have worked with me and whom I've known from birth, as we were all from Rolwaling. I needed to be sure my partners were strong, technically skilled, courageous, and most importantly they should think like me. I wanted to see the Nepalese flag on the 8,000-meter winter first ascent list, so it was important that someone from my team make it to the summit—it didn't matter if I made it.

In 2019, when I was on Everest, I got sick, and in 2019–'20, on my first winter attempt on K2, I was sick too. [*The author led a team of seven—four Sherpa and three clients—that struggled with poor conditions, injury, and illness; they made it only to 6,600 meters.*] This made me think over and over about this project and how to improve our chances. Since March 2020, we were under lockdown because of COVID-19, but one of my family members is very conscious of exercising and training, and, following her, I started running, cycling, and climbing, which helped me lose lots of weight and get back in shape. As a result, this time on K2, I was physically fit and not sick at all.

A few days before our departure for Pakistan, one of my Sherpa partners decided not to come. He worried he might lose fingers or feet to frostbite or might not return at all, and his family pressured him not to join. His disappointing decision put my other partners, Dawa Tenjin Sherpa and Kilu Pemba Sherpa, in a dilemma, because their wives also were pressuring them not to go K2. Both Dawa and Kilu work in Norway in the summertime, and Dawa's wife kept telling me that his Norwegian boss also didn't want him to go. This filled me with worry, because it takes four to six weeks to get a climbing permit in Pakistan, and I couldn't change my climbing members at the last minute. If getting a permit were easier, I could have found new partners, because there were many interested in my project, and I was not only covering all the expenses but also paying them for their hard work, plus some climbing gear sponsorship. Fortunately, I convinced Dawa and Kilu's wives, and we three traveled quickly to Pakistan before they changed their minds.

We reached Skardu on December 10. Sirbaz Khan from Imagine Climb Tours had made all the arrangements for trekking to base camp. We left Askole on December 13 in falling snow.

All of our porters were from Baltistan, and they were very strong. Though we had better food to eat and carried light loads, they were happier and faster than us in the snow. They slept on thin mattresses, most of them sharing a single sleeping bag between two persons, and they did not carry any extra clothes to avoid adding weight to their loads, and still they did not complain. Starting on the second day, we had to find and break the trail in deep snow, which was tiring work; we all lost some weight before we reached base camp after six days of trekking. I gave each of the porters extra tips and fresh meat to eat on their way back home. They prayed and asked blessing for our success in return. And they are the ones who made our expedition successful from the beginning.

We took a complete rest on December 19 and 20, and the reason was the never-ending debate on what season to follow for winter ascents: the meteorological season (December 1 to February 28 or 29) or the astronomical season (December 20 to March 20). We didn't want any controversy, so we chose to start our climb on the 21st of December. We believed we could finish the expedition within three weeks if the weather remained stable. The route to Camp 1 had been completed the day we arrived in base camp by Muhammad Ali Sadpara, Sajid Ali Sadpara, and John Snorri Sigurjónsson. We were climbing without clients, which means we had lighter loads and didn't have to climb up and down repeatedly for acclimatization. Above Camp 1, we were not expecting any help from other climbers—we had that much confidence in our team. [*In addition to the Sadpara-Snorri team, a very large commercial group organized by Seven Summits Treks and a smaller all-Nepalese team led by Nirmal (Nimsdai) Purja soon would arrive at base camp.*]

On December 21, we climbed to Camp 1 carrying 1,200 meters of rope, snow pickets, a tent, food, and our personal gear. The next day, we fixed the rope from Camp 1 to Camp 2 in a single day, and on December 23 we carried up 800 meters of rope and a tent and deposited them at Camp 2, returning to base camp the same day. The forecast for the next three days was bad. By then, the other all-Nepalese team, led by Nimsdai, had arrived.

With a forecast for perfect weather from December 28 to 30, we started back up the mountain on the 27th. On the 28th, we moved up to Camp 2, and on the same day, after setting up our camp at 6,800 meters, Kilu and I went ahead and fixed rope to 7,000 meters. On the 29th of December, we moved our camp up to 7,000 meters, so we could sleep higher. There, we realized we had only 900 meters of rope, of which 600 meters were very lightweight, high-quality 6mm rope, which we wanted to save for summit day. The remaining 300 meters was not enough to fix to Camp 3, so I decided to ask Nimsdai to collaborate.

Nims knew about me and I knew about Nims, but we never had met or talked before. I made radio contact with Chhang Dawa Sherpa, Seven Summits' manager, at base camp, since he was coordinating Nims' expedition, and I asked if Nimsdai's team could help us carry rope to 7,000 meters. Nims and his team were in the lower Camp 2 (6,700 meters). In a few minutes, Dawa radioed that Nims and team would move up and help us fix the line.

The next day, December 30, we started fixing the rope we had, plus some old ropes from previous climbs. We continued above the Black Pyramid to just below the icy section at Camp 3. Near this point, Mingma Tenzi from Nims' team arrived and helped us fix another 90 meters to the icy section, where we deposited the remaining ropes and gear and started back down.

About 200 meters below, we met Nims, who was carrying 200 meters of heavy 10mm rope. It was great to see Nims and Mingma Tenzi, who had not acclimatized but still came almost all the way to Camp 3, bringing rope to help us. The five of us descended to our camp at 7,000 meters, where we made formal introductions over some tea and discussed our plans. We only spoke for a few minutes, but that was the moment in which Nims' team and my team became one team on one mission. We both were climbing, not guiding, and we were climbing for our nation.

On the way down to base camp on December 31, Nims invited us to a New Year's Eve party at his camp. After dinner that night, we started walking toward their camp, which was about 10 minutes away, and we met two guys who had been sent by Nims because he wanted to be sure we were still coming. It gave us a warm feeling. The party continued until 3 a.m., and the hangover we had the next day was awful. It was a good environment to get to know each other, and it

K2 WINTER ATTEMPTS: A BRIEF HISTORY

IN FEBRUARY 1983, Jacques Olek and Andrzej Zawada made a spirited reconnaissance of winter conditions on the Baltoro, confirming that K2 and the nearby mountains were likely to be much harsher in winter than the Nepal 8,000ers. The Pakistan government was reluctant to give anyone a permit to attempt K2 in winter, and the first real attempt did not come until 1987-'88. Since then, and before 2020-'21, six more expeditions had attempted K2 in the "cold" season (versus strict calendar winter): 2002-'03, 2011-'12, 2017-'18, 2018-'19 (two expeditions), and 2019-'20.

Prior to the 2021 success, no one had climbed above 7,650m, an altitude reached first by Piotr Morawski and Denis Urubko on the north ridge (Japanese Route) on February 12, 2003, then again two weeks later by Marin Kaczkan and Urubko. These two were making a summit push but retreated when Kaczkan came down with cerebral edema. — *Lindsay Griffin*

Moving up toward the Bottleneck, above the usual Camp 4 site. *Mingma Gyalje Sherpa*

created a very strong bond between our two teams.

Since we had already fixed lines to Camp 3, our next plan would be for a summit push. We would need very good weather, but the forecast showed high wind until January 8, so we had to spend a week inside the tents doing nothing. On the 10th, some climbers from Nims' team headed back to Camp 2 to deposit some loads, but when they reached Camp 2, they discovered that all of their gear had blown away. Nothing remained. They returned to base camp late that night.

Next day, I walked down to Nims' camp and we discussed what to do. Given the current forecast, the best day to go to K2's summit would be January 15. Nims decided he would have to leave a day earlier than us for Camp 2, because they would be carrying replacement gear for everything that had disappeared in the storm, as well as food and oxygen for the upper mountain. My team would start on the 13th and meet Nims the next day at Camp 3. Since we already had most of our gear at 7,000 meters, plus 600 meters of rope, ice screws, and four bottles of oxygen at 7,300 meters, we had light packs, so I told Nims we would carry more rope to Camp 3. At this meeting, Nimsdai surprised me by saying that everyone should climb without supplemental oxygen. I had hoped to summit K2 without oxygen, and so did Kilu and Dawa from my team. But I didn't want to let them try, because I had promised their wives to bring them home safely.

As per plan, Nimsdai's team went to Camp 2 on the 12th, and we started on the 13th to reach our camp at 7,000 meters, below the Black Pyramid. On the 13th, Nims' team couldn't make it all the way to Camp 3, so they set up camp just above the Black Pyramid. That night, our camps were quite close, about an hour and a half apart. They were planning to stay there for two nights because they had received a weather report showing extremely high wind on January 14.

That night, Nims, Dawa, and I discussed the plans by walkie-talkie. Nims said he now wanted to summit on January 16, as the forecast showed better weather then. In the meantime, I received my own weather report, which showed good weather on the 14th and bad weather on the 15th. I told them about this report, but they didn't believe it—my weather forecast was from Nepal, and theirs were from foreign experts. I thought it would be a mistake to spend two nights without moving up. We ended the discussion by saying we would reconsider the situation in the morning and make a decision.

The next morning, my forecaster again predicted better weather for that day, the 14th, than for the following day. We both could see there was sun and no wind above us, which meant my report must be right. Nims and I agreed that we all could move up to Camp 3 and use the next day for fixing line to Camp 4 and checking the condition of the upper mountain. When we got to Camp 3 at about 7,350 meters, some of Nims' Sherpa already were setting up the camp, and Nims and two others had continued fixing rope above.

The next morning, on the 15th, the weather at Camp 3 and above turned out to be fine. [*Other teams had stayed lower on the mountain, at Camp 2, and were unable to move up in time to take advantage of the good weather on the upper mountain.*] Kilu and Dawa Tenjin went down to retrieve the gear and supplies at our deposit and carry them up to Camp 3. Mingma Tenzi, Mingma David, and I, along with Sona Sherpa, who had joined our combined teams from the Seven Summits expedition, started fixing more ropes toward Camp 4.

At this point, we were still following the normal summer route, but when we started up the wall below Camp 4, we discovered a big crevasse that was impossible to cross. We tried on the right, but the crevasse was still impassable. Then we descended a little and tried to find a way on the left side, but again it was same. We had to drop all the way back to just above Camp 3 and move farther left, toward the Česen Route, before we finally found a narrow spot in the crevasse, partially filled with fallen ice. I was afraid I might fall in, but with Mingma Tenzi belaying me from behind, I took courage and crossed the crevasse. Afterward, the climbing was very steep, with deep, soft snow, and I worried it might slide off in an avalanche. Ice axes were useless, so I plunged snow pickets into the deep snow and climbed up about 20 meters, and then the way above was easier.

It had been a very tiring day, and I asked Mingma Tenzi to lead the last few meters to the site of Camp 4. The way from Camp 3 to Camp 4 usually takes two to three hours in summer, but it took us more than eight hours. At around 4 p.m. we finally made it. Our first reaction was: *Winter K2 will be ours!* We knew we would make the summit the next day.

By the time we got back to Camp 3, it was already getting dark. Summit day would begin in just a few hours, and we needed some rest. Instead of leaving for the summit at 11 p.m., we decided to start at 1 a.m. on January 16. We woke at around midnight and started gearing up inside the frost-filled tents. I was still feeling tired from the previous day, and I gave up my plan to climb without oxygen. Kilu, Dawa Tenjin, Sona, and Mingma Tenzi left first. I couldn't get my oxygen regulator to fit, and I had to get a spare from friends. By then my hands were very cold, so I went back inside to warm up. Nims and Dawa Temba started climbing around 2 a.m. By the time I got ready, some of the climbers were already nearing Camp 4. I started up with Mingma David, Pem Chhiri, and Gelje. We had very good fixing teams ahead, so I was not worried and didn't try to catch them.

When we started climbing there was no wind, but as I got closer to Camp 4, a high wind started blowing. We did not have a thermometer, but the forecast had called for -50°C (-58°F) at this altitude, and the wind made it feel colder. My body was OK, but my left foot was so cold that I started losing hope—I worried about losing it to frostbite. I also worried I might put my team-mates in difficulty, so I wasn't sure whether to continue or abort. I tried to call Dawa Tenjin, but his radio was off. I kept kicking the ice to make my feet warmer, which actually worked.

Around 6 a.m., above the site of Camp 4, we got our first sunshine, which was enough to warm my feet and body and keep me going. The wind also dropped as the day brightened. We could see our friends climbing above us. Mingma David, Pem Chhiri, Gelje, and I met the rest of the team right at the traverse after the Bottleneck. Mingma Tenzi was leading the way, and we climbed behind him, carrying the rope and other gear.

Until about 300 meters below the summit, I hadn't realized Nimsdai was climbing without oxygen. When I saw him with no mask, I asked if his oxygen was finished and Kilu replied that Nims had not used oxygen all the way from Camp 3. It was almost unbelievable. He was not well acclimatized at all; the summit push was just their second rotation on mountain, and still he took the risk. Later, I checked my pictures from the Bottleneck and above until the summit. In all the pictures, Nimsdai was without oxygen. I told myself, *This guy can do anything in the mountains.*

When we reached the small plateau 200 meters below the summit, we had a tea party and deposited the extra rope. Everyone took a rest for a while, and then again Mingma Tenzi started fixing ahead. From there to the summit, we took almost four hours.

Before leaving base camp, we had made a plan to stop ten meters before the top and wait for everyone to arrive. Then, all the Nepalese brothers joined shoulder to shoulder and we walked together to the summit, singing the national anthem. At 4:43 p.m., we stood on top of K2. This was an historical ascent, and every member in the team had worked equally, so we wanted everyone in the team to feel equal. There were no individual agendas, only solidarity and a shared vision. When we unite, nothing is impossible, and that is the way it was on K2.

SUMMARY: First winter ascent of K2 (8,611 meters) by Dawa Temba Sherpa, Dawa Tenjin Sherpa, Kilu (Kili) Pemba Sherpa, Gelje Sherpa, Mingma David Sherpa, Mingma Gyalje Sherpa, Mingma Tenzi Sherpa, Nirmal Purja, Pem Chhiri Sherpa, and Sona Sherpa; the ten were members of three separate expeditions who joined forces to complete the route. They followed the Abruzzi Spur (southeast ridge), with a small variation above Camp 3, using new or existing fixed ropes all the way to the top. All ten climbers went from Camp 3 (ca 7,350 meters) to the summit on January 16, 2020. Nirmal Purja reached the summit without supplementary oxygen; all other climbers used oxygen on summit day.

ABOUT THE AUTHOR: *Born in Rolwaling, Nepal, in 1987, Mingma Gyalje Sherpa is an IFMGA guide and operates the Imagine Nepal guide service. He wrote about the solo first ascent of the west face of Chobutse in AAJ 2016.*

[Top] **Nirmal Purja on summit day.** [Bottom] **Mingma Gyalje and Dawa Tenjin on top.** *Expedition Photos*

EDITOR'S NOTE: *The 2020–'21 winter season was marked not only by the Nepalese success on January 16, but also by several tragedies. Sergi Mingote (Spain) died in a fall low on the mountain the same day the Nepalese summited, and Atanas Skatov (Bulgaria) died in a fall on February 5. That same day, Muhammad Ali Sadpara and Sajid Ali Sadpara (Pakistan), Juan Pablo Mohr Prieto (Chile), and John Snorri Sigurjónsson (Iceland) began their push from Camp 3. After his oxygen regulator failed, Sajid descended from the Bottleneck while the other three continued up. They did not return, and search efforts—severely constrained by the altitude and winter conditions—turned up no evidence of the men.*

The labels on the image, from left to right, read:

Aguja de l'S

Aguja St. Exupery

Aguja Rafael Juárez

Aguja Kakito

Aguja Poincenot

Cerro Fitz Roy

THE MOONWALK

THE FIRST SOUTH TO NORTH TRAVERSE OF THE FITZ ROY MASSIF, SOLO

SEÁN VILLANUEVA O'DRISCOLL

I arrived in El Chaltén, Argentina, at the beginning of January 2020 with my climbing partner Nicolas Favresse. We had a great season, climbing two new routes and freeing a third (*AAJ 2020*). Nico returned to Europe around mid-March. My plan was to stay until the end of March, but by then the pandemic had hit. Travel was complicated, and Argentina was in lockdown. At some point, I could have found a way home, but things in Europe seemed bad, and I was in one of my favorite places on the planet. After the initial confinement period, with no COVID cases, things became more relaxed in El Chaltén. I felt like I was locked in a giant playground. I spent the fall, winter, and spring taking long hikes, bouldering, sport climbing, ski touring, ice climbing, training, and playing music—there wasn't a dull moment.

Inspired by the approach and philosophy of my friend Sílvia Vidal—who has climbed many big walls solo, sometimes without any outside contact for more than 30 days—I had dreamed of doing a solo ascent for years. But when you are spoiled with the best climbing partners imaginable, it is not easy to find the opportunity to go off on your own! During

Aguja Val Biois

Aguja Mermoz

Aguja Guillaumet

The Moonwalk Traverse went from left to right (south to north) over the Fitz Roy Massif, crossing nine major summits in about five kilometers. *Rolando Garibotti*

the long winter nights in my camper van, I imagined trying the Fitz Traverse, Tommy Caldwell and Alex Honnold's traverse of Fitz Roy and its satellite peaks (*AAJ 2014*). The route is incredibly aesthetic, but the idea was absurd, too big, totally unrealistic. But it never hurts to dream. I leafed through the guidebook, taking notes, making photocopies, and seeing if I could put all the pieces of the puzzle together. Whereas Tommy and Alex climbed from north to south, I imagined doing the traverse in reverse, mostly because it was something new. One day, I started believing it was actually possible, and that was enough.

Roped solo climbing is laborious and time-intensive. Realistically, I planned on 10 days. My prerequisite was a six-day weather window, which is very rare. Regardless, I started to prepare by training, visualizing, and arranging gear and food. A six-day window appeared over my 40th birthday, February 7, 2021. I was bubbling with excitement.

I had not yet told anyone my plans, for fear they would think I had lost my mind, but now I did. "At least tell us which direction you are going, so we know where to look if you get into any trouble," my friend Juan Collado pleaded. I told him I would start on Aguja de l'S and get as far as I could. I asked Rolando Garibotti for some last-minute advice on the weather. Convinced he would try to talk me out of my plan, I was surprised when a smile appeared on his face. "That's a great idea!" Rolo said, immediately pulling out his own gear to replace some of my worn-out stuff. He insisted I take his brand-new, top-of-the-line rope. "For a project like this, the right rope is essential," he said. I felt like he was giving me the keys to his Ferrari. I later learned that both Juan and Rolo thought the summit of Fitz Roy was my ultimate objective. It had not occurred to them that I was going to try a full traverse of the massif.

I approached from the southeast, via Laguna Sucia, sleeping at the cave near the edge of the glacier. On February 5, the east face of the Aguja de l'S lit up with the golden glow of morning light as I started climbing the Cara Este route. I felt at home. Every move felt precise and efficient, the summation of years of big-wall free climbing. I reminded myself, *This is a marathon, not a sprint! Don't rush. Keep a rhythm. Stay in the present. Enjoy every moment.*

My gear—with ten days of food, a small tent, sleeping bag, and tin whistle—was too heavy to carry while climbing, so I brought both a light pack and a small haul bag, which I would haul with a thin tag line on technical pitches. On ledges and sections with easy scrambling, I just stuffed everything into my pack. This strategy was very inefficient. I often had to repack my bags depending on the terrain. On the other hand, I had not prioritized efficiency or achievement, just experience.

While I was hauling on Aguja St. Exupery, a few loose rocks slid off a ledge. When I pulled up my main lead rope, it had three core shots. I felt like I had just crashed Rolo's new Ferrari! The sight of the core shots pierced my heart like a needle, so I covered them with climbing tape.

[Left] The author celebrates atop Aguja Guillaumet, the final summit of his traverse. [Right] The rope after the final rappel. *Seán Villanueva O'Driscoll (both)*

Out of sight, out of mind, I thought. The tape got stuck in cracks, carabiners, and the Grigri. On rappels, when possible, I unweighted the rope to move the damaged sections through my device. I spent my first night on the north shoulder of Aguja St. Exupery, maybe a couple of rappels from the ridge leading to Aguja Rafael Juárez.

On day two, the long ridge traverse between St. Exupery and Rafael Juárez demanded a good nose for route-finding. With a sea of clouds below, small waves danced between the summits. The breeze was icy cold. Crossing to the east face, I noticed major difficulties, so I turned back to the west face. When I spotted a red cam lying on the ground, I instantly knew: One of my harness gear loops had broken (probably from a diet of too many offwidths). I backtracked for 100 meters, just in case, and found more cams lying around, but not all of them. At least there was now less weight to carry. After reaching the summit of Aguja Rafael Juárez, I descended the Piola-Anker Route to reach the base of the south face of Aguja Poincenot. I then climbed the Fonrouge-Rosasco (700m, 6c) to a bivy near the junction with the Whillans-Cochrane Route.

On day three, I continued to the summit of Aguja Poincenot and rappelled north via Invisible Line. From the col, I tackled Aguja Kakito, climbing a few new pitches to reach the summit from the east. When I arrived at Brecha de los Italianos, below the southeast side of Cerro Fitz Roy, it was still early afternoon, but I was worried about strong winds predicted for that night. (At least that was the last forecast I had seen before leaving El Chaltén; I did not carry an inReach or phone.) I wanted to avoid being benighted on Fitz Roy with no decent bivouac. There was still a long way to go, but it was important not to burn out. I was still doubting my plan when I saw two friends rappelling the Franco-Argentine—due to a waterfall on the route, they explained. I relaxed the rest of the afternoon in my tent, protecting myself from the sun and glad for my luck.

On the morning of day four, the Franco-Argentine linkup was dried out and protected from the wind. The climbing flowed, and I focused on keeping a rhythm. The topo describes the last 200 meters as a "50° slope, not difficult." Expecting an easy walk to the top, I was surprised by sections of hard ice. My approach shoes, aluminum crampons, single ice axe, and one ice screw did not feel like the appropriate equipment. The slightest misstep would have been fatal. Once on Fitz Roy's summit, I spent an hour there, enjoying the view, playing my trusty tin whistle, and eating some trail mix. It was still early, and I had plenty of time to descend the big north face. Though I live in Belgium, my nationality is Irish, so when the tune "An Poc Ar Buile" came to mind, I started dancing and singing aloud about the mad, ferocious goat who symbolizes the indomitable spirit of the Irish.

It was windy, which made the rappels down the Casarotto Route dangerous. After a few rappels, I found myself 100 meters above the Goretta Pillar, just above a big waterfall. I had hoped to reach the top of the pillar and bivy there, but I wanted to avoid a wet rope at all costs, as wet nylon would wear out even faster. I waited on a small ledge, hoping for the wind to ease. I started cleaning the ledge, more to stay warm than with the thought of a potential bivouac. However, once all the ice and rocks were cleared, the ledge looked about the size of my tent, and it was protected from the wind! For the second day in a row, I stopped early and spent the evening admiring the magical sunset. The shadow of the Fitz Roy Massif appeared on the plains and slowly dissolved into a pyramid of strange lights.

On the fifth morning, the wind had died, the waterfall had stopped, and I could continue the descent to the Col del Bloque Empotrado without incident. Once again, things had fallen into place. It was still early as I climbed Aguja Val Biois and then did the traverse to Aguja Mermoz. The whole ridge up to Mermoz was longer and more complex than I expected. Every time I climbed a small peak, I found several more separating me from Mermoz. But, this moment was *it*. There was no longing. I stayed present, moved, and relished it. I arrived on the summit of Mermoz as the light faded and pitched my tent for my fifth and final night on the traverse.

In the morning, the 10th, I made a few rappels down the upper part of the Pilar Rojo, then two rappels straight down to a big ledge system. I then climbed up the Cumbre Sur (Bresba-Dominguez-Lüthi) of Aguja Guillaumet. Around noon, as if in a dream, I strolled onto the main peak of Guillaumet, the last summit of the Fitz Roy Massif. I burst out my tin whistle and celebrated with an extra handful of trail mix. However, the wind grew stronger, and I reminded myself of the importance of keeping focus until the end. After seeing some rockfall on the sheltered Amy-Vidailhet Route on the lower east face, I decided it was safer to take my chances with the wind and rappel the Brenner-Moschioni Route on the north ridge.

The rope, which in less than a week had received the equivalent of a lifetime of climbing, looked like a rag. By my last rappel, the six days of intense effort and concentration had added up. The ground was near, but the weight of my backpack was crushing. There were now many patches of tape on the rope. Suddenly, the sheath cut loose and I slid down quickly, exposing more than a meter of core! Miraculously, the rope I had damaged on day one had survived to the end. I continued quickly to firm ground at Paso Guillaumet. From here on, it was only walking.

A few hours later, I arrived at Piedra Blanca, a green meadow with a large, white boulder, a small, howling torrent, and a beautiful view down the valley. Big, dark clouds rolled through quickly. I had visualized the final descent to Piedra del Fraile so many times. *But why go down?* The afternoon was young, and I had plenty of time to reach the village of El Chaltén. I had seen only three parties of climbers during the entire traverse, and I did not feel ready to face the world below. Rolo and Juan, the only people I had dared tell my plan, probably would be worried. *They could wait until tomorrow*, I thought.

I planted my tent under the granite boulder. Freed from my clothing, I dipped into the small glacial stream to feel the cold and life passing over my skin. Then I walked around naked and picked wild berries while the wind served as a towel. I spent the rest of the afternoon lying beneath the boulder, admiring the view, and absorbing the experience I had just lived.

SUMMARY: The Moonwalk Traverse (+4,000m, 6c 50°), climbed from February 5–10, 2021, was the first south to north traverse of the Fitz Roy Massif in Argentine Patagonia. Climbing solo, Seán Villanueva O'Driscoll self-belayed and hauled on all but easy pitches and climbed everything free except for rappels; the majority of the traverse was climbed onsight.

ABOUT THE AUTHOR: *Born and raised in Belgium to an Irish mother and Spanish father, Seán Villanueva O'Driscoll still resides in Belgium but says, "Home is wherever I put down my duffel bag, really." He spoke about the Moonwalk Traverse in episode 38 of the Cutting Edge podcast.*

VIRTUAL UNKNOWNS

TWO WEEKEND WARRIORS' YEARLONG SABBATICAL CULMINATES IN THE FIRST ASCENT OF K6 CENTRAL

PRITI WRIGHT

The sun was setting behind distant Nanga Parbat as Jeff and I ascended the seemingly endless ice face on the western flank of K6, searching for a bivouac spot in the fading alpenglow. It was October 5, very late in the season to be climbing a 7,000-meter peak in the Karakoram, and we wanted to be warm in our tent when the temperatures plummeted with nightfall. I had led four long simul-climbing pitches on the steep face, placing a screw every 30 meters, and now Jeff, my husband and climbing partner, took over for the last hundred meters to the shoulder of K6's southwest ridge. This 900-meter face presented the most direct line up to the ridge but with no flat spots to rest along the way. Our calves were burning from kicking our crampon frontpoints directly into a skim of névé over hard blue ice.

We were holding on to hope for the luxurious bivouac that we expected to greet us at the top of the face, as promised by Graham Zimmerman in his article describing the first ascent of K6 West's southwest ridge (*AAJ 2016*). I looked up into the dark as Jeff disappeared around the ridgeline. Finally, I heard him give a joyful shout as he reached a grand flat spot. We gratefully set up our tent at 6,600 meters around midnight. I warmed Jeff's feet

After weeks of poor weather, February 8 was a perfect day to summit Cerro Torre. The previous day, Fabian Buhl became the first person to paraglide from the top after climbing the peak (see photo on p.1). *Jeff Wright*

on my stomach, and we huddled close through the frigid night. It was one of the hardest days of our climbing careers.

Jeff and I had been alpine climbing for only seven years, and this was our first expedition to the Greater Ranges. Certainly no one expected us to make the first ascent of K6 Central, a 7,155-meter peak, with such slim résumés. (The *Rock and Ice* news story about our eventual success labeled us "virtual unknowns.") K6 was to be the literal high point of an extended climbing sabbatical, using our saved earnings to live and climb abroad for a full year. We had carefully researched and planned every destination, starting with Patagonia, then the Alps, followed by the Karakoram, and finally recovering with some sunny sport climbing in Southeast Asia. We could not have anticipated a global pandemic.

In December 2019, Jeff put his aerospace engineering job at Boeing on hold, and I left behind my software development position in Seattle. We flew to Argentina in early January, arriving in Patagonia for the austral summer season. It was our fourth visit to El Chaltén. In February 2019 we had summited Fitz Roy, and we had attempted Cerro Torre in 2016. On this trip, after climbing Aguja Poincenot and a couple of other peaks in Patagonia's typically awful weather, a perfect window arrived and we joined a crowd on Cerro Torre's west ridge (Via dei Ragni), finally reaching the summit of this dream peak. With several parties behind us waiting to summit as the sun was about to set, urgency compelled us to accept a top-rope for the final pitch on the summit mushroom.

At the beginning of March, we arrived in France with grand aspirations. COVID-19 was in the news, but even at this point, we still had no premonition that normal life in Europe soon would come to a complete halt. Chamonix was still lively, and travel was unrestricted. On March 18, at the tail end of winter, we squeezed in an ascent of the 1938 Heckmair route on the Eiger's north face, just as France began enforcing a nationwide lockdown.

For weeks we watched out the windows of our rented apartment as beautiful weather rolled through Chamonix. Our goal had been to climb the "six great north faces of the Alps" described by Gaston Rébuffat in his 1954 book *Étoiles et Tempêtes* ("Starlight and Storm"). France's lockdown lifted on May 11, and soon we were able to climb the Allain-Leininger Route on the Petit Dru. Having lost eight weeks of our precious year, we worried that we would run out of time and weather to complete our goal.

Jeff and I had a lot of experience with the waiting and watching game. Before our sabbatical, we would optimize our limited vacation time by using a "smash and grab" style, watching the weather and conditions from Seattle and then traveling at the last minute to grab a summit in quick alpine style. In this way, we had climbed Fitz Roy and Denali's Cassin Ridge. In Chamonix, we used the same tactics for the remaining four of the six classics: the Matterhorn, Grandes Jorasses, Cima Grande

K6 from advanced base camp on the East Nangmah Glacier. The mixed southwest ridge on the left was climbed to (A) K6 West in 2015. The 2020 route followed the same long snow slope, then traversed farther west to ascend directly to the upper ridge, before traversing over the west peak to (B) K6 Central. *Priti Wright*

di Lavaredo, and Piz Badile. In a way, COVID-19 worked in our favor: Because Pakistan, our next destination, remained closed to foreign tourists throughout the summer, we could extend our stay in Europe. We summited Piz Badile on July 21, completing the six classic north faces in a single season.

However, we had still another, bigger goal. Each of our climbs had successively prepared us for the ultimate challenge of summiting an unclimbed 7,000-meter peak.

K6 Central doesn't appear on most lists of unclimbed peaks due to its prominence of only 200 meters, but when viewed from the south or north, this central nub is striking amid the broad massif of K6. The K6 group is located in the Masherbrum Range of northern Pakistan, in Gilgit-Baltistan, flanked by several major glaciers: the Charakusa to the north, Nangmah to the south, Lachit to the southeast, and Kondus to the east. The mountain's three main summits run along a two-kilometer ridge. K6 Main (7,281m) was first climbed in 1970 by an Austrian expedition led by Eduard Koblmüller. We got in touch with one of the original members of the young team, Fred Pressl, who graciously shared pictures and stories from a half-century ago. The mountain had already been attempted by three expeditions, including a 1969 Italian team, led by Luigi Barbuscia, which attempted the west side of the south face of the massif, with hopes of completing the high traverse to K6 Main. We found some old gear, likely from a reconnaissance by this 1969 expedition, along the southwest ridge.

In 2013, Canadians Raphael Slawinski and Ian Welsted made the first ascent of K6 West via a highly technical route from the Charakusa side, for which they won a Piolet d'Or. In 2015, Scott Bennett and Graham Zimmerman from the United States completed the second ascent of K6 West, starting from the Nangmah Glacier to the south. They too had hoped to traverse the ridgeline, but an impending storm forced them to retreat before starting toward K6 Central. It remained unclimbed.

Expeditions to Pakistan's highest peaks usually start no later than midsummer, and we had planned to arrive in July. However, in 2020, Pakistan didn't reopen its borders until late August.

Jeff and I were convinced we could still have a productive adventure in September and October, and we both still felt passionately about embarking on the expedition, despite the delay.

We had been discussing our Karakoram plans with Colin Haley, our Seattle pro-climber hero and friend of several years, since January when we were all in Patagonia. Shortly before we were to depart for Islamabad, he decided to join our expedition to attempt some solo objectives. We were glad to have his massive amount of experience (this would be his seventh Karakoram expedition) and his great company at base camp.

We dusted off the visas we'd obtained in December, bought plane tickets, and got the COVID tests required for entry. Our expectations for a smooth arrival in Pakistan were low. However, when we got to Islamabad on August 23, we were able to fly to Skardu within hours, without even leaving the airport. We were practically the only tourists in the country, and we were getting the royal treatment. Ali Saltoro (our tour operator from Alpine Adventure Guides) navigated our caravan from Skardu to Kanday, smoothly getting us through two military checkpoints, where officers checked our COVID test results, visas, and climbing permits. The same day that we reached the trail head, we hiked into the Nangmah Valley to choose a suitable base camp location. The following morning, 49 porters dropped their 25kg loads at our home for the next two months. We set up camp, and it poured rain for three days straight, immediately flooding our tents.

At first, we simply acclimatized to the altitude of base camp (about 4,000 meters), admiring Ishaq and Azhar, our cooks, who were running around gathering firewood, making food, and playing sports, while we just rested and created red blood cells. When the weather improved, Colin introduced everyone, including Ishaq and Azhar, to Japanese calisthenics, which we performed as a group in the mornings. We played chess, learned some Urdu, practiced our chapati making, paraglided from slopes above base camp, and watched movies at night, settling in like the family we would be for the next two months. Ishaq and Azhar's cooking was superb, and they impressed me with their repertoire of recipes, working around Jeff and my vegetarian diet, and Colin's dairy- and gluten-free diet.

After a week at camp, we started moving higher to acclimatize and scout out the area. Heading up the West Nangmah Glacier, we bivied at 5,600m on Kapura Peak, where we got a good view of the west face of the K6 group. Colin, Jeff, and I identified three potential alternatives to Graham and Scott's southwest ridge route, avoiding the hardest mixed climbing on their line. We bailed on a summit attempt on Kapura when I fell ill, but after descending we moved our ABC to the East Nangmah Glacier before returning to base camp.

During the next weather window, we explored two variations on the west face of K6 in order to acclimatize, identify potential bivouac sites, and choose the most efficient route for our final assault. On this venture into the mountains, we slept for five nights above 5,700 meters and climbed up to 6,200 meters. We found only one poor bivouac option, situated on a precarious corniced ridge.

Jeff and I then received an inReach message from Colin down at ABC. He had fallen ill and made an excruciating descent to base camp. We hurried back to see how we could help. As it turned out, there was not much we could do, except to bring his gear down from ABC.

On October 1, we all sadly bid farewell to Colin as he departed for home after a week of high-altitude diarrhea. In spite of our fear of the daily dropping temperatures, Jeff and I were determined to stay and make a summit attempt on K6 Central.

We headed back up to ABC on October 2, a 10-hour trek that climbs 1,200 meters over moraine and loose scree. We were completely self-supported above base camp during the expedition, and as we hiked up the valley, we were very glad to have put in the effort to stock an advanced base. This meant that we could climb until the very end of good weather and hunker

A 900-meter day up the west face of K6 gained Camp 2 on the upper southwest ridge and then snow slopes leading first to (A) K6 West and then (B) K6 Central. In all, the climbers spent six nights at or above Camp 2 (6,600 meters) in frigid October weather. K6 Main (C) is at far right. *Colin Haley*

down at ABC if the weather turned poor. On the off chance that weather and conditions would allow us to complete a full traverse from K6 West, over the unclimbed central summit, and on to K6 Main, we packed a rack of rock gear, even though we knew we'd only need it after summiting Central. It was a heavy gamble just for the small chance of continuing on toward K6 Main.

Our route started from the East Nangmah Glacier on a prominent ramp up the southwest flank of the peak, following 45-degree snow and ice for about 600 meters. In this way, we avoided the icefalls of the lower west face. We crossed over the southwest ridge to reach a broad campsite we dubbed "Sunny Knob" at 5,700 meters. Newly fallen snow had wiped out our previous steps, and we waded through waist-deep snow. The next day was dedicated to plowing a path over to the crux of our route: the direct line up the ice face (55° snow and ice), the same line Graham and Scott had rappelled in 2015, using 19 V-thread anchors, during their descent from K6 West. This direct line would bypass our reconnaissance routes and the only bivouac option on the face.

On October 5, we committed to the unrelenting line up the west face, climbing into the night and setting our tent up at 11 p.m. atop the southwest ridge in the crushing cold. The next morning, exhausted from our big effort on the west face, we followed the southwest ridge to the upper slopes of K6 West, postholing and wallowing through deep snow along the upward traverse. Progress was slow, and we made two more bivouacs between our 6,600-meter camp and the summit ridge at 7,000 meters. Miraculously, the good weather continued, although our forecaster had warned us we would encounter the jet stream near the summit, with sustained winds of 45 km/h (28 mph). He was absolutely correct.

When we reached the summit ridge, on October 8, we were greeted with high wind blowing incessantly from the southeast. Setting up a tent in that wind would have been impossible, so we scouted for a cozy crevasse. Once a suitable site was secured for our Camp 5, we left our backpacks and headed toward the summit of K6 West, at 7,140 meters.

Returning to the Sunny Knob camp after laying a track for an early start on the west face. *Jeff Wright*

The wind raged around us, whipping a few scattered clouds through the dark blue sky and blasting the cold into our summit puffies, ski masks, and giant mittens that felt like boxing gloves. We crested two snowy mounds that each revealed another, taller one behind it before we reached the true top of K6 West at 4:20 p.m. on October 8, completing the third recorded ascent. Beyond, K6 Central reared up, so close it dispelled all doubt in my mind: We *had* to try for it. But it was nearly sunset, so we descended back down to our homey crevasse and set up the tent for a very cold and windy night.

We awoke to a frost-covered sleeping bag, with huge gusts of wind blowing spindrift into the gaps in the tent door and windows. We huddled under clumps of wet feathers, wearing every piece of clothing we had. When the sun hit the tent, we roused ourselves and packed our gear, leaving the tent in place. By this point, we had abandoned thoughts of the complete traverse to K6 Main. It was too cold, too windy, too far, too late.

We reascended K6 West against crippling cold and whipping wind. Could we climb the technical terrain of K6 Central's final slopes in these conditions? "Let's just go take a look at it," Jeff said. "Just go to the base." After traversing the ridge to the foot of K6 Central, we stopped and looked up. The face appeared to be in great condition: a concave, wave-shaped wall, gently sloping at first, then steep and icy, and finally capped with a cornice.

We dropped our packs, and Jeff led across a tall bergschrund, which luckily had good ice at its lip. The slope gently increased in angle, and protection was sparse in the loose snow, but Jeff managed to place a stubby ice screw halfway into a small patch of ice before burrowing into the cornice, the last crux before the summit. At 3:45 p.m. on October 9, Jeff stopped at a rocky outcropping on the summit of K6 Central and anchored us in. Reaching the top, I sat straddling the rock, with one leg over the Lachit Valley and one leg hanging over the sheer vertical drop to the Charakusa. We gazed around the incredible panoramic view: 7,000- and 8,000-meter peaks spread around us, the four 8,000ers of the Baltoro Glacier visible only 20 miles to our north, poking into the thin atmosphere, while the sun set directly behind Nanga Parbat, on the horizon over 100 miles away. We felt so isolated and blessed to be amid these lonely, giant peaks.

The heights of K6 West and Central have never been officially surveyed, but estimated to be 7,040m and 7,100m, respectively. After crossing the broad saddle between the two peaks and ascending the west face of K6 Central, we observed that we were approximately level with the summit of K6 West. Some years ago, Eberhard Jurgalski of 8000ers.com used SRTM data (from the Shuttle Radar Topography Mission of 2000) to more accurately estimate K6 West at 7,140m and K6 Central at 7,155m. His findings aligned with our GPS data and our observations.

We still had one more windy night to endure in our high-altitude crevasse home. The following two days were spent retracing our steps to ABC, first rappelling back down the west face (counting the exact same number of rappels that Graham and Scott had made). We then traversed back up and over the southwest ridge and soloed down to ABC, wearily arriving around 10 p.m.

The next morning we relayed our success to Ali by InReach and told him we would be back for dinner at base camp that evening. As we made our way back down the grotesque moraines, I heard a familiar whistle. I shouted and heard it again: It was the same whistle that woke us every morning at base camp for breakfast. From around the corner, Ishaq and Azhar appeared: our cooks, our friends! They had hiked all the way up to the valley and waited for hours with hot tea, cheese, and crackers.

We had been away from base camp for 10 nights, but it felt like eons. That night we sang and danced by a bonfire, sharing songs, banter, and a congratulatory cake. (I still don't understand what magic makes baking possible in base camp.) I was filled with joy, not to mention with Ishaq and Azhar's amazing cooking.

A couple of days later, we packed up camp and headed down to Kanday and civilization. The whirlwind of people, places, and sudden attention for a couple of "virtual unknowns" was overwhelming. After 52 days without access to the internet, we returned to Skardu, back to distractions, back to routines, back to Earth from the Heavens.

[Top] Traversing to K6 Central's summit fin, which was climbed directly up the snowy face. [Bottom] Priti (left) and Jeff Wright atop K6 Central, with K6 Main's summit tower behind. *Priti and Jeff Wright*

SUMMARY: First ascent of K6 Central (7,155 meters GPS) from the west by Jeff and Priti Wright (USA), October 3–11, 2020. The two climbed the southwest face of K6 West, making the third documented ascent of that summit on October 8, then traversed to K6 Central on October 9. The route gained about 2,000 meters from the East Nangmah Glacier. The pair reversed their route of ascent. An interview with the Wrights was featured in episode 35 of the Cutting Edge podcast.

ABOUT THE AUTHOR: *Born in 1988, Priti Wright grew up in Florida, where she met her husband, Jeff. They became alpine climbers after moving to Seattle in 2013; weekend trips into the Cascades led up to bigger successes in further ranges. The 2020 sabbatical marked a breakthrough in their climbing careers, and they hope to take a similar break in a few years.*

ACKNOWLEDGMENTS: *Jeff and I owe thanks to Steve Swenson, Graham Zimmerman, and Ian Welsted for their helpful beta, to Colin Haley for his great advice and wonderful company in Pakistan, and to Ishaq Jee, our base camp manager and cook, Azhar, Captain Zohaib Iqbal, our liaison officer, and Ali Saltoro, our expedition manager.*

AGAINST THE ODDS

AN AUTUMN ASCENT OF SANI PAKKUSH IN THE KARAKORAM

SYMON WELFRINGER

We had hoped to go to Nepal in the fall, but the pandemic decided otherwise. Pierrick Fine and I were forced to modify our plans just two weeks before our departure. The choices were limited—the only country that opened its doors to us was Pakistan.

Once the destination was confirmed, we had to find a new goal very quickly. We were looking for a peak of around 7,000 meters to reinforce our high-altitude experience. With great help from Fatmap and Google Earth, our eyes finally turned toward Sani Pakkush, which rises to 6,953 meters. The summit had only been reached once, in 1991, by a German team who climbed the upper north ridge above Tilman's Col, approaching from the west; the rocky west buttress of the mountain was attempted in 1998. The south face, 2,500 meters high and very steep, was still virgin.

Sani Pakkush rises near the west end of the long ridgeline formed by the Batura group. The mountain's south side is accessed by the Toltar Glacier, which branches to the north near the snout of the Baltar Glacier. It is unclear if any previous climbing expedition had ventured to the head of the Toltar, though locals certainly have. Even more than usual, we set out on this adventure with a lot of uncertainties!

Ours was one of the few international expeditions to the Karakoram last fall. In addition to COVID-19, this is also explained by the fact that autumn weather in the Karakoram is nowhere near as stable as in Nepal. The temperature is too low and the faces too snowy for rock climbing. However, we felt the south face of Sani Pakkush might offer great possibilities for mixed climbing.

As it turned out, the month of September was particularly rich in precipitation in the Karakoram, and in October the weather became milder. Thus, the mixed and ice conditions were very interesting.

The approach up the Toltar Glacier took two days; crossing the glacier to reach our base camp site was tricky with our porters. We arrived on September 26 and established a campsite on dry ground at around 4,100 meters. Almost all the mountains around us were unclimbed, offering amazing potential for future expeditions.

Once at BC, we were stuck in our tents for a few days, watching the snowflakes come down. After all the effort to get here, we were quite disappointed to see such bad weather, and these days were really hard to bear. It's not like we hadn't been warned: Everyone had told us you can't climb big mountains in Pakistan in October!

With all the tent time, it was comforting to think back on the experiences that had led the two of us to this remote glacier in the Karakoram. After some successful studies in science, Pierrick had decided as a teenager that he preferred ice axes to pencils and calculators and had devoted himself to the mountains. He was a member of the French ice climbing team, traveling the World Cup circuit for a few years and achieving some great results. After that, he applied his skills to the real mountains with some good ascents in the Alps. In 2019, we traveled to Pakistan together with two other climbers and completed the first ascent of a nearly 6,000-meter mountain in the Hindu Raj, near the border with Afghanistan, at the head of the wild and unknown Risht Glacier.

On my side, nothing had predestined me to alpinism. A former indoor climbing competitor, I went quite late to the mountains, as I was born and raised in the city of Metz, in the flat northeast of France. It was only after moving across the country to finish my meteorological studies at an engineering school in Toulouse that I discovered alpinism in the nearby Pyrenees. After school, I moved to the Alps and devoted myself almost full-time to the mountains. Now I split my time between meteorological engineering, mountain guiding, and climbing. Pierrick and I are only in our mid-20s, but we've both developed a deep love for the expedition life.

[Top right] **Acclimatizing with a superb view over the Toltar Glacier.** [Middle] **Pierrick Fine follows a strip of good ice past a rock band at 5,800 meters.** [Bottom] **High camp at 6,400 meters on Sani Pakkush.** *Symon Welfringer | Pierrick Fine*

Meanwhile, at our campsite by the Toltar Glacier, the sun had finally appeared. The battle was now on.

It was difficult to find technically easy terrain on which to acclimatize—all the faces surrounding us were really steep. But we managed to climb to about 5,500 meters on snow slopes, spending one night at our high point. After five days of acclimatization, we returned to base camp, hoping this would be enough to go up to nearly 7,000 meters on technical terrain. At least we managed to do some good hangboard sessions at base camp.

Back home in France, we had envisioned a steep line in the center of the broad south face of Sani Pakkush, where massive rock buttresses are split by complex, twisting couloirs. But given the weather conditions and the ambient cold, our only option was snow and mixed climbing, not rock, and the left side of the face held the most obvious line. We spent the days of acclimatization observing this side of the wall for objective hazards and planning how to avoid them. In the end, we followed exactly the line we imagined from base camp—only the bivouacs were in different spots than we expected.

After two weeks we felt ready to go, but poor weather made us wait a few days more. The upcoming forecast was good, however: The sun was expected to shine for almost a week, which would give us a proper try on the face.

We left base camp at 2 a.m. on October 16 and met the first difficulties at the very bottom of the face, at 5,000 meters, with some sustained ice pitches. Big avalanches were rolling down the face, and we nearly got caught in one. On the very first pitch, a spindrift avalanche smashed into my pack as I was leading, cutting a big hole in the fabric. Luckily, we managed to find a safer line to avoid the slides. We repaired the pack as best we could, but we could no longer carry heavy loads in it.

Some easier terrain on snow and mixed followed. At around 5,600 meters, we completed one of the hardest pitches (M4+/M5) and found a little platform for an uncomfortable bivy. It was impossible to find a good spot for our tent, and we could only use one of the poles to put it up. It was not a restful night.

On the second day we managed to get high on the face, passing through the rock band at around 5,800 meters that was obviously going to be one of the hardest parts of the climb. The rock band is vertical to overhanging, but two awesome pitches of ice broke right through the middle. For me, this was the best moment of the ascent, with dreamy ice conditions.

At around 3 p.m., at 6,200 meters, we began another desperate search for a bivy site. After hours of looking, we could only sit and wait for morning, one of us on a small snow ledge and the other sitting in the tent, which was hanging from the belay anchor like a hammock.

After two bad bivies, we were really exhausted. We were happy the face got sun early, because the nights had been very cold, dropping below -20°C (-4°F). We decided to climb only to the summit ridge that day and to find a spot to stop as early as possible. At an altitude of 6,400 meters, we located a nice, comfortable crevasse in which to put up the tent and have a proper rest.

Early on October 19, we started for the summit. We left our tent and extra gear at the crevasse bivy and slowly climbed the last 500 meters on the snowy southwest ridge. The snow constantly changed in consistency, and sometimes we had to dig through deep powder. It became harder and harder to continue. In such moments, you understand how significant it is to climb with the right person. Pierrick and I have different skills, and that was one of the keys to our success. I led the technical pitches, but for sure he was the master above 6,500 meters, getting stronger and stronger as the altitude increased. Leaving for a big and committing expedition with only one teammate is risky, but when everything goes right, it creates a very special bond. "L'esprit de cordée," as we say in French, the partnership between two friends linked by a rope.

Sani Pakkush (6,953 meters) showing the 2020 route up the south face and upper southwest ridge. The climbers spent a second night at their high camp before descending the route. *Symon Welfringer*

After seven hours of hard work, we arrived on top at 2 p.m., completely exhausted. We descended to our camp at 6,400 meters and spent another night there, relaxing before the long descent to base camp. We spent our last day on the mountain going back down the same route we had climbed, alternating between rappelling (20 to 25 rappels) and downclimbing. Late in the afternoon of October 20, we made it safely back to base camp, empty of all energy but with lots of emotion in our minds.

We called our route Revers Gagnant, a name that translates somewhat poorly in English as "winning setback." It refers to the fact that we played against all odds by going to Pakistan without much notice and at a season supposed to be bad for alpinism. As a result, we had the chance to discover a completely wild place and stunning mountains.

During all that time I spent on Google Earth and Fatmap, looking for virgin mountains and steep walls, I was amazed to see so many interesting places and objectives in the Himalaya and especially in northern Pakistan. This was my third time in Pakistan and eighth expedition in all, and the discovery of new places and new people remains fascinating to me. The search for unclimbed steep faces at higher altitudes is now my main goal. The potential is still gigantic.

Summary: First ascent of the south face and upper southwest ridge of Sani Pakkush (6,953 meters) in the Batura Muztagh of Pakistan, by Pierrick Fine and Symon Welfringer (France), October 16–20, 2020. Their route is called Revers Gagnant (2,500m, WI4+ M4+ 90°). This was the second ascent of the mountain.

About the Author: *Symon Welfringer lives in Grenoble, France. He thanks North Pakistan Adventure and Ishaq Ali for organizing this expedition.*

RUNNING
IN THE SHADOWS

A FOUR-DAY ADVENTURE
ON YEXYEXÉSCEN

ETHAN BERMAN

I first laid eyes on the Emperor Face in October 2018. Winter had already arrived, and lines of snow and ice shimmered in the afternoon light. The wind whipped snow over the ridgeline and clouds spun around the summit. A prominent gully system left of the classic route Infinite Patience (Blanchard-Dumerac-Pellet, 2002) immediately captured my attention. First because it was a logical weakness that looked like it would suit a fast-and-light style, and second because I knew nothing about it. I left Mt. Robson that day feeling equal parts inspired and intimidated.

I later learned that striking line was, in fact, a variation of the route envisioned on the first serious attempt at Robson's Emperor Face by Americans Pat Callis and Jim Kanzler in 1974. The

Ethan Berman starting the 3,000-meter descent off Yexyexéscen (Mt. Robson) in the Canadian Rockies. Berman and Uisdean Hawthorn made a rare car-to-car ascent of the Emperor Face to the summit of Yexyexéscen , without helicopter assistance. *Uisdean Hawthorn* pair climbed high onto the face through "The Jaws"—a two-pitch choke point where three major gully systems converge—before deciding, after two bivouacs, to escape horizontally to the north face, having misjudged the ice conditions on the upper face.

The gullies above The Jaws received little more attention until 2010 when, on their third attempt of the year, Canadians Jason Kruk and Jon Walsh more or less followed the middle gully to reach the Emperor Ridge, Robson's northwest ridge, bounding the right side of the concave Emperor Face. They descended the ridge without going to the summit due to incoming thunderstorms. I wondered if it would be possible to climb through The Jaws and aim for the right-hand gully above.

After a couple of winter seasons in Canmore and expeditions to Bolivia and Alaska, I felt ready to revisit the Emperor. In June 2020, Peter Hoang and I made an attempt but quickly deemed the face out of condition. After spending a warm night watching the face cleanse itself of its winter weight, the decision to bail was easy. The reconnaissance did provide valuable information, though, and I figured the copious amount of fluffy snow, stuck to the steep face like cotton candy, might solidify into solid ice by the fall season.

The short Canadian summer quickly passed, and soon I was back to checking the weather forecast daily, taking notes of freezing levels and snowfall amounts, and scouring social media for tourists' photos of the face, which sits conveniently in the backdrop of one of the most popular hiking trails in the Rockies. A window appeared just a week before I was due to head south to the United States. A few days later, Uisdean Hawthorn (Scotland) and I were on the trail to Berg Lake, bags packed for four days in the Canadian wild.

Four days of clear weather is a lot to ask from the king of the Canadian Rockies. So when we started the approach in a drizzle, with the mountain completely shrouded in fog, we weren't totally surprised. Halfway to Berg Lake, we stopped for shelter under the dense forest canopy. We brewed a coffee and I closed my eyes, already noticing the sharpening of senses that accompanies each alpine ascent. It was Uisdean's first trip to Robson, and he had yet to lay eyes on the peak. I wondered if he could feel its presence. I appreciated the trust he had in me. This would be by far our most significant undertaking together.

When the alarm went off at 1:30 the next morning, we got our first full view of the face from our bivy by the Robson River, which serves as the toe-numbing threshold between approach hike and mountain climb. The sky had cleared overnight, and a bright moon wrapped us in a blanket of stars. We were concerned about the quality and level of the freeze on the face, but after discussing all the reasons not to go climbing, we laced up our boots and packed our bags.

The rope stayed in the pack as we scrambled through broken rock bands, avoiding the drainages still running with water low on the face. We crossed the freezing threshold and roped up just before The Jaws, which turned out to be a pitch of unprotectable near-vertical snow. Conditions improved as we climbed into the right-hand gully. We fell into a familiar rhythm, stopping to belay tenuous pitches of thin ice blobs over steep and compact limestone slabs, and moving together over large sections of lower-angle alpine ice.

In the early afternoon we reached the first of several crux rock bands. I twice tried to work my way up a thin ice strip that didn't feel like it would hold my weight, and then backed off. The flow state we found earlier had dissipated, and the daunting reality of retreat began to penetrate our mental armor. Uisdean took the lead, sniffing out an overhanging snow-choked corner, and with slow and deliberate craft worked his body upward. The clearing of snow was laborious, and he had to rest and pull on a few pieces of gear as he progressed. He howled as he reached the belay above, and I joined him shortly thereafter. "You can take the boy out of Scotland, but you can't take Scotland out of the boy!" he said, the fire back in his eyes.

Berman launching into one of the crux pitches on the Emperor Face. A discontinuous thin ice runnel split the rock buttress above and took the climbers through several steep rock steps. *Uisdean Hawthorn*

After a couple more pitches, we stood below another steep rock band, the last big question mark of our route. I found a thin, vertical ice runnel, which I followed for nearly 60 meters and through several overhanging rock steps. I took an abrupt fall onto the leash of one ice tool (thankfully with the best protection of the pitch at my waist), then tied off my final ice screw, hammered in two mental pitons, and made delicate moves to the ice slope above. One more long mixed pitch brought us to easier ice, which we followed for several pitches to the Emperor Ridge, topping out the face after 19 hours of climbing.

We hacked out a decent tent platform on the edge of the abyss and began rehydrating and refueling. We had gained about 1,800 meters of elevation from our bivy in the valley, half of which was over new ground, comprising around 14 long and sustained pitches of the highest quality ice and mixed climbing. But the summit was still far away—only 500 meters higher but more than a kilometer horizontally over convoluted calf-burning terrain.

We woke dizzy from dehydration, a sea of clouds swirling outside the tent. With only 30 meters of visibility, we decided to make our summit bid via the "Patience Traverse" across the upper west face, bypassing the infamous rime-ice gargoyles that guard the Emperor Ridge. The route-finding was difficult, but as we neared the end of the traverse, the clouds broke just enough to help us locate the final ice pitches, which led us through a "tube" separating 20-meter rime towers. We topped out to an auspicious full moon rising, just above the cloud ceiling that had tested our mental fortitude all day. We howled to the moon and sat on our packs, savoring the realization of our vision and the comfort of horizontal ground, before putting up our tent, elated to shiver away a cold and windy night at the highest point of the Canadian Rockies.

The pre-dawn hours were rough, as our strung-out bodies struggled to stay warm. But the morning sun thawed our numb fingers and toes and energized us for the arduous 3,000-meter descent down the Kain Route and Patterson Spur. We trudged down glaciers, snow slopes, ridgelines, talus, scree, and water-worn rock to reach the ancient forests below. My feet were a mess, but I welcomed a newfound sense of clarity and awareness in the vast landscape. I felt like I could see each ripple of rock on the towering limestone walls lining the valley, and hear the sound of each droplet of water cascading down the nearby falls.

It is hard for me to imagine what Jamie Logan and Mugs Stump must have experienced when they made the first ascent of the Emperor Face in July 1978. My own climbing experience has been fully shaped by modern ice climbing equipment, ultralight gear, and up-to-the-minute weather forecasts. Yet our ascent bears a familiar resemblance to theirs. "The real key to climbing the Emperor Face was making the firm decision to try, regardless of the obstacles that nature and our imagination might place in our path," Logan wrote in the 1979 AAJ. That much certainly still rings true.

We named our route Running in the Shadows as reference to the song that blasted from our car speakers as we turned onto the Yellowhead Highway and sped away from Robson. This

The Emperor Face of Mt. Robson (Yexyexéscen) in October 2018. Approximate lines of: (1) Cheesmond-Dick, 1981; (2) Logan-Stump, 1978, first ascent of face; (3) Haley-House, 2007 (approached from the Helmet-Robson col below the north face; this line shares some ground with the 1978 route near the top); (4) Kruk-Walsh, 2010; (5) Running in the Shadows (Berman-Hawthorn, 2020); 6. Infinite Patience (Blanchard-Dumerac-Pellet, 2002; and (7) Emperor Ridge (northwest ridge), Perla-Spencer, 1961. *Ethan Berman*

will perhaps be my most treasured memory of the whole experience, when the climb, already completed, was still our secret, only a conglomerate of raw sensory experience and consciousness, all of which was released to the wind as we lowered the windows and sang and danced our way to pizza and beer.

SUMMARY: Running in the Shadows (2,300m, VI AI5 M6, with a smattering of aid), a new route up the Emperor Face on the north side of Mt. Robson (Yexyexéscen) in the Canadian Rockies, by Ethan Berman and Uisdean Hawthorn, September 30–October 2, 2020. On the lower face, the pair climbed previously traveled ground through "The Jaws," then broke right for about 14 pitches of new terrain, to the right of the 2010 Kruk-Walsh route, exiting in a similar location on the Emperor Ridge. They traversed alongside the upper Emperor Ridge and across the northwest face to reach the summit. Berman and Hawthorn walked about 20km to approach Robson and hiked back out, only the second party (after Dave Cheesmond and Tony Dick in 1981) to climb a new route up the Emperor Face and also reach Robson's summit, without using a helicopter for the approach or descent. They told their story in Episode 34 of the AAJ's Cutting Edge podcast.

ABOUT THE AUTHOR: *Born in 1990, Ethan Berman lives in Canada, splitting his time between Squamish and Canmore, and works as an environmental and data science consultant.*

THE MOUNTAINS WERE CALLING

LOOKING BACK AT THE EARLY DAYS OF ADAPTIVE CLIMBING

WAYNE WILLOUGHBY

C limbers with disabilities have accomplished extraordinary feats in recent decades. Hugh Herr, Mark Wellman, and other adaptive climbers made international news with their ascents in the 1980s and '90s, and in the 21st century, climbers with disabilities have summited Everest, climbed El Capitan in a day, flashed 5.13, and bouldered V11. Some even have become household names. But there's an earlier chapter to the history of adaptive climbing—the story of climbers who made impressive ascents long ago, yet whose names and accomplishments have been forgotten by many climbers today.

Speculation about the first adaptive climbers leads my imagination to run wild with possibilities. In 327 B.C., Alexander the Great's troops used mountaineering skills, with cords of flax and tent pegs for pitons, to conquer a fortress in what is now Uzbekistan. In the Southwestern United States, examples of people living on cliffsides go back to the 10th century. The idea that some of these early climbers might have been injured from a fall or battle wounds yet continued to climb is not at all unlikely.

In the 19th century, accounts of technical ascents by climbers with disabilities began to appear in newspapers and books. In 1868, John Wesley Powell, a Union officer who had lost most of his right arm in the Civil War, made the first well-documented ascent of 14,259-foot Longs Peak in Colorado, one year before his famed descent of the Colorado River through the Grand Canyon. The one-armed explorer and his party followed an arduous multi-day route that involved 3rd- and 4th-class scrambling over several peaks.

More than a century before Erik Weihenmeyer began climbing high peaks around the world, Sir Francis Joseph Campbell, who was born in Tennessee and lost his vision after running into a thorny bush at age three, climbed Mont Blanc in the Alps in 1880, at age 47. He went on to summit many mountains in the Alps, including the Jungfrau, the Wetterhorn, and the Eiger.

"At first the guides expected to drag me up," Campbell wrote in a letter to *The Times* in England, describing the Mont Blanc ascent, "but...I was resolved to make an honest climb or give up the ascent. I took my place on the rope in the ordinary way, except that the distance between my son [who also climbed the peak] and myself was only a few feet. This enabled me to follow his footsteps closely.... With the exception of cutting very extraordinary steps for me, the guides during the ascent did not assist me in any way."

Geoffrey Winthrop Young in 1934. He lost a lower leg in World War I, then climbed for another two decades. *Alpine Club Photo Library, London*

In his adopted home of England, Campbell established a school for the blind that was unlike anything that had previously existed. The Royal Normal College and Academy of Music for the Blind was created at a time when society considered its blind citizens to be essentially useless. Sir Francis dedicated his life to erasing these stereotypes, and believed strongly that being both physically and mentally fit would lead to greater self-confidence and subsequently a better quality of life for his students. Helen Keller described his impact by saying: "Wherever he went he started things moving, he always knew what to do, and before the sun of his spirit obstacles melted away."

Like John Wesley Powell, the British mountaineer Geoffrey Winthrop Young lost a limb in wartime. Before World War I, Young was among the most accomplished alpinists from Great Britain, with impressive first ascents including the huge south face of the Täschhorn in Switzerland, climbed in 1906 and not repeated until 1943. He was 38 when the war broke out and was a conscientious objector; instead of fighting, he joined the Friends' Ambulance Unit. In the mountains of the Italian-Austrian front, in 1917, an explosion necessitated the amputation of his left leg above the knee.

Young had climbed in the Alps with his good friend George Mallory, and just a fortnight after losing his leg, he wrote to Mallory of his plans to continue climbing with an artificial leg: "Now I shall have the immense stimulus of a new start, with every little inch of progress a joy instead of commonplace. I count on my great-hearts, like you, to share in the fun of that game with me." His ascents post-amputation included the Matterhorn, the Dent du Requin, the Dent du Géant, the Zinalrothorn, and Monte Rosa, and he continued climbing until 1935, then aged nearly 60. He was perhaps the first mountaineer to create prosthetic legs suitable for various climbing applications, with variable lengths and attachments for rock or ice.

In 1920, Young co-authored *Mountain Craft*, an instruction manual that was the *Freedom of the Hills* for a couple of generations of mountaineers. A lifelong educator, Young collaborated with German emigrant Kurt Hahn on the formation of the prestigious Gordonstoun international school in Scotland, and later helped Hahn with the creation of the Outward Bound program. From 1941 to 1944, Young was president of the Alpine Club in the United Kingdom, and was instrumental in the formation of the British Mountaineering Council (BMC).

In the United States, the most experienced climber with disabilities of this era may have been Jim Gorin, who lost his right leg at the hip to bone disease when he was nine years old. In 1941, then in his mid-20s, he went to a Sierra Club climbing meetup at Southern California's Stoney Point, where he was encouraged to find another sport. He watched two of these opinionated fellows struggle on a boulder problem and then promptly scrambled up it. He later figured out the moves on a problem no one had been able to climb. In time he became the chairman of the club's Southern California climbing chapter. Gorin owned a television and radio shop, and often scrambled around on the roofs of his customers to install antennas. His most impressive accomplishment may have been a speedy ascent of Nez Perce (11,901 feet) in the Tetons.

Gorin frequently was featured in newspaper and magazine articles, one of which, in breathless prose, gives some insights into his minimalist adaptive techniques: "His crutch gives him firm footing in ascending or descending steep mountain trails. Roped up for a high-angle climb over bare rock, he suspends his crutch from a sling around his neck and swings his leg and body from one hold to another by means of his arms. When asked what he gets out of toeholing his way up to heights usually reserved for airplanes, Jim replied, 'It's mainly a matter of meeting a challenge.... You just see a mountain and you want to climb it.' "

Two of the most accomplished and best-known adaptive climbers of the 1960s were Frenchwoman Colette Richard and Briton Norman Croucher.

Richard grew up in Versailles and lost most of her sight at age two. From an early age, she had an interest in the outdoors, and in 1953, as a teenager, she visited the Mer de Glace above Chamonix and, as she wrote later, "My dream of becoming a real climber never afterward left me. In all of us there is a sleeping star which, consciously or unconsciously, we seek to grasp." After taking a brief, intensive mountaineering course in her early 20s she was off.

During the summers of 1960 to 1962, Richard climbed numerous times out of Chamonix, usually moving directly behind her partner or guide, with one hand on the leader's pack for guidance. (One of her friends, Arthur Richard, climbed Mont Blanc without any eyesight in 1959.) Her climbs included Mont Tondu and Mont Blanc du Tacul. Richard also became an accomplished caver, often partnering with the well-known French caver Norbert Casteret.

In her book *Climbing Blind*, published in 1965 as *Des Cimes Aux Cavernes ("From Summits to Caves")*, she writes of overcoming her fears, the exhilaration that followed each success, and the galvanizing effect that each one had, propelling her forward and allowing her to develop a sort of sixth sense for finding her way. Friends, she wrote, wondered why she was so fascinated by mountains when they were invisible to her. "We do not need to see moun-

[Top] Jim Gorin. *Courtesy of Cole Gibson* [Bottom] Colette Richard near Chamonix. *Climbing Blind*

tains in order to love them," she responded in the preface to her book, "any more than we need to see, or even hear, a person who is dear to us. Their presence is enough." In the foreword to Richard's book, Maurice Herzog wrote, "She shows us that no difficulties are insurmountable, that it is a matter of challenging the world, challenging ourselves, and conquering our weaknesses."

In 1960, at age 19, Norman Croucher lost both legs below the knee after he fell down an embankment while drunk and a train ran over him. He had begun rock climbing the year before, and once he was fitted with artificial legs, he began cragging again, but he dreamed of doing high peaks. After a frustrating experience on a small mountain in Wales, "finishing like a

[Top] After losing both legs below the knee at age 19, Norman Croucher climbed dozens of large peaks. *Croucher Collection* [Bottom] Wayne Willoughby on Lurking Fear, El Capitan, 1994. He has climbed El Cap 24 times. *Steve Schneider*

pilgrim, crawling on my knees through the snow," he vowed to get into better shape so he could pursue his mountaineering dreams. In 1969, Croucher solo-hiked about 900 miles from the northern tip of Scotland to Land's End in far southwest England. He then began climbing in the Alps and summited the Matterhorn, Mont Blanc, the Eiger, and a score of other peaks. On a trip to Peru in 1978, he and his team climbed Huascarán Norte and two other mountains. In 1981 he climbed his first Himalayan peak, White Needle (6,600 meters) in Kashmir, and eventually, in 1995, Croucher summited 8,188-meter Cho-oyu in Tibet.

"Obviously, keeping your feet warm in alpine climbing is a problem—but only if you have feet," he joked. On a more serious note, he wrote, "One difficulty was choosing targets that were ambitious and at the same time realistic. I achieved my ambition of climbing a mountain of 8,000 meters by many stages and over many years as I explored my physical and mental limits. Time and again there were knock-backs, but winners must have the courage to fail, must get up again and go back to the mountain with a positive attitude.... There has been an added bonus that my climbing has been the base for campaigns promoting access, integration, and adventure sports for people with disabilities." (Croucher wrote half a dozen books about his experiences, including *A Man and His Mountains* and *Legless But Smiling*.) Sir Chris Bonington said of Croucher: "There is no one like him. His extraordinary achievements have earned him a place in climbing history."

My own climbing story began in Yosemite Valley in 1977. As I learned the ropes and met the locals, Jim Bridwell and others told me about a seemingly mythical character, who, like me, had contracted paralytic polio as a child. With a permanently weakened right leg, Roger Breedlove's capabilities on certain styles of climbs were limited, yet, in less than a decade he had put together a climbing résumé that would be impressive for anyone. While primarily focused on free climbing routes in the Valley and Tuolumne, he swung leads on an early ascent of the Salathé Wall in 1973 (likely the first adaptive ascent of El Capitan) and guided the Regular Northwest Face on Half Dome several times. Roger's disability was well-known among Yosemite climbers at the time, but, unlike mine, his polio was not so severe as to be a defining characteristic. Nonetheless, after hearing of Roger's accomplishments, my own dreams of climbing big walls were no longer abstract concepts. [*Turn the page for an essay by Breedlove about his experiences in Yosemite Valley.*]

I have dealt with post-polio syndrome since 1962 (though it was undiagnosed until the mid-1980s), as well as many other challenges. I have had 11 surgeries related to my polio, the first when I was an infant. One was botched so badly that it required an 18-inch rod inserted in my femur for a year and a half; four of those months were spent in a body cast. These events left me ill-prepared for the big-wall arena. But the fact that someone with a similar—albeit less restrictive—disability had found a way to make it up El Capitan was incredibly reassuring.

Through the assistance of some of the best friends a man could ever hope to find, I have managed to climb El Cap 24 times, the first time in 1990, by the route Zodiac. More than half of those climbs were done in a day, and a handful of others in a push—all of them first adaptive ascents. I have done other first adaptive ascents on the Diamond in Colorado, the walls of Zion, the Chief in Squamish, and other places.

There is nothing easy about these adventures, but everything about them teaches lessons I would never learn otherwise, and they keep the world looking much brighter. Their greatest meaning is knowing someone else might find strength and faith in hearing my stories, as I did upon hearing Roger's. This thought has carried me through many grueling workouts and a great many difficult times, and at age 68 it continues to do so.

As humans, it is in us to seek adventure, to challenge ourselves and find out what we are capable of doing. As this article has shown, adaptive climbers have been embodying positivity in the face of adversity for well over a century— almost as long as mountaineering has been a sport. It is my fervent hope that these stories will encourage others to carry their own visions forward. Though living with a disability is not *un*-challenging, making vertical progress while disabled is a challenge that comes with a great many rewards, and, if you have the right mindset, a great deal of joy.

ABOUT THE AUTHOR: *Wayne Willoughby was born in 1952 and lives with his wife, Becky Sands, in Seattle. He is an oil painter, writer, and big-wall climber.*

MODERN ADAPTIVE CLIMBING

BY CRAIG DEMARTINO

1981 Nine climbers with blindness, deafness, or other disabilities summit Mt. Rainier.

1983 Hugh Herr, who lost both legs below the knee to frostbite, is one of several climbers to free Vandals (5.13-) in the Shawangunks. Three years later, using custom feet for thin cracks, Herr climbs City Park (5.13c) at Index, Washington.

1989 Mark Wellman, who has paraplegia as a result of a fall in 1982, completes an eight-day ascent of the Shield on El Capitan with Mike Corbett, using a jumar and pull-up rig.

1995 Erik Weihenmayer, who developed retinoschisis as a teenager and eventually lost his eyesight, summits Denali at age 26. In May 2001, he earns worldwide fame (and a *Time* magazine cover) by summiting Everest.

1998 Welsh climber Tom Whittaker, whose right foot was amputated, summits Everest on his third attempt.

1999 Adaptive Adventures is founded, offering outdoor sports to people with physical disabilities. In 2007, Paradox Sports is founded by climbers Malcolm Daly, Timmy O'Neill, and D.J. Skelton to foster adaptive climbing.

2005 Brad Zdanivsky, who lives with quadriplegia, climbs Stawamus Chief in Squamish, B.C., using a custom-designed cart to move up fixed ropes.

2006 Wayne Willoughby, a polio survivor, climbs the Nose of El Capitan in 22 hours with Hans Florine and Tico Gangulee. Willoughby did his first of 24 El Cap ascents in 1990.

2006 The first international paraclimbing competition is held in Ekaterinburg, Russia. At the 2019 paraclimbing world championships, 158 athletes representing 24 countries compete.

2007 Craig DeMartino, who lost his right leg below the knee and fused his spine after a 100-foot ground fall, becomes the first amputee to climb El Capitan in less than 24 hours (via Lurking Fear). In 2009, DeMartino, Pete Davis (who is missing one arm below the elbow), and Jarem Frye (an above-the-knee amputee) make the first all-adaptive ascent of El Cap.

2007 Misty Mountain creates the ARC (Adaptive Ropes Course) harness. In 2010, TRS develops a climbing-specific foot with a shoe by Evolv, which eventually develops its own climbing system, the EAF (Evolv Adaptive Foot).

2010s Rand Abbott, who lives with paraplegia, begins leading crack climbs in Joshua Tree using aid systems he developed. In 2013, Sean O'Neill, a paraplegic climber, leads a Yosemite crack climb.

2017 Spanish climber Urko Carmona, who lost his leg above the knee from childhood cancer, flashes 5.13. Maureen Beck, who was born without one arm below the elbow, leads 5.12a outdoors. Ronnie Dickson, who lost his leg above the knee after a childhood illness, boulders V10.

2018 Justin Salas, who lost sight progressively from a young age, climbs V11.

2019 Jesse Dufton, a blind climber, leads all four pitches of the Old Man of Hoy (trad 5.10) in Scotland.

2021 Solenne Piret, a Frenchwoman missing one hand and part of her arm, boulders 7B (approx. V8) in Fontainebleau.

ALL CLIMBING IS ADAPTATION
THOUGHTS ON DISABILITY AND INABILITY

BY ROGER BREEDLOVE

In the early 1970s, Roger Breedlove was a full-time climber in Yosemite: teaching climbing, doing big walls, and putting up classic routes like the Central Pillar of Frenzy and Free-wheelin' on Middle Cathedral Rock, and the first free ascent of Beverly's Tower at the Cookie. Roger had contracted polio as a baby, and his atrophied right leg forced him to adapt his climbing to succeed. In this essay, he reflects on how the Yosemite experience shaped his thinking about disability and capability.

Roger Breedlove in the 1970s.
George Meyers

When my friend Wayne Willoughby asked me to contribute an essay on adaptive climbing, I resisted: With a relatively mild disability, and having never used adaptive equipment, I do not consider myself an adaptive climber. But I've realized that while a physical disability is not the same as having a limited capability in climbing, overcoming either one requires a process of adaptation. Based on my own experience and on my knowledge of Yosemite climbing history, personal adaptation applies to all climbers at every skill level in every style of climbing.

When I started climbing in the mid-1960s, climbing gave me opportunities I could not find in any other sport. I had contracted polio in 1951 when I was 14 months old. The disease wiped out about 40 percent of the muscles in my right leg. When I was seven and nine years old, an orthopedic surgeon rebuilt my right leg from the knee down, rearranging everything that still worked so I could push down with my big toe—still the only motion I can control below my right knee. He also slowed the growth of my left leg, reducing my adult height by three or four inches. After the surgeries, I stopped wearing braces. I learned to ride a bike. But I cannot run fast, cannot jump high, and cannot stand on my leg without something for balance. I dance terribly. While my hip and knee work well enough, I cannot raise my foot or twist it, so, from a climbing perspective, my right leg contributes only about 3rd- or 4th-class capabilities to my overall ability. It turns out that in technical climbing that is plenty good enough. I climbed because it was the sport at which I could excel.

I moved to the Valley in the spring of 1970. Jim Bridwell and the Park Service had just formed the first Yosemite climbing rescue team in exchange for year-round camping. He had noticed me climbing at the base of El Cap the previous year—he admired my tenacity but did not think much of my technique. Nonetheless, he invited me onto the rescue team.

My ah-ha moment came in 1971 when I belayed Peter Haan on his first ascent of Secret Storm. Peter tried to talk me through the short offwidth crux. But I could not heel-toe with my right foot and did not yet have the skills to turn around or chimney against the corner or stem—all sensible adaptions, even if they would increase the climb's rating—so I flailed. It wasn't fun. While I could support my weight on my right leg, I could not really stand up on small holds, and crack climbing often involves actively twisting your foot, so climbing well required finding alternatives to these sorts of moves.

I learned to take advantage of all of the available holds, smearing with my right foot, pushing down with my hands, stemming against opposing face holds, creating chimney moves with my shoulders against small corners and my feet on the face. I was not the first climber to use moves like this: Chuck Pratt had been doing it for years.

But sometimes nothing worked. As an illustration, Moby Dick, at the base of El Cap, has a low-angle, straight-in, four-inch crack mid-pitch. With good heel-toe jams, this is easy 5.9. Since I couldn't do the heel-toe jams with my right foot, this part was always the crux for me; I could easily stand on my left foot but could not move up. Ahab, the corner just to the right, is a flared chimney, mid-5.10, which can be climbed with heel-toe jams in the back and with chimney techniques farther outside. In pre-cam days, Ahab had a fearsome reputation, but there were lots of ways I could move up without using my right leg in an insecure way. So, Moby Dick was very strenuous and not very secure, but on Ahab, my disability did not have an appreciable effect on my climbing. This also illustrates why I rarely rated any of my climbs: My climbing adaptations created havoc with my personal relationship to the grading system.

What is the point of these observations? In my opinion, they show the mashup of adaptations available—and often required—to get up hard climbs. Whatever distinction a climber makes between disability and *inability*, I think that climbing itself blurs the line: Everyone has to adapt. If I had to learn new techniques to get up something, I was just like everyone else. If I found climbs that were beyond my capability or will, I was just like everyone else. To say that my disability kept me from climbing Mark Klemens' offwidth routes or Barry Bates' thin cracks begs the question of what kept most climbers from doing those fearsome early 1970s routes. My disability did not put me into a special category.

We all know that some climbs fit our bodies and capabilities well and others do not. I was tall, skinny, and very strong—positive attributes on many climbs. But I could not put my left foot under my hand while manteling. (This was not a result of polio; my left leg was unaffected.) Steve Wunsch could do this kind of move, and I was envious of his capability. I had to learn other ways to do such moves.

Like everyone else, as I reached my limits, I specialized. I learned to spot high-potential free climbing lines and work out the details of getting up them. I learned to keep a quiet mind on run-out slab climbs. While I do not think of myself as an adaptive climber, I am in a good position to sing the praises of adaptation.

Breedlove leading on the Third Pillar, Dana Plateau, California. *Roger Breedlove Collection*

The zinger is that the very best climbers, in every generation, drive climbing standards by focusing on what they do best. This is easy enough to see by comparing Tommy Caldwell and Alex Honnold. They are good friends, they climb together, and they are among the best ever. However, by their own admission, each cannot do everything the other does. They are both highly adapted to maximize their own capabilities. And, clearly, no one thinks either is in any way diminished.

So, would I have been a better climber if I had not had polio? Of course. But I would not have been a climber. Without the limitations of polio, I would have more likely been a basketball player!

ABOUT THE AUTHOR: *Roger Breedlove lives in Cleveland Heights, Ohio, with his wife, Marsha Dobrzynski, whom he met in Yosemite in 1975. He owns and runs a consulting business solving complex technical problems for manufacturers of highly engineered products.*

'ARD CORE

THE LEGENDARY ICE CLIMBS OF WESTERN NEWFOUNDLAND

ALDEN PELLETT

When people talk about world-class ice climbing, Newfoundland rarely comes up in the conversation. As a New Englander, in the late 1990s and early 2000s, I had chased steep ice in the Canadian Rockies, Québec, Montana, Wyoming, and Colorado. But Newfoundland wasn't on my radar.

Then, in 2006, I sat with Ryan Stefiuk, my frequent climbing partner, to watch a slide show with a crowd of ice climbers packed into a gymnasium in Keene Valley, New York. The speaker was Joe Terravecchia, who told tales of spindrift pouring down rock walls, thigh-deep bushwhacking through tuckamore (thick, gnarly spruce growth), near-fatal avalanche scares, heavy snowmobiles stuck in deep snow, and vomit-inducing ferry rides just to reach western Newfoundland. He wasn't exactly selling it. But the routes! They were huge. Joe clicked through photo after photo of 750- to 2,000-foot ice lines spilling into the fjords. Clearly, first ascents waited for anyone willing to make the long journey and brave the nasty elements.

Probably most people went home that evening thinking Joe was nuts. Alaska sounds easier than Newfoundland, they said. Not us—we were hooked. But there was one big problem: There was no guidebook, and no one who had been there, not even Joe, would give us additional information. "It'll be great," he told me over the phone. "Just go up there." Ryan and I ordered a topo map of Gros Morne National Park. We pored over Google Earth. I found a big summer waterfall several miles into the backcountry. That's where we would start.

Ice-draped Pissing Mare Falls above Western Brook Pond. Several routes have been climbed alongside this 1,000-foot waterfall, the most recent, Dreamline (WI6+), in 2017. *Joe Terravecchia*

The following winter, Ryan and I packed a car with skis, snowshoes, climbing gear, extra crampons, tools, beer, and single malt and headed for Newfoundland. We left my old farmhouse in Vermont, and after 14 hours of white-knuckle winter driving, we pulled into the ferry dock in Sydney, Nova Scotia. An overnight ferry dropped us and our car full of gear in Channel–Port aux Basques, Newfoundland. January is not a hospitable time to be on the big island. Driving the four hours from the port toward Rocky Harbour, near Gros Morne, road signs warned of winds over 100 km/h. Branches on the stunted roadside trees all pointed in the same direction.

The next morning, with the thermometer reading -15°F under rare clear and windless skies, we drove to the village of Trout River, parked out at Birchy Head, and trekked across frozen Trout River Pond, hopefully toward the climb I had found using Google Earth. A warm sunrise crested the horizon as we trudged around a bend at the Narrows. The entire face came into sight. There it was: a big ribbon of yellow ice, just as Google had promised. Eight hundred feet and maybe WI6, or so we imagined. Intimidation crept in. The second lake we needed to traverse to reach the climb was not frozen, and we were forced to boulder sideways along a steep, icy wall above open water. Once at the base of the climb, elated, we started up a pitch of unprotectable thin ice. After a couple more pitches of beautiful ice with a fun WI5 section, we stood on top of our first big route in Newfoundland.

Was it a first ascent? We had no idea, and we didn't care. It was an amazing day of adventure. We celebrated with cold beer and a hot shower back in town. The lack of shared information hadn't dampened our spirits. If anything, it boosted them.

[Top] Steve Larson and Karin Bates navigating Western Brook Pond, which seldom freezes solid enough for easy approaches to climbs. Larson had carried a small outboard motor on the plane to Newfoundland. [Middle] Bates at the rim overlooking Western Brook Pond after climbing White Drift (1,000', WI6) on Pissing Mare Falls. [Bottom] Will Carey encounters one of the locals. *Joe Terravecchia (all photos)*

NEWFOUNDLAND IS AN English-speaking island nearly the size of Ohio in the Gulf of St. Lawrence, north of Nova Scotia and south of Labrador. Gros Morne National Park, a UNESCO World Heritage Site, preserves 697 square miles of the Long Range Mountains along the west coast. Centuries ago, Vikings settled on these western shores and the native Beothuk tribe eked out a rugged existence

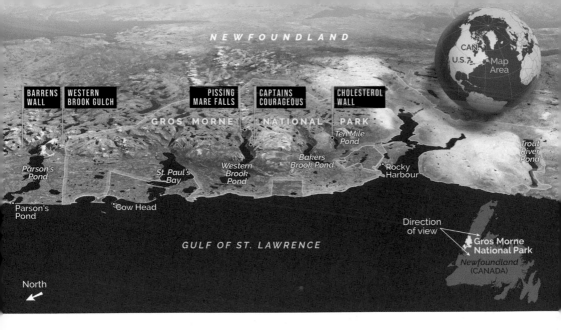

The ponds of Gros Morne National Park from the west. "Gros morne" is old French for an isolated large mountain. In modern French: "big gloomy." *Marty Schnure | Maps For Good. Data: Esri, Parks Canada*

along the many bays. In the summertime, tourists flock to hike the trails and take boat tours through the dramatic terrain, where steep-walled freshwater fjords were scooped out of the surrounding tablelands by ice age glaciers.

In winter, the gawking crowds are gone. Fishing boats and lobster traps line the shores in small villages, stored on dry land and waiting for warmer weather to return. In the scenic fjordlike ponds, winter climbing in Newfoundland really got started—albeit very late in North America's ice climbing history.

In the summer of 1994, Terravecchia traveled with Jeff Butterfield and Chris Kane to southern Newfoundland to climb rock in Devil's Bay, near the town of Francois. The next fall, he went back with his future wife, Karin Bates, and put up Leviathan (9 pitches, 5.12a), the classic of the big cliff called Blow Me Down. He also climbed rock on Newfoundland's south coast with Casey Shaw. Terravecchia, now 60, is a highly accomplished rock and alpine climber who runs a carpentry business in Portsmouth, New Hampshire. Shaw, 59, works with Patagonia's R&D department and now lives in New Mexico. During their spring trip, the pair started talking about the possibility of big ice further north in Newfoundland. They made plans to visit Gros Morne that coming winter, hoping to find ice routes above Western Brook Pond, the largest of the miles-long freshwater fjords. But that winter proved to be too mild on the maritime island.

The following winter, in February 1997, the pair boarded the ferry in Nova Scotia, heading to Newfoundland. During the ride, they saw photos of Pissing Mare Falls, a free-falling waterfall that drops about 1,000 feet to Western Brook Pond, in a tourist brochure. Once in the vicinity, they met a local man, Rex Hewlin, and pointed to the brochure photos: "We want to climb that!" Hewlin agreed to take them to the Big Level, the flat, tundra-covered tablelands above Western Brook Pond. Hundreds of feet deep, the pond below rarely freezes, making it nearly impossible to ski or snowmobile across the surface to reach climbs. Shaw and Terravecchia spent 12 days in their alpine camp, climbing five major routes up the walls below.

Even on the first new route of this trip, the duo learned of the dangers that lurk on Newfoundland ice climbs, many of which follow chimney or gully systems from the talus along the shoreline

Northeast-facing walls above Trout River Pond. (1) The Gutfounded (900', WI5, Pellett-Stefiuk). (2) Trout Fishin' (WI3+), put up by Neil Pilgrim, Jesse Terry, and Kenny Tuach. Unusually, these three were able to kite-ski across the frozen pond to quickly reach their route. *Alden Pellett*

to abrupt finishes on the tundra. The pair climbed in heavy down parkas as wind swirled around the high walls. Partway up the route, a massive chunk of brittle ice spontaneously broke off a wall high above, smashing apart as it fell. Ten-foot-thick sections of ice hurtled through the air. Shaw, who was leading in the back of a 15-foot-wide groove, hugged the steep ice. He had nowhere to hide. Like cars dropped from a crane, the frigid blocks smashed into the icy face, breaking up just before they shot past him. Belaying from a niche in the ice below, Terravecchia watched the cold chaos careening 500 feet down the wall onto the talus below. They dubbed the route Fear of Frying (650', IV WI5+), a tongue-in-cheek reference to the ubiquitous deep fat fryer in every Newfoundlander's kitchen, as well as their fear of dying. Up top, they crawled back into the only shelter they had on the open terrain, a small Bibler tent they had brought. Shaw had frostbitten his nose.

Paul Fenton, who then lived in Rocky Harbour and is now a guide in Nain, Labrador, called Shaw and Terravecchia to congratulate them on the first ice routes ever climbed above Western Brook Pond. He then immediately called Jim Bridwell, urging him to visit. The pair headed straight into Ten Mile Pond, where they did the first ascent of Spirit of Beothuk (1,000', WI5), an obvious classic route that has seen at least five ascents now.

Over the next few years, more climbers trickled in to southwest Newfoundland. Canadian Tim Auger and American Joe Josephson arrived and headed immediately for the back end of Western Brook Pond, where they put up Undaunted Courage (650', WI4) on the most obvious moderate flow there. In 1999, Shaw, Bates, Terravecchia, and their friend Steve Larson arrived for a six-week visit, aiming to reach a massive gully and chimney system above Western Brook Pond by Zodiac inflatable boat; Larson had managed to bring a small outboard motor and a gas tank as carry-on luggage on an Air Canada flight! The temperature was too warm for climbing, however, and Bates and Larson eventually headed home. Shaw and Terravecchia stayed for another three weeks, and when the temperature dropped, they flew to the Big Level with bush pilot Rick Adams, rappelled down to Western Brook Pond, and made the first ascent of Captains Courageous, a 2,100-foot WI5+ route [*see story on p.53*].

By 2003, word was slowly leaking out. Québecois ice climbers Bernard Mailhot, Benoit Marion, and André Laperrière headed up to Newfoundland and lucked upon cold conditions that left Western Brook solidly frozen over, allowing them to ski ten miles into the base of the cliffs and camp there. They returned to Québec with three new routes...or so they thought. Upon arriving back home, they learned each one was a second ascent [*see story on p.57*].

The lack of information about Newfoundland's early ice routes was soon to create a little stir among the Northeastern climbing community. Shortly before Ryan and I first visited Gros Morne in 2008, Canadian climbers Louis Philippe "LP" Menard and Yan Mongrain had been up in the area. Not realizing they could hire a local resident to snowmobile them into Ten Mile Pond, they had skied the 10 kilometers up and over Gros Morne Mountain via the summer trail, across the tundra flats, down into the fjord, and back up and out again. Camping out, the duo sent a couple of hard lines on the Cholesterol Wall, then excitedly reported their achievements to the climbing magazines.

Unfortunately, their routes had already been done. Baby Beaver (700', WI5 M6+) and Tundering Lard (700', WI5+ M5) were established by earlier climbers, one of whom exclaimed anonymously online they had "climbed the place silly." An online debate ensued over the ethics of keeping first-ascent information private, only to claim the ascent once another unsuspecting party reports it.

The lesson learned was, when it came to Newfoundland, it might be safest to assume that most routes in the area had already been done. However, Gros Morne was—and still is—far from climbed out.

Ryan Stefiuk weaving through ice umbrellas on the Barrens Wall. *Alden Pellett*

AFTER I CAUGHT the Newfoundland ice climbing bug, no other place mattered as much. I had been to the Canadian Rockies, climbing routes like Polar Circus, Weeping Wall Direct, Curtain Call, and more, but I have not returned since. Stefiuk and I keep going back to the island, drawn by the unknown and by the friendly Newfoundlanders.

Over three different trips starting in 2008, with the help of local residents and their snowmobiles, we put up a couple of first ascents and did second ascents of established Ten Mile Pond classics, ticking off Stratochief, Weather Vein, Fat of the Land, Hide the Baloney, and Spirit of Beothuk.

In 2014, Stefiuk, on his fourth winter trip to the area, this time with Bayard Russell and Chris Beauchamp, headed into a back gulch off Parson's Pond. The trio, accompanied part of the way on snowmobiles by a crew of friendly beer-drinking locals, found several large ice flows that Stefiuk had seen in online photos of summer waterfalls. The trio established a broad 1,000-foot WI5 they called Newfin'ized. (A few days before that climb, Russell had informed the friendly locals, with whom they had partied late into the night, that the visitors had been left destroyed. One of the locals quipped, "You've been Newfin'ized!") A few weeks later, Terravecchia and Will Carey visited the same gulch, establishing the seven-pitch mixed classic The 'Arding Slot (WI5+ M6) and a steep ice route, Got Me Moose B'y (WI5+). They also put up Drop of the Pure, a 600-foot WI5+, in Bakers Brook Pond.

In 2016, starting from a hunting cabin at the back of Parson's Pond, Stefiuk, Beauchamp, and I snowshoed for an hour to reach the Barrens Wall, a quarter-mile-long cliff that offers a half-dozen 400- to 500-foot ice routes which, if located anywhere in the United States, would see numerous ascents each winter. Knowing the obvious routes had been done, we spied a striking line that had formed partly as spray-foam ice on the right end of the cliff. Starting on blobs, I led up the slightly overhanging first pitch, stemming to ease the pump. Strong winds had sculpted big fans of ice hanging over the top of us, leaving a perfect nook for a sheltered belay. The air was calm under these umbrellas, but we could hear the wind whistling around the corner. Leading out, Ryan teetered on one foot, wind whipping his jacket like a luffing canvas on a tall sailboat. With each lull in the blasts of wind, he made more progress up the 180-foot pitch. Another moderate lead brought us to the top. Later, Terravecchia confirmed a first ascent. We named the route Between Wind and Water (600', WI5), the climb on the cover of this edition.

A few days later, with direction from Terravecchia about a sure-thing FA, Stefiuk and Beauchamp put up a wild 350-foot WI6, which they named Dangerously Weak, at Bakers Brook. At the top of the overhanging flow, Stefiuk chopped a hole barely big enough to squeeze through to

Nick Bullock begins pitch two of The 'Arding Slot. The belayer wrote: "Watching Nick squirming helplessly in the jaws of this great beast, for easily an hour, was at once hilarious and terrifying." *Guy Robertson*

Casey Shaw in Captains Courageous' huge chimney, the dark slot in the lower half of the route photo. Higher, the climbers traversed to thicker ice to finish the 2,000-foot route. *Joe Terravecchia | Bernard Mailhot*

PUSHING ME 'ARD
THE FIRST ASCENT OF CAPTAINS COURAGEOUS

BY CASEY SHAW

"FEEL FREE TO get involved, Jimmy," says Joe: a classic exchange between Joe Terravecchia and me when the ropes are tangled and one of us is momentarily distracted by time and place. We are three pitches up the 2,100-foot ice line that will become Captains Courageous, and we are in an outrageous position. We are enveloped by rock, 80 feet inside a giant cleft that runs 800 feet above us. Looking out at Western Brook Pond from the back of the chimney gives a sense of viewing the scene from inside a telescope. With the open ocean in the distance, air, water, and walls merge, instilling a profound sense of isolation and commitment.

It's 1999, our third winter coming to western Newfoundland, and we've imprinted some exciting moments in our gray matter, but this route, in this place, on this day, is about to burn an indelible stamp into our memories. Captains will become the longest ice route on the east side of North America, but I'm getting ahead of myself. Joe and I are far from certain that the line connects, and this uncertainty is part of the reason we keep coming to this uncharted land.

Carved by glaciers, Western Brook Pond is a landlocked fjord that is 10 miles long and 541 feet deep. In places the shoreline is framed by massive rock walls that drop directly into the water. The locals call it Whistling Pond (or "Pand" in the local dialect) because the wind can be heard to whistle as it rips down from the Big Level. The Big Level is a plateau 2,600 feet above sea level, and in the winter it is a monochrome landscape where it is easy to become lost. As the wind descends off the Big Level, it accelerates and creates a low-pressure vortex that can break up the frozen lake surface and blow giant sheets of ice a quarter mile on shore.

On our first trip to Newfoundland, in 1997, Rex (Rix) Hewlin from nearby Sally's Cove guided us onto the Big Level, where we planned to camp and scout for routes on the walls below. Rix stood up on his snow machine with his jacket unzipped, taking the full force of the wind. A hand-rolled cigarette hung from the corner of his mouth, the fur ear flaps of his hat porpoising with the wind. He yelled over the roar of the two-stroke engine when we pointed to a place on the topo map, "Yiss, b'ys, I know right where she's to," then navigated along the flat, white landscape, past Two Rock Pond and other barely discernible landmarks, delivering us exactly where we had pointed. The Hewlin family have become close friends over the years, and Joe and I feel blessed to know them.

Casey Shaw and bush pilot Rick Adams.
Joe Terravecchia

Midway through our stay, Rix came out to deliver fuel and freshly baked bread from Irene, his wife. Rix had made the delivery as an excuse to check on us. He yelled our names and shook the tent, and when we didn't answer, he later said, he was afraid to unzip the door and look inside for fear we had frozen to death. It was a rare day of good weather, and we were out climbing.

When we arrive in Newfoundland in 1999, Rick "FA" Adams is months out from a hip replacement and still insists on flying us into "Dub-e-yah Bee" (Western Brook), even though he is unable to load his own plane. Rick's verve for life and flying is infectious, and he leaves us with a legion of classic expressions, including "pushing me 'ard, b'ys, pushing me 'ard." This is quickly shortened to "PMA" and incorporated into our lexicon. We once asked Rick about the payload of his Super Cub, and he replied, "Two men and a moose, b'y." When Rick realized that Joe and I loved bush flying, he made a point of buzzing the landscape, hugging the contours from 50 feet up. We had to ask Rick if he'd ever had an engine-out emergency landing. "Oh, yiss, b'y, several times!" It was from Rick's plane that we had spotted the line that would become Captains Courageous. With no way to reach it from below, only a committing series of rappels will allow us to attempt it.

I arrive at the belay after my third stop to purge a stomach unsettled from bad kippers and the sheer audacity of the place. I help sort the ropes after Joe's rejoinder to get involved, and then meander upward, weaving under and then belaying on top of a giant chockstone lodged in the chimney. Darkness arrives and the apprehensive feeling I always have during the sunset evaporates into the night. Joe, always the ace, leads an engaging pitch along a thin ramp, with a soaring rock wall leaning overhead and long gaps between pro. "What's the issue up there, Jimmy?!" I yell. Code for, *I'm with you, but I'm getting cold.* All day we've been carrying the extra weight of uncertainty: It might not be possible to climb to the rim, but we are absolutely certain that going down is a bad idea.

Joe and I have certainly experienced the far side of adventure in Newfoundland—snapping ice curtains, broken bones, an avalanche ride, and frostbite—but this day will be different. A Holy Grail kind of day, when the magic aligns and something rare and special emerges.

Joe's lead of this committing pitch links the upper and lower sections of the wall, and we climb cautiously into the night. Somewhere, in the arc of pitches, the moon rises above the opposite side of the fjord and lends a distant comfort; we feel less alone. Later still, when our minds float in the interstitial space between lucidity and ghostlike delirium, a brilliant display of Northern Lights appears, shimmering like an ephemeral blessing. There has been no wind, and it remains calm throughout the night, a rare occurrence and much appreciated in the bitter cold at the back of Whistling Pand. We enjoy time in the quiet dream-state of the belays, kept company by the incredible light show.

At the upper ice sheet, the ice is thinner than expected and we occasionally hit the underlying rock with our dull points; we keep a firm grip on our situation, and on the tools. When the ice ends, we carefully wallow up a steep snow slope. As we arrive at the tent, the sky is streaked in the pastels of dawn. We look at each other with the wordless acknowledgment that something magical has just happened. We celebrate with a wee dram of the amber restorative, but with the waning of adrenaline it is impossible to resist sleep.

ABOUT THE AUTHOR: *Casey Shaw loves climbing as much today as he did on his first day, and is fortunate to enjoy his job as an innovation designer at Patagonia.*

The 1,200-foot Crepitating Wall (left) and 800-foot Cholesterol Wall are south-facing cliffs above Ten Mile Pond. (1) Triple Flutter Blast (WI5+ M5+). (2) Thundersprake (WI5 M5). (3) DP (WI5-). (4) Repeat After Me (WI5). (5) Baby Beaver, aka Len's Route (WI5 M6+). (6) Fat of the Land (WI5+). (7) Tundering Lard (WI5+ M5). (8) Apocalypse Now (WI7 M9). (9) The Lion, The Witch and the Wardrobe (WI7+ M12). (10) Pellett-Stefiuk start to Stratochief. (11) Stratochief (WI5 M6). (12) Right Shinnicked (WI5 M5). (13) Hide The Baloney. (14) Brace Yourself Mary (WI5+). (15) Take It to the Base (WI4). *Alden Pellett | Annotated by Joe Terravecchia*

finish his lead. The day was bitter cold, and with wind chill hitting -25°F, I had decided a party of three would be inappropriate on a hard route. So, with my partners' approval, I opted to solo a 2,000-foot azure blue WI4/4+ ice line I had seen nearby. Predictably, my two-hour solo climb, a hopeful first ascent, turned out to be the second ascent. Fenton had done it with a partner more than ten years earlier.

With the weather closing in fast, our snowmobile ride arrived after we all had descended from our climbs. Visibility narrowed from a quarter mile to a hundred feet. Walt Nichols, our snowmobile operator from Rocky Harbour, urged us to be quick. After a long, blinding ride back across the pond, he stopped the machine in the woods, out of the dirty weather. We were thinking he needed to relieve himself, but he surprised us by grinning and pulling out a small flask of whiskey. "Yis, b'ys!" he exclaimed in a thick Newfie accent. We all toasted the fact we wouldn't be spending the night out in an emergency snow cave.

IN RECENT YEARS, action has centered on Ten Mile Pond, the most easily reached and densest collection of routes in Gros Morne—and specifically on the steep and intimidating Cholesterol Wall. Prone to spontaneous ice fall, the Cholesterol Wall has had its share of accidents.

In the early 2000s, a huge section of ice collapsed with a roar like a cannon when Terravecchia and Shaw were climbing up an icy gully below the center of the wall. Shaw escaped injury, but Terravecchia suffered a broken leg and bruises from head to toe. With no rescue services in the area, the pair self-rescued the six miles to their car. Shaw recalls that Terravecchia didn't want to go straight to the hospital. "No, they're gonna cut off my Gore-Tex suit!" he said. With help from Shaw, he changed out of the pricey one-piece suit at their rented cabin, showered, and got into more expendable clothing before getting treated for the fracture.

Then, in 2003, higher on the Cholesterol Wall, this time climbing with Andy Tuthill, Terravecchia's lead rope was snagged by a many-ton dagger of ice that broke off above him. The heavy ice pulled out slack in the rope and then suddenly released it, dropping Terravecchia a hundred feet, down past Tuthill. Impact from the huge fall snapped his arm and fractured his hip, knocked him unconscious and lacerated his face. Tuthill, a Yankee hardman, continued to hold tight as the rope zipped through his belay device, melting through his insulated glove and burning down into his palm, but keeping Joe off a ledge 20 feet further down. "I'd be dead right now, if it wasn't for him," said Terravecchia.

In 2015, properly warned of the dangers, Americans Will Mayo and Anna Pfaff started work on a new route up the overhanging center of the Cholesterol Wall. A large section of the upper hanging flow had already fallen off, leaving the wall theoretically a bit safer. After several days of ground-up climbing, Mayo and Pfaff aided and then freed the burly mixed route Apocalypse Now (720', WI7 M9). Maintaining the clean-climbing precedent set by earlier winter climbers in Newfoundland, the duo installed no bolts and removed any fixed pitons and hooks they had placed in thin seams after their ascent. Mayo returned in 2016 with Ben Collett and Chelsea Rude and put up a harder variation: The Lion, the Witch, and the Wardrobe (720', WI7+ M12).

When Mayo and Pfaff returned to Newfoundland in 2017, Terravecchia, the old master, asked them to help him complete a longtime dream. Still fueled by his first trip to Gros Morne two decades earlier, Joe wanted to climb the steepest line yet at Pissing Mare Falls. He and Casey Shaw had climbed The Last Beothuk (1,000', WI5), left of the famous waterfall, in 1997. In 2000, Joe, Casey, and Karin Bates climbed White Drift, the island's first WI6, and in 2010 it was Spray-lordius (also WI6). Now, with Shaw having headed home after waiting out a week of bad weather for an attempt, Terravecchia teamed up with Mayo and Pfaff to tick off Dreamline (1,260', WI6+), with Joe leading the crux pitch of overhanging spray ice, two decades after his first climbs above Western Brook Pond.

Joe Terravecchia leading the crux of Dreamline in 2017, twenty years after his first visit. *Will Mayo*

Clockwise from left: André Laperrière heading in on Western Brook Pond; Benoit Marion at the crux (pitch five) of Captains Courageous; Clarence Roberts (front) to the rescue! *Bernard Mailhot | André Laperrière*

ICE OUT
A MEMORABLE LATE-WINTER TRIP WITH A SOGGY ENDING

BY BERNARD MAILHOT

IN THE LATE 1990s and early 2000s, the holy grail of ice climbing in the Northeast was rumored to have been found in western Newfoundland, where the Vikings first landed in America nearly 500 years before Christopher Columbus. But the Southern Knights had sworn a secret oath and were keeping a tight lid on it. So the Northern Knights had to start from scratch, reminiscing about their summer travels and sightings of high, damp walls in the area, and checking for clues on topo maps. Deep in Western Brook Pond, they found cliffs nearly 700 meters high that might yield the secret.

When a pond is 16 kilometers long, it gives you an idea of the scale in Newfoundland. The finicky coastal weather usually leaves the fjords' inland walls inaccessible, protected by deep, open-water moats that rarely freeze. I hired bush pilot Rick Adams and armed him with a penciled fly-by route to search for steep ice. It was found. As a bonus, the pond surface appeared to be frozen solid to permit an over-ice approach.

At the time, in March 2004, I happened to be working in Corner Brook, less than two hours away, so I drove on up. Coincidentally, a lobster fisherman named Clarence Roberts from nearby St. Paul's had just ventured—for the first time in 43 years—onto the Western Brook Pond ice with his snowmobile, checking the thickness with an ice auger. I happened to spot him pulling into his driveway with a snowmobile in the box of his big pickup, and I asked on the spot if he would mind giving me a lift. Within five minutes we were zooming back out for a reconnaissance. He would later prove to be one of the legendary kind souls of Newfoundland.

Photographic proof of big ice climbs and a fast and safe approach was shared with Benoit Marion and André Laperrière, two brave and faithful knights from the *Hochelaga bourgade* (Montréal). But by the time we all made it to Newfoundland, a thaw cycle had undermined the pond ice and Clarence didn't want anything to do with ferrying us out there. We were on our own, but had planned for it with skis and a large fiberglass sled to haul our gear for a week of exploration.

The climbing was truly awesome, and we got up three major lines, thinking they were all first ascents, but it turned out they were all second ascents when the Southern Knights shared their secrets. Benoit and I first climbed Angishore (275m, WI5), a route at the south entrance to the pond. All three of us got six pitches up what turned out to be Captains Courageous, but veered left too high and had to rap down. Benoit and I then climbed a spectacular 300-meter route (White Drift, WI6) on Pissing Mare Falls, soloing the three bottom pitches to avoid hangfire from the two-meter-wide ice umbrellas above. Finally, the knights Laperrière, Marion, and Mailhot gave their best in an epic battle up Captains Courageous, climbing 11 full 60-meter pitches (660m, WI6 M6, according to us—we never got to see the Southern Knights' secret saga book). There were large spindrift avalanches on the last three pitches; we rappelled in the dark; and we weren't able to cook supper because we were holding tight to the tent, battered by high winds.

The warm weather blowing in—and early April on the calendar—was a clear sign we had to break camp on the breaking pond ice at daybreak. Soon afterward, as I was scouting the route ahead, with over 165 meters of water under the clear black ice, the hangman's trap opened and I fell into the drink. My rapidly deployed outstretched arms held me at armpit level at the edges of the gaping hole. I was wearing crampons because the high winds had completely cleared the snow from the ice surface, and this might have been a blessing—easier to deal with than submerged skis.

I was out like a cork and rolled my right hip onto the surface in an effort to distribute my weight on the thick but decaying ice. I yelled back to my partners to don skis and bring mine. We were trapped by huge walls on both sides of the fjord, with many kilometers ahead to firm ground. We beelined for the shortest way to the lowlands, ultimately hopping on moving ice sheets near the shore, but frankly not getting any wetter that I already was. I don't remember being cold—likely I'd dried up quite a bit just from moving along on a fine spring day.

We sure were glad to be on land again, sitting on big rocks in the bare grass with that near-freedom grin of escaped convicts. The going was easy for a long while until we arrived at a large stream of rapidly flowing water. The only option was tight, snow-free bush, where we certainly could not haul our sled. André had a tiny bit of battery power left in his cell phone, and I called Clarence.

"Oh, hello, Jacqueline, this is Bernie. How are you?" "Oh, I'm fine, how are you?" "Oh, I'm fine, we had an awesome time and climbed these three world-class ice routes in your backyard. May I speak to Clarence, please?" "Sure!" "Hello, Bernie, how are you? We were worried about you with this warm weather." "No worries, we are fine, but we're stuck behind the Parks Canada boat hangar; the river is open water and we cannot cross." "Ohhhh!" "Clarence, do you have a canoe?" "Bernie, let me think about this...."

After about 90 minutes, we heard the sound of incoming motor vehicles. Clarence's brother, Malcom, appeared first, clad in fishing waders and hauling a 16-foot canoe, which he quickly paddled over to us, solo, like a pro. (He was a quick learner, we later learned.) A first load was ferried across the river, along with a safety line made with one of our climbing ropes, and after a few crossings, all of us had reached the far side. They had towed in a huge log-hauling sled, on which we installed the canoe and all our gear, with our sled on top, all cinched together with straps.

André hopped behind Malcolm on a four-wheeler while Benoit and I sat behind Clarence on his snowmobile, and off we went over the wet, beige ground, all five of us with big happy grins on our faces. I leaned closer to Clarence's ear and yelled, "There is no more snow, you are gonna damage your machine!" To which he replied with the classic line, "Oh don't worry, Bernie, I just imagine it's all white!"

ABOUT THE AUTHOR: *Bernard "Bernie" Mailhot, 62, is a retired mechanical engineer reincarnated as an outdoor guide, mostly backcountry skiing in the Chic-Chocs of Québec's Gaspé Peninsula.*

March of 2019 saw the first known free-solo ascent of the Cholesterol Wall. Ryan Stefiuk, Lindsay Fixmer, and I had snowmobiled to the park boundary on the far side of Eastern Arm Pond, using snowshoes the remaining two and a half miles to reach the climbs in Ten Mile Pond. We were aiming to do the second ascent of He Speaks for Rain (650', WI6), a line of steep columns that spill down the western end of the long cliff band. But I was restless. Conditions were also good on Fat of the Land (950', WI5+), which climbs leftward on the Cholesterol Wall, avoiding the more dangerous and overhanging central wall. After some inner struggle, I decided this would be my best chance to attempt a solo of this route.

I walked the three-quarters of a mile back to the Cholesterol Wall alone. I had brought a 60-meter rappel cord and a 15-liter Mammut speed pack. After digging a neck-deep trench through the snow to reach the base of the ice, I started climbing. A little less than halfway up, I stopped on a snow ledge below the crux for a sip of tea and to enjoy the blue-sky view over Gros Morne Mountain. I had it all to myself. A little over an hour later, I placed a tool in the tundra grass at the top. Leaving nothing behind, I used a long screw to make naked threads in the ice for rappel anchors. Hanging out as I slid down the rope, I could fully relax and enjoy the steepness of my surroundings—the rat had been fed.

[Top] **Ryan Stefiuk on Hanger Management (400', WI6), Parson's Pond.** *Christopher Beauchamp* [Bottom] **The author after soloing a 2,000-foot WI4+ route above Bakers Brook Pond.** *Alden Pellett*

As I walked back up the frozen pond to meet my partners, I looked at the incredible collection of routes lining the cliffs, some already done and worthy of repeat, others offering tempting first-ascent candy. The fact is, despite how much has been done, first ascents are usually completed every year in these fjords. Often, the easier routes have been ignored by visiting expert climbers, leaving WI4s just waiting for the first touch of tools and crampons. There are unclimbed routes at Ten Mile Pond, Trout River Pond, Bakers Brook, Parson's Pond, and perhaps other places where a topo map or Google Earth might lead you in the wild northland. Just pick a spot, head in, find an appealing line, and start climbing. Someone will let you know if it's a first ascent…or maybe not. If the climbing is good, and if the adventure feels the same, does it even matter?

About the Author: *Alden Pellett, 59, is an ambassador for Mammut and part of the product development team for CAMP. He has been a professional photographer for over 30 years. Pellett recently built his own home 10 minutes from the ice climbing at Lake Willoughby in Vermont.*

Editor's Note: *The online version of this story includes helpful information and contacts for travel to Gros Morne National Park, permits, lodging options, and snowmobile access to the climbs. Find the complete article at publications.americanalpineclub.org.*

CLIMBS & EXPEDITIONS reports generally are arranged geographically, from north to south, and from west to east, within a country or region. Unless noted, reports are from 2020. The complete AAJ database, from 1929 to present, can be searched at *publications.americanalpineclub.org*. Online reports frequently contain additional text, photos, maps, and topos—look for these symbols indicating additional online resources:

FULL-LENGTH REPORT	ADDITIONAL PHOTOS	MAPS OR TOPOS	VIDEO OR MULTIMEDIA
≡	📷	🔍	▶

UNITED STATES

WASHINGTON / CASCADES

VEGAN TOWER, WEST FACE, BEYOND REDLINING

GROUND-UP FIRST ASCENTS are ephemeral experiences, like steep turns in perfect powder, burning briefly and brightly before flickering from fantasy to memory. Top-down route development is a long, dirty, and masochistic affair, like fighting through steep, wet brush on the approach to an obscure Beckey route, with just enough glimpses of alpine glory to keep you going.

Kurt Hicks and I have done first ascents in both styles. Looking for a line with the potential to become a popular classic, we were drawn to the 1,200' west face of Vegan Tower, whose shorter southwest arête Darin Berdinka and I had climbed via Mile High Club (*see AAJ 2016*). Vegan Tower is the northernmost tower along a jagged ridge running north from Morning Star Peak (6,020'). In September 2018, Kurt and I began a top-down exploration of the west face and spent hundreds of hours over three seasons to unlock and equip the formation's king line, which eventually would require only a rope and 17 quickdraws to lead.

On May 29, 2020, as the pandemic raged, we set out to climb our route, Beyond Redlining, from base to summit. We leaped over a raging river swollen with spring snowmelt, post-holed up steep snow, and stemmed across a 20-foot deep moat to reach the start of the route. After many hours of aid and free climbing, we reached the snowclad summit. Two days later, George Floyd was killed by Minneapolis police and the world exploded in rage.

In climbing, redlining might mean getting pumped or otherwise pushing beyond our physical limits. In the United States, redlining was used by the Federal Housing Administration, cities, banks, and others to demarcate inner-city areas, typically Black neighborhoods, where residents were systematically denied home loans, insurance, health care, and other services, even if they were more qualified than whites outside these areas. Thankfully, we have moved beyond redlining, but we still have a long way to go before our country lives up to the principle that "all men are created equal."

On July 11, we made a team free ascent of Beyond Redlining, the cruxes feeling increasingly desperate as we fought our way up the steep headwall, hanging on for the route's hardest crux on the final pitch. In the midst of 2020, this first ascent felt like a miracle. It still does. We hope people will climb Beyond Redlining (1,200', 11 pitches, IV 5.10+) and also find a way to help make the world a more just and equitable place. 📷

— RAD ROBERTS

MT. INDEX, NORTH NORWEGIAN BUTTRESS, JÖTNAR

RIGHT ABOVE HIGHWAY 2 and the town of Index lives one of the biggest walls in the Lower 48: the North Norwegian Buttress on Mt. Index. The buttress received its first ascent back in the '80s, solo by Pete Doorish. His line has remained unclimbed ever since. In the early 2000s, Blair Williams, with help from Todd Karner, Roger Strong, and William Thorpe, put up an also-unrepeated direct start to this line that he named the Voodoo Proj (*see AAJ 2003*).

In 2019, I convinced my friend Lani Chapko to attempt the Doorish line. We climbed about 800', but turned back after a partial anchor failure. It looked like all the bolts and rivets would need replacement. Over the winter, we contemplated the wall and decided climbing a new route would require no more work.

The next June we set off, having chosen a continuous crack system on the left side of the buttress, about 100 yards to the left of the Doorish line. We had enlisted our over-stoker friend Kyle Willis to help out. The winter before had an above-average snowpack, and the lower half of our line climbed through a seasonal water streak. Occasional light drizzle amplified the situation and made for heinous, often hilarious conditions as we climbed through a waterfall. The climbing

The North Norwegian Buttress, part of the northeast face of Mt. Index, showing (1) Jötnar (2,000', 16 pitches, VI 5.9 A3+), (2) Doorish Route (Pete Doorish, 1980s), and (3) Voodoo Proj (VI 5.10 R A4, Williams-Karner-Strong-Thorpe, 2002). *Sam Boyce*

was chossy and hard nailing, and even in full Gore-Tex, the leader would only be able to sustain a pitch or so of water torture before returning to camp. After five days we had climbed only 700'.

Our next window was three weeks later in late July. On the first day, Lani and I fixed lines to our previous high point. The next day we set up a portaledge camp, and, after dinner, Lani set off on the first pitch of new terrain. This pitch overhanged about 40' over the course of 100' and required a fixed line descend. Kyle arrived the following day and hauled our remaining gear while Lani and I pushed the route higher through a surprisingly high-quality band of gneiss.

After moving our camp the next day, I led an extremely exposed pitch of natural hooks and rivets on the prow of the southeast ridge. Kyle set off on the next pitch, free climbing with questionable beaks for protection, leading to a chossy wide crack. He sent down multiple toaster- to microwave-size rocks, eventually ripping a blind offset cam and taking a pretty sizable fall. We all descended to camp to find a rock had pierced a portaledge fly.

We packed for a summit push the next morning, but a miscommunication meant half of our water for the day was forgotten. Kyle's hand was a little messed up from his fall, so I went up to finish his lead. At this point we were all starting to feel a little delirious from dehydration. We managed to keep each other in check and pushed onward to the top. Having long been out of water, we decided not to climb the moderate terrain to the summit of Middle Index. After descending to camp, we each drank at least six liters of water before passing out. The next day we descended a few pitches and then executed a 1,000' lower of Kyle riding the haul bags; Lani and I rappelled the route.

Jötnar (2,000', 16 pitches, VI 5.9 A3+) took seven days of climbing to complete to the top of North Norwegian Buttress. We named the route after the race of giants in Norse mythology.

– SAM BOYCE

AXIS PEAK, ARCTIC AXIS

ON OCTOBER 29, 2019, Adam Butterfield and I completed a likely new route on the northeast buttress of Axis Peak (7,550'), above Eightmile Lake in the Stuart Range, near our homes in Leavenworth. Arctic air had spread south into the region, and the Pacific Northwest experienced a rare window when ice formed anywhere there was previously water, but snow had yet to fall in the mountains. Many routes that often get covered by early season snow were in prime form.

After two reconnaissance missions, we completed Arctic Axis (1,300', WI4+ M4+ R). We found an enjoyable mix of ice, rock, and even a pitch of frozen moss in a chimney. Later in the season, this climb would be easier though still quite enjoyable, with a descent on snow rather than talus.

– MATT PRIMOMO

MT. RAINIER NATIONAL PARK, LITTLE TAHOMA PEAK, NORTH FACE, LAWLESS

I BECAME INTERESTED in Little Tahoma Peak (11,130'), a satellite peak on the east side of Mt. Rainier, while talking with Matt Christensen, my stepfather, about his first ascent of the west ridge with Paul Cook in 1980. We found it interesting that the third-highest peak in Washington has only a few routes, and only two routes on its steep north face (see AAJ 1960 and 1980). Curious about this face, I teamed up with my friend Jay Lyons, who had been wanting to climb something on the north side for a while.

At 3:30 a.m. on March 3, we started from a camp at around 8,800' on the Cowlitz Glacier. We crossed below Cathedral Rocks and got onto the Ingraham, then headed west up-glacier. Eventually, we made it to the start of the west ridge and descended the Winthrop Glacier to below the north face of Little Tahoma. By that time the sun was fully out. We scanned the north face for a weakness and chose a line beginning on the right-hand lower snowfield, to the right of the original north face route. We encountered a significant bergschrund, which took two rappels using V-threads to get across and to the base of our route.

The climb started out on lower-angle snow and ice leading to fun ice and mixed pitches. Pitch five was more serious: steep mixed climbing with a thin layer of snow over what appeared to be cement mix with cobblestones protruding. I was able to find a pin placement low on the pitch, but the majority of the lead was unprotected. Jay took the crux sixth pitch: a short crack system leading to difficult moves pulling around an overhanging bulge. At the top of this pitch, we gained the west ridge, where we started to climb a series of gendarmes, mostly on good rock. From the last major gendarme, we rappelled into the notch below the final buttress of the west ridge.

By this time it was dark and weather had moved in, causing whiteout conditions. We decided to bail on our original plan of climbing a distinct vertical chimney system directly up the final buttress and instead traversed around to the south face until we found a large couloir that brought us to the standard route up the east ridge. We were only about 150' below the summit, but being exhausted and with no bivy gear, we decided to descend from there. We returned to camp 24 hours after departing. We named our route Lawless (1,400' climbing distance, 11 pitches, V AI4 M6 5.8). 🗎 🞑

— RYAN DOUGHERTY

CALIFORNIA / YOSEMITE NATIONAL PARK

FIFI BUTTRESS, THE NEXUS (A.K.A. THE NIELS TIETZE MEMORIAL ROUTE)

IN EARLY NOVEMBER, Nick Sullens of Yosemite Valley Search and Rescue and Eric Lynch, a Yosemite climbing ranger, completed the long-awaited free ascent of a new route on the Fifi Buttress in Yosemite Valley—the culmination of vision and determination by several Yosemite community members.

In the spring of 2017, Brandon Adams and Adam Ramsey established an aid route in the middle of the wall called Make It So (5.8 A4). Around the same time, Niels Tietze began envisioning a free line that shared many of the same features, and that autumn, Tietze and Adams ventured onto the route together. As with many of the difficult modern routes on Fifi Buttress, Tietze planned to link crack systems with technical climbing on intricate face holds. Tietze pointed out the features to Adams, and the two debated bolt placements needed for a free ascent. With fixed lines on the route, Tietze began the work of equipping, cleaning, and perfecting the line.

The Nexus (10 pitches, 5.13-) on Fifi Buttress, just to the southwest of Leaning Tower. Other routes are not shown. *Eric Lynch*

Just a few weeks later, on November 13, 2017, Tietze fell from the route in an apparent rappelling accident, and for the next few years the project sat silent with his memory.

Tietze had established around two-thirds of the route, and in 2019, Adams returned to see if he could complete the vision. By the spring of 2020, he had installed more than a dozen bolts and attempted the free moves. But by fall his motivation had shifted away from the project. With Adams' blessing, Lynch and Sullens teamed up to finish the route, though they had never climbed together before. They finally coordinated schedules on November 5, a day they remember as perfect for climbing, though Yosemite's first winter storm, predicted for the next day, added a bit of pressure.

The two flowed up the route, a climb they describe as sustained and beautifully varied. Above the first pitch, rated 5.10+, the route has three pitches of 5.11, four pitches of 5.12, and two pitches of 5.13a/b. Like all the Fifi Buttress routes, it was named with a Star Trek theme: The Nexus (10 pitches, 5.13-). Both Sullens and Lynch credit Adams' hard work on bolting and cleaning, but for Adams the route's ultimate credit lies with Niels Tietze. "I never would have done it without his vision," he said. 🗎 🔍

— LAUREN DELAUNAY MILLER

EL CAPITAN, GOLDEN GATE, ONE-DAY FREE ASCENT

ON NOVEMBER 4, Emily Harrington (USA) became the first woman to free El Capitan's Golden Gate (37 guidebook pitches, 5.13a) in a single day, the fourth person to free this route in a day, and the fourth woman to free any route on El Cap in a day. Golden Gate, established by Alexander and Thomas Huber in 2000, shares the same line as Freerider before breaking right from El Cap Spire (after the notorious Monster Offwidth). A one-day ascent is notably difficult as the route's hardest pitches are all in the last ten.

Harrington first redpointed Golden Gate over six days in 2015, and returned in November 2019 to attempt a one-day ascent, but she took a serious fall while simul-climbing the Freeblast slabs, low on the route, resulting in a trip to the hospital. On her successful ascent in 2020, Harrington took another bad fall, on the Golden Desert pitch, leaving a deep gash on her forehead. She persevered and topped out the route after 21 hours and 13 minutes.

Previous one-day free ascents of El Cap by women include Lynn Hill's groundbreaking climb of the Nose (harder than Golden Gate) in 1994 and two ascents of Freerider (considered easier overall than Golden Gate) by Steph Davis and Mayan Smith-Gobat.

– ANDY ANDERSON

CALIFORNIA / EASTERN SIERRA

CROFT'S BIG FOUR BY FOOT AND BICYCLES

LAST SUMMER, WITH travel not an option, Chris Natalie reached out to me with an intriguing proposition: to link Peter Croft's "Big 4" via human power. We knew multiple parties who had done these four classic Sierra climbs, highlighted in Croft's *The Good, the Great, and the Awesome* guidebook, as a 4x4, climbing back-to-back days and driving between each trailhead. Linking the mountains by our own power added enough novelty and uncertainty to pique my interest.

Starting on July 31, we walked the first half our route through a gorgeous section of the northern Yosemite wilderness, climbing the Red Dihedral on the Incredible Hulk and the southwest face of Mt. Conness en route to our bicycles, parked on Tioga Pass. That's when the challenge began in earnest. Neither Chris nor I had cycled in preparation, and it showed. The combined toll of 100°F heat and the unrelenting steepness of the Glacier Lodge Road from Big Pine to the Palisades trailhead nearly ended our adventure. But we gave in to the suffering and found new life among the craggy peaks of the Palisade Crest, climbing Dark Star on Temple Crag.

Our last two days consisted of a pleasant morning ride to Lone Pine, another steep grind to the Whitney Portal, a meandering ascent through off-route choss on Keeler Needle's Harding Route, and the relief and release of the summit. All told, we hiked 62.5 miles, biked 160 miles, and climbed a total of 52 pitches or 5,700' in six days and 11 hours. The Sierra Nevada has never felt bigger.

– ERIC LYNCH

ROYCE FALLS, FIRST KNOWN ICE ASCENT

ROYCE FALLS IS notable for being perhaps the highest of the large waterfalls in the Sierra. This obscure horsetail falls descends approximately 700' vertically over its 1,200' length, fed by the drainage of Royce Lakes atop the 11,000' Merriam plateau. The unique combination of a sun-exposed lake plateau at high elevation provides a ready supply of running water to be frozen into a pure water ice climb. The route only forms in the very depths of winter, and wind-deposited snow collects in the large approach basin. In the relatively dry January of 2021, I observed knee- to waist-deep powder for nearly four miles of the nine-mile, 4,000' approach from Pine Creek trailhead. The long approach, limited daylight, and the frigid temperatures required for the ice to form made this ascent a committing 14-hour day, car-to-car.

The climb itself is no harder than WI3, though plenty of opportunities exist for harder variations. The lower 300' are the steepest, where the falls emerge from a large dihedral and cascade down a series of steps to the valley floor. The upper dihedral is like a standard 30–50° Sierra goulotte, but filled primarily with ice steps and slabs rather than snow. With its moderate climbing, striking form, and spectacular position, Royce Falls has the potential to be a more widely sought objective in the High Sierra. 📷

– JONATHAN LAI

PEAK 12,640'+ (SEVEN GABLES NORTH), HOT CHERRIES

WITH AN EXTRA day off over the Fourth of July weekend, Johnny Lomas and I decided to push over the Sierra crest to see what we could find on the imposing east face of Peak 12,640'+, a.k.a. Seven Gables North. After a long hike to a camp just below Seven Gables Lakes, armed with a topo for the Direct East Face (Clevenger-Fiddler, 1981), we gawked at the looming black wall above us while gorging on a big bag of Grocery Outlet cherries.

The following morning we started climbing in a recess left of a pillar and did two long, easy fifth-class pitches to the base of the east face proper. We quickly realized we were well left of our intended route, and were standing below an ever-steepening headwall filled with ominous cracks and corners. After deciding that traversing back onto the original line might be too hazardous, we began our vertical quest into the unknown. [*Editor's Note: The Direct East Face description in the Secor guide mentions climbing the right side of the central pillar. This new route climbs the left side of the pillar, between the Direct East Face and Consolation Prize (5.9, Cable-Tipton, 1998).*]

Peter Throckmorton on the approach to Seven Gables North, showing the line of Hot Cherries (9 pitches, 5.10). The route shares the final three pitches along the ridge crest with the Direct East Face (Clevenger-Fiddler, 1981). *Johnny Lomas*

We delighted in the continuous climbing, bobbing and weaving up a surprisingly vertical line through a number of right-facing corners. After three quality 60m pitches, all 5.9 to 5.10, Johnny freed the crux overhanging flared corner in style and propelled us onto the crest of the east ridge. After six new pitches, we climbed the final three pitches of the Direct East Face along the ridge, landing us right on the summit prow. We named our route Hot Cherries (1,700' climbing distance, 5.10) for the bag of cherries that fueled this magnificent excursion across the high country. 📷

– PETER THROCKMORTON

Andy Wyatt traversing east toward Mt. Gilbert during the Evopal Traverse. The slab in the background, on Mt. Gilbert's west side, had the only roped (simul-climbing) pitches the climbers did—an "awesome" stretch of 5.7. *Bernd Zeugswetter*

THE EVOPAL TRAVERSE

IN 1996, PETER Croft completed an awesome eight-mile traverse along the crest of the peaks surrounding the Evolution Lakes basin, defining the classic Evolution Traverse. Some ten miles to the south, the jagged Palisades span from Bishop Pass in the north to Taboose Pass in the south, with seven peaks above 14,000' as well as a number of classic linkups and traverses. After flying around on Google Earth one night, I realized how well-defined and rugged the Sierra crest was between these two well-traveled ridgelines. I thought it'd be a super-cool adventure to try to connect them.

In 2016, I tried to solo the route but got stormed off two days in. Austin Siadak and Andy Wyatt tried it a couple of years later, but were too late in the season; after encountering early-winter conditions, they completed the full Evolution Traverse instead of bearing south at the Clyde Spires. In the summer of 2020, looking for a cool adventure close to home, I decided another attempt was in order.

At midday on July 7, Andy Wyatt, Bernd Zeugswetter, and I hiked over Lamarck Col and on to the beginning of the Evolution Traverse. By evening we reached a bivy on top of Mt. Gould. On July 8, we climbed the first half of the Evolution Traverse and bivied at the col between Mt. Wallace and the Clyde Spires.

The middle of the traverse—between the Evolutions and the Palisades—includes seven prominent peaks and many smaller summits along nine miles of the Sierra crest. On July 9, we left the Evolution Traverse, climbed over the Clyde Spires, and continued south, climbing the various subpeaks of Powell and Thompson, and reached a bivy on the summit of Mt. Gilbert.

The next day we climbed over Johnson, Goode, and several smaller peaks and ended the day at Bishop Pass, where we had cached some food, fuel, and whiskey. Bernd hiked out that evening. On July 11, Andy and I continued into the Palisades, climbing over Agassiz, Winchell, and on to the Thunderbolt-to-Sill Traverse. We ended the day with a bivy below the east face of Sill, and the next day we hiked out to Glacier Lodge.

The options and variations for ridge traverses in this area of the High Sierra are seemingly endless, with myriad natural start and stop points. It's worth noting that this traverse could extend through the entirety of the Full Palisades Traverse or even farther south along the Sierra crest. [image icon]

– DYLAN JOHNSON

MT. HITCHCOCK, ALFRED'S TOOTH, PRESSURE DROP

AT THE END of July, Mike Pond and I made the trek into the northeast face of Mt. Hitchcock. We approached via the Russell-Whitney col and set up camp at beautiful Hitchcock Lake, directly beneath the mountain. After some scouting, we decided to try to find our way up what looked to be the steepest buttress, rising from the southern edge of Hitchcock Lake. This feature was named Alfred's Tooth, presumably by Mike Pennings and Jimmy Haden, who in 2010 climbed the only recorded route on the feature, Pleasure Garden (5.12). [*Editor's Note: This route was never reported in the AAJ, but appeared in a feature story entitled "Storming Castles" in Rock and Ice 195.*]

We started left of Pleasure Garden in a shallow right-facing dihedral. The route came together beautifully, with most pitches checking in at 5.10, plus a few harder moves here and there. We climbed some unbelievable cracks through headwalls, corners, and arêtes. The crux tenth pitch was a steep, featured finger crack that slowly closed up just as a curving hand crack came within reach—a four-star pitch! A few pitches later, we were packing up the rope and scrambling a rather long, exposed ridgeline to the top of the tooth. Pressure Drop (1,800', 12 pitches, 5.11c) is an excellent route and deserves to be repeated. [image icon]

– ANDY STEPHEN

MT. LE CONTE, IRIDESCENT WALL, IRIDESCENT FLOW

IRIDESCENT WALL IS a distant south-facing point on a southwest spur of Mt. Le Conte (about 13,960'). The wall, which rises above an idyllic lake in the Miter Basin area, can be reached by a strenuous cross-country route up the South Fork of Tuttle Creek or a longer, more leisurely hike from the Cottonwood Lakes trailhead.

On July 17, Andrew Oesterreicher and I climbed Iridescent Flow (9 pitches, 5.10), which follows the right margin of what could be called the Iridescent Pillar, a massive white feature on the left side of the formation that offers a way to avoid the prominent red shield of lower quality rock on the upper wall. [*Editor's Note: This route is to the right of Space Force (5.11b; AAJ 2019), likely the first route up the wall, and may share some terrain with it near the top.*]

Iridescent Flow is steep and mostly on clean rock, with the exception of one short section of bush wrestling, which only adds to the character of the route. Each belay is on a comfortable ledge and bolted. The final ridgeline to the crest has extremely poor rock and still leaves you a long way from the actual summit of Le Conte. A reasonable option is to descend from the top of the pillar by scrambling west and down to the lake or by rappeling our route with a single 70m rope. [search icon]

– DAVE NETTLE

The Iridescent Wall on Mt. Le Conte showing (1) Space Force (5.11b, 2018) and (2) Iridescent Flow (5.10, 2020). *Dave Nettle*

Mt. Corcoran's south face, showing For the Love of Men. *Vitaliy Musiyenko*

MT. CORCORAN (PEAK 4,151M), SOUTH PILLAR, FOR THE LOVE OF MEN

"WATCH ME!" I yelled to Connor Chilcott and Derek Field as I climbed above a sharp flake that would mangle me if I fell. I did not have the right gear to protect the 5.10 offwidth and could not allow a slip. We were six pitches up the south pillar of Mt. Corcoran, just southeast of Mt. Le Conte. I had envisioned an aesthetic route up the obvious prow on the peak's south face, left of the original route climbed in 1998 by Bart O'Brien and David Harden. Now I was scared, but by this time in our climb, I felt comfortable sharing my fears with my two partners, which allowed me to focus on the task, continuing up the steepening crack until I reached a good piece of protection.

Though this climb ended up being an enjoyable adventure, it was close to being called off, as all three of us—Derek, Connor, and I—were going through tough times. It was very fortunate we didn't bail, however, because during the approach we all slowly opened up about the troubles in our lives—things men usually don't talk about. We lamented how unfortunate it is that men are under so much pressure to be stoic and not share things that might make us appear weak. In opening up, we all found we felt stronger. Feedback from buddies in similar situations led to greater understanding of the things troubling us, acceptance, and, after the trip, at least partial resolution.

Connor took over on the following pitch and did a brilliant job at connecting thin finger cracks through bulges, topping the pitch with a bouldery crux of overhanging baggy fist jams. After two more pitches and then simul-climbing and soloing for a few hundred feet, we stood on the summit an hour and a half after dark. The descent was one of the cruxes of this taxing day, as we faced 500' of technical down-scrambling in an extremely loose and steep gully.

Because we'd had such a therapeutic session, opening up about what was on our minds, we dubbed the route For the Love of Men (10 pitches, 5.11b), after a recommended book on the topic.

— VITALIY MUSIYENKO

LOCKE ROCK, LOCKED AND LOADED

IN AUGUST, BRANDON Thau invited me out to the southeast face of Locke Rock, northeast of Courtright Reservoir, to climb a line he had been eyeing. We started to the right of the rarely done, run-out classic Best of the West (1,000', 5.11c R, Laeger-Leversee-Seiden, 1986) and did several sustained pitches of face climbing before I was able to execute some improbable moves and gain a steep splitter. On our second day of work on the route, we were joined by Brian Prince, who boosted morale and helped divide the load of bolting and leading improbable terrain. We topped out after seven pitches, five of which included sustained 5.11a-ish climbing on perfect rock—Locked & Loaded (1,100' climbing distance, 5.11a).

During this trip, we also climbed Best of the West and replaced all of its bolts. 📷 🔍

— VITALIY MUSIYENKO

CYCLORAMA WALL, EXTRATERRESTRIAL VORTEX; LANGILLE PEAK, THE PRODIGY

IN 2013, JON Griffin, Scotty Nelson, and I slogged 18 miles back to the "netherworld between the Palisades and Le Conte Canyon" (*AAJ 1980*), home to the Cyclorama Wall. The only recorded route here was done by Vern Clevenger, Claude Fiddler, and Galen Rowell in 1979 and has a vague and intriguing description; they rated it F10 A1. Our goal was either to free their route or establish a new line. We picked a route near the center of the wall and found a fixed hex around the fifth pitch. It must be theirs! We placed a two-bolt anchor atop the first pitch and a piton on pitch five (above the hex), but otherwise added no hardware. Despite our best efforts, however, we did not free the route.

This past summer, I recruited Vitaliy Musiyenko to join me for another free attempt on the 1979 route. I told him I had freed all the moves individually and that there was one really good pitch that probably would go at 5.12a. My memory served me well, and we were able to free the route in a push, calling our free version Extraterrestrial Vortex (1,000', 9 pitches, 5.12a).

On our way to the Cyclorama Wall, Vitaliy and I stopped by Langille Peak. Previously, he and Brian Prince had made an attempt to repeat the East Buttress Direct (IV 5.10b, Rowell-Wilson; *see AAJ 1989*), but, as reported in *AAJ 2019*, they were shut down by blank rock five pitches up, and later determined they were likely on new terrain.

Armed with a few bolts this time, Vitaliy and I were able to equip and free the blank section at 5.11. In all, we climbed 18 pitches, encountering one more section of 5.11 and several pitches of 5.10, followed by endless simul-climbing to join the Beckey-Jones Route (*see AAJ 1972*) to the top of Langille's southeastern summit. The rock quality was excellent on the entire route, which we called The Prodigy (3,000', 5.11). 📷

– SHAUN REED

LAKE BASIN, PEAK 12,358', THE FABLE OF HEDWIG

LAST SUMMER, MY friend Tess Smith and I got increasingly involved in route development in the Eastern Sierra, mostly sport climbs. After figuring out that drills should be set to hammer mode and that rocks don't make good hammers, we decided it was time to up our game. I spend an inordinate amount of time hangboarding. Tess spends an inordinate amount of time adventuring in high mountains. With our combined finger strength and expertise in alpine shenanigans, we felt we had the skill set to put up free routes in the Sierra.

We were tipped off to a gorgeous unclimbed wall above Lake Basin, the north face of Peak 12,358', in the remote Cirque Crest region of Kings Canyon. [*Editor's Note: This wall is just southeast of Marion Lake and looker's right (west) of a formation climbed in 2019 by Vitaliy Musiyenko and Brian Prince, which they dubbed Alexandra's Arête. See AAJ 2020.*] In late August, after a strenuous approach consisting of 8,000' of gain, just under 20 miles, and one bear encounter, we found ourselves staring up at 1,000' of untouched granite. Unfortunately, it soon became clear that climbing this route would be an exercise in avoiding death by rockfall.

Pitch two of our line was the crux, with well-protected, discontinuous 5.10+ finger cracks, spiced up by the loose rock. Pitch three was a long dihedral, which ended about 20' below a body-length roof, avoided with a short traverse pitch to the right. Better rock led to the summit of Peak 12,358'. Despite fun climbing and solid protection throughout, omnipresent loose rock warrants an R rating for the route. Luckily, the descent was very mellow—a walk-off down a scree slope climber's right of the summit. We named the route The Fable of Hedwig (1,000', 6 pitches, 5.10+), after my snowy-white chicken Hedwig, a sweet girl who was taken from this life too soon by Fable the dog shortly before our trip began. 🖹 🖻

— TAIMUR AHMAD

TEHIPITE DOME, ONE FOR THE HOMIES

ON JULY 4, Damien Nicodemi and I completed a new route on the upper portion of Tehipite Dome and named it in memory of friends and family lost this past year. Two weeks prior, Rett English, Damien, and I had attempted a different line, but bailed 400' up. Once back at our camp on top of the dome, we spied a beautiful corner about 900' tall on the upper east side, to the right of Astro-Gil (5.11).

Damien and I returned a couple of weeks later and completed a bolted rappel route (two 60m ropes) to the base of our line, which begins on ledges about 1,000' below the summit. (Previous parties climbing this aspect of Tehipite Dome have reported it's preferable to approach by rappel rather than descending the loose, brushy terrain east of the dome.) We then climbed back to the summit, following a single crack system capped by a final run-out slab pitch, completing One for the Homies (1,000', 6 pitches, 5.10c R). 🖹 🖻

— RYAN EVANS

EL COMANDANTE TURRET, THE HONEY BADGER EXPERIENCE

IN JULY, DANIEL Jeffcoach and I hiked over to the Gorge of Despair from Kings Canyon to check out a wall we had seen a few years prior while descending from the Watsi Wall near Tehipite Dome (*see AAJ 2017*). We approached from the Lewis Creek trailhead in Kings Canyon and hiked over Harrington Pass, then descended to approximately 8,200', where we slept near a creek with great views of the striking peaks of the lower gorge. Getting an alpine start the next day, we hiked over a col from the south and into a gully between Cobra and El Comandante turrets.

We dropped to Crystal Creek and started up the huge east face of Comandante Turret, which transitions into a knife-edge northeast ridge as it gains elevation toward the summit. The climb was sustained, demanding, quite long, and of very good quality. As far as we know it was the first route up any of the spires in the Gorge of Despair from the Crystal Creek drainage.

Paired with a long approach after a difficult work week, finishing the route at 2 a.m., and a big hike out with the need to be at work at 6 a.m. the following day, it seemed like the ultimate Honey Badger Experience (2,000', 14 pitches, 5.11c A0). 🖻

— VITALIY MUSIYENKO

BUBBS CREEK WALL, EAST FACE, IKIGAI

THE 2,000' BUBBS Creek Wall has seen a fair amount of recent development on its main southern face, but the east face had yet to see an ascent. During the socially distanced summer of 2020, that's where I set my sights: a massive unclimbed face to explore and try to piece together a line.

Throughout the summer, Dave Meyer, Cassie Reed, Marec Serlin, and I made frequent week-end trips to the wall, carrying loads nearing 70 pounds. Starting in the big chimney that marks the east end, we climbed ground-up with a mixture of free climbing and aid tactics. Slowly but surely, we fixed 1,200' of rope to the top of the headwall. On August 22, we pushed into the unknown. We were ecstatic to find highly featured golden granite reminiscent of nearby Charlotte Dome. We completed the first ascent, then rapped the route.

Our goal was a completely free route, so we still had our work cut out for us. Using modern solo top-rope techniques and our remaining fixed lines, we figured out the best free line. The rock required little cleaning, and the cruxes tended to be short, mostly no harder than 5.11, with one section of around 5.12a (or super-fun 5.11 A0).

Winter was starting to move in, so our trip on October 24 would likely be our last chance to free the route. With the beta still fresh in our minds, we completed an all-free ascent with daylight remaining. To follow the samurai theme of the wall, and because we'd felt we had purpose during these unprecedented times, we named the route Ikigai (1,800', 18 pitches, 5.12a), which means "a reason for being" in Japanese. 📷 🔍

— SHAUN REED

Dave Meyer on pitch 10 of Ikigai, the first route up Bubbs Creek Wall's east face. *Shaun Reed*

PANDA EXPRESS FREE ASCENT: *In 2020, Christian Black and Vitaliy Musiyenko made the first free ascent of Panda Express (2,000', 5.11b) on Bubbs Creek Wall, a route Musiyenko and Daniel Jeffcoach first climbed in 2018. They found a variation to the route's one aid pitch, with overhanging face and varied crack climbing above the bivy ledge. This is now the easiest free route on the main wall.*

MT. BAGO, TOWER OF DELPHINA, DEE-BEES RIB DIRECT

DOING RESEARCH FOR a High Sierra guidebook, I was able to recruit my friend Sean Sullivan with the aim of finding an obscure climb on Mt. Bago (11,870') called Dee-Bees Rib (5.7, Boyd-Hurd; *see AAJ 1975*), on a formation they named the Tower of Delphina. Because Mt. Bago is composed of multiple dome-like fins and pillars, the exact line of this long-lost climb, described as a gem by the first ascensionists, was unclear at first. The AAJ report sounded quite specific, but once below Mt. Bago, on the north side of the Bubbs Creek drainage, many of the "towers" appear to fit the description.

I spied some steep-looking cracks and face features that appeared interesting, to the left of what we decided was likely the original route up the path of least resistance. The following day we found sustained 5.9/10 climbing for close to 1,000' before we reached an obvious gap and found the piton mentioned by the first-ascent party, which they had used to rap into a wide gully below. I clipped the pin for pro and was able to do a huge stem and wild dynamic move instead of the rappel to gain the other side. We continued for about 300' until we could unrope and continue over the top of the tower: Dee-Bees Rib Direct (1,300' climbing distance, 5.10c).

The summit of Mt. Bago was still about an hour of bushwhacking away, so we opted to descend a loose gully on the west side to return to Bubbs Creek. Plenty of loose class 4 and 5 was required, but it still seems like a better option than climbing over Mt. Bago, which would add several miles of cross-country walking to the day.

— VITALIY MUSIYENKO

Milestone Mountain's beautiful east face. *Vitaliy Musiyenko*

GREAT WESTERN DIVIDE, NEW ROUTES

IN JUNE, CHAZ Langelier and I made one of the longest approaches possible in the High Sierra in order to climb a few gems on the Great Western Divide. We approached via the Shepherd Pass Trail, crossing the 12,000' pass and descending to an unnamed lake on the Kern River at around 10,700', where we camped after 22 miles of hiking. It was another three to five miles to the walls we hoped to climb.

First, we climbed a beautiful corner system and steep cracks up the east face of Milestone Mountain (13,641') to reach one of the coolest summit pinnacles in the range—Western Divine (750', 5.10b). After two days attempting an unclimbed wall that remained that way, we managed the first ascent of a steep wall that Doug Robinson had spotted on one of his trans-Sierra ski trips. The southeast face of Peak 13,228' sits directly across from the striking northeast face of Table Mountain. Chaz and I found a clean route littered with splitters and juggy dikes that led directly to the top: Fear Inoculum (800', 5.10c).

The view of Table Mountain from that route encouraged me to repeat the long approach later in the summer with Tad McCrea. We climbed the most striking pillar on the northeast face of Table via Pass the Courvoisier (1,000', 5.10) as well as the north ridge of Thunder Mountain, which we named Thunder Thighs (1,000', 5.7). Unfortunately, both of these routes are aesthetic lines more than good climbs; Thunder Thighs is more of a chossaneering adventure than a technical climb. 🖼

— VITALIY MUSIYENKO

SPRING LAKE WALL, CENTRAL BUTTRESS, NEW ROUTES

SPRING LAKE WALL is a beautiful formation about a four-hour hike from Mineral King. The best approach is over the old Glacier Pass trail. All of the reported activity (*see AAJ 1976, 2016, 2020*) had focused on the main wall, but the two lesser buttresses to the left (east) offer impressive climbing potential. In June, Clayton Helzer and I climbed the first known routes on the central buttress.

Spring Fling (7 pitches, 5.10) takes a line of least resistance starting just left of the prominent overhangs at the base of the wall and aiming just right of the obvious "great roof" feature. Angels and Demons (10 pitches, 5.10+ C1 or 5.11), named after the whiskey Clayton brought along, takes a line through the right side of the base overhangs via a wild hand-to-fist crack, which you can wrestle with, à la Indian Creek's King Cat, or surmount with a single French free move on a large cam. The climbing is varied, and each pitch has a comfortable two-bolt belay.

Both routes can be descended by hiking up and around the south side of the main wall and joining the faint Glacier Pass trail, or by rappelling Angels and Demons with a single 70m rope. 🖼🔍

— DAVE NETTLE

BASIL HAYDEN'S ON THE CENTRAL BUTTRESS: *In August, on a tip from Helzer and Nettle, Townsend Brown and Reuben Shelton added a third route to the central buttress. They set off to the right of Angels and Demons, finding mostly high-quality crack and corner climbing, with a mid-route crux through some small roofs. An "incredible face" crack linked them into Angels and Demons at the top: Basil Hayden's (6 pitches, 5.10+).*

UTAH / ZION NATIONAL PARK

KOLOB CANYONS, TUCUPIT POINT, NORTH FACE, STAR PLANET

NEAR THE END of August, Zion National Park finally lifted the pandemic-related climbing ban, and I was able to revisit Kolob Canyons for the first time since the scenic drive closed for construction in early 2018. I headed straight to a potential line I had photographed before the closures in the center of the north face of Tucupit Point, deep in the North Fork of Taylor Creek.

I knew there were beautiful splitters high up on the wall, but I wasn't sure if the bottom would allow passage without extensive drilling. On closer inspection, I found a hairline seam that ran to the ground, the first of a series of seams that cut through a clean, gently overhanging wall.

The first pitch was 200' and took me six days to complete! I almost wrote it off as too thin. In the beginning, only number 1 Pecker tips would work. I'd get up a few placements, then the beaks would rip and I'd tumble down the hill. This went on for an hour or so until I had some luck and managed to string together a series of beak tips that held. I got a bolt in around the 18' mark.

On day two, I ripped all the beaks down to the first bolt and jammed my thumb. I gave it one more try before bailing—bolt two went in around 30'. Motivated by self-preservation, I would drill a catastrophe bolt every time I approached ground-fall terrain. Aside from these fail-safe bolts, the occasional hook, and a few small cams at around 140', the entire first pitch was beaks. The remaining wall offered vertical to overhanging aid climbing, including seven pendulums, for over 1,000', before it kicked back to just under vertical for the last two pitches.

I recruited Cedar City local Christian Cattell to help finish the route on day 13. Up to this point, I had done everything solo, fixing ropes and returning to the ground each night. The final 400' was less steep and the cracks widened to chimney size. Christian and I were on the summit by sunset. We rappelled the wall, first from a tree and then down the route using fixed anchors. In all, I placed 24 lead bolts and 14 belay bolts.

The wall is approximately 1,300' high, but due to its wandering nature and all the pendulums, it ended up involving over 1,600' of climbing—what a ride! Star Planet (VI 5.11 A3+). 📷

– KARL KVASHAY

KOLOB CANYONS, BEATTY POINT, BIG GAME HUNTER

IN NOVEMBER OF 2019, Lane Mathis, Collin Turbert, and I set out to attempt a new route on Nagunt Mesa in Kolob Canyons. After hiking three fully loaded bags almost three miles over rough terrain, including some fifth class, we found our intended route had already been climbed by an unknown party. So, we hiked back down the canyon and up the other side to the base of the south face of Beatty Point. On that wall, a sun-soaked buttress promised a worthy—or at least warmer—plan B.

After two days of ground-up climbing, we were only a couple of hundred feet off the ground. Pitch three proved to be very difficult and required a handful of lead bolts near the top where the crack vanished. Collin had to return to work, so Sam Stuckey was called in to fill the spot.

After six total days and around 1,100' of climbing, we topped out the route just shy of the rim of the mountain. It felt amazing to reach a high point, but the thought of freeing the route weighed heavy on my mind.

It wasn't until January that Lane, Sam, and I could return to free it all from the ground. The pitch three crux, which had been difficult just to establish, featured all sizes from fingers to chimney and required very strong ringlock and face climbing skills. This 45m pitch went all free at 5.12d, but can be done at 5.10+ A0. At the same length, pitch four is almost entirely a 5.11 stembox/corner that has stellar rock and great gear. Big Game Hunter (1,100', 9 pitches, 5.12d) finishes on a high note with a 55m chimney that is remarkably clean and easy to protect with mostly hand-size pieces. We established two additional pitches to the top, but we found them to be lower quality and dangerous—we'd recommend future parties rappel from the top of pitch seven. 📷 🔍

– DAKOTA WALZ

KOLOB CANYONS, NUGGET MESA, NEW EWE

The west face of Nugget Mesa, a subpeak of Nagunt Mesa. (1) New Ewe (1,450', 11 pitches, 5.11+). (2) New Ewe Direct (5.12- R). (3) Sheehe Buttress (V 5.10 A3, Cosgrove-Dicker, 1999). *Dakota Walz*

ON THE WEST end of Nagunt Mesa is a prominent subpeak known as Nugget Mesa. The origins of this name stem from a 2000 AAJ report by the late Scott Cosgrove, and it may or may not have been a simple misspelling. Regardless, the name fits well. Although Nugget Mesa is dwarfed in comparison to Nagunt, its cliff face starts hundreds of feet lower in the canyon, allowing for nearly as much technical rock climbing with a much shorter approach.

Lane Mathis, Sam Stuckey, Felipe Tapia, and I arrived in early November, planning to spend a full week establishing a route up the huge, triangular west face. Climbing ground-up and onsight, we encountered strenuous offwidths and much unprotected face climbing (that we would later bolt). After two days of this, we were only 40m from the end of the technical climbing. Unfortunately, a rainstorm hit the canyons for the remainder of our trip.

We made three subsequent weekend-warrior trips from the Colorado Front Range in order to finish the route, equip rappels, inspect a direct variation, and tag the summit of Nugget Mesa. On the last trip, with only one day available before an incoming snowstorm, we opted to split the team after pitch four in order to climb both our original line and the direct variation in the same day. Sam and Felipe traversed Forest Ledge to finish on the well-protected New Ewe (1,450', 11 pitches, 5.11+), while Lane and I cast off on the more severe New Ewe Direct (5.12- R). Both lines finish on the beautifully exposed broad arête of pitch eight, with a final face crux a mere body length from the last anchor. From there, we scrambled to the summit (another 550') as a team of four.

According to Cosgrove's 2000 report, he and Kathy Dicker left a register marked by cairns after reaching the summit in 1999 via their route Sheehe Buttress (V 5.10 A3), which is to the right of our lines. Disappointingly, we were unable to locate a register, but were happy to enjoy a sunset on top.

While Sheehe Buttress is the only known route up this face, we did find evidence of other climbers as high as the ledge at the base of pitch seven on New Ewe. A Gatorade bottle so old it was beginning to degrade was found in the dirt, as well as a bleached sling around a pine tree with the initials "TB" written in Sharpie. These artifacts are likely remnants of an undocumented route or attempt up the less technical north side of the mountain. ▤ ◙

— DAKOTA WALZ

SPRING CANYON, ITALIAN COWBOY

IN FEBRUARY, JACOB Dickhausen, Andrew Park, Pasquale Verrastro, and I headed up Spring Canyon, a seldom-visited portion of Zion National Park, east of the Altar of Sacrifice and behind the old Zion History Museum. After hours of bushwhacking through rough terrain and examining options for new free routes, a beautiful southwest-facing wall with an obvious line screamed, "Climb me!"

After a few feet of vegetated rock at the base, the dihedral crack was clean for hundreds of feet. Higher, we repeatedly deployed four- and five-inch cams as the crack headed into a monster chimney ending with a short roof. (*See photo on p.7.*) Above was a comfy belay and the crux of the route: 45m of tips to hands taking us through a short lieback crux and onto an exposed face and arête sequence to the final belay stance. The last pitch begins in an overhanging dihedral protected by two bolts and sporty moves, transitioning onto a dead-vertical panel with a one-inch crack. Italian Cowboy (1,000', 5.12+) is a striking line that stops just short of the top of the wall, due to deteriorating rock and lack of cracks. The route has five protection bolts in seven pitches.

After several days establishing the line, and on the last day before the park was shut down due to COVID-19 restrictions, I freed every pitch while Pasquale supported the ascent. ◙

— ROB PIZEM

NEW ZION-AREA WALL ROUTES

IN THE SPRING, Mike Dunn and Matt Ward climbed two new routes in the Canaan Mountain Wilderness, south of Zion National Park. Resurrection of General John Wayne (10 pitches, V 5.9 A3) is located on the southern end of the sprawling west flank of Canaan Mountain and took four days in late April to complete. The pair spent two nights on the spectacular Hamsa Bivy at the top of pitch six and topped out on the evening of day three.

In early May, the two spent five days establishing another route to the right of Resurrection called Too Much Sex, Too Little Jesus (12 pitches, V 5.10 A4). They fixed to the top of pitch three before establishing an advanced camp below pitch seven. The crux eighth pitch required 16 consecutive beak placements. They summited in the evening of day four, returning to the ground the next day.

In early November, after the park reopened, Dunn and Ward completed a new route on the east face of Angels Landing: Dancin' with the Devil (1,200', 14 pitches, 5.9 A2+). This route climbs the first three pitches of the "unknown 5.10" listed in the Bird guidebook, after which it breaks right and follows cracks, corners, and chimneys up the east face's prominent tower. The eighth pitch through a gaping maw and the tenth pitch, which tops out on the tower, both went at A2+ and required many beaks and small gear in soft rock. The route finishes on a short, previously climbed 5.7 pitch. Every pitch has bomber bolted anchors and a nice belay ledge. ◙

— ANDY ANDERSON, *WITH INFORMATION FROM* STEFFAN GREGORY *AND* MATT WARD

BITTERROOT MOUNTAINS, MYSTERY DOME, WEST FACE AND FIRST FREE ASCENT

The west face of Mystery Dome in the Bitterroot Mountains of Idaho, showing the line of Bitter Fruit (1,650' climbing distance, 10 pitches, 5.11-). The original route, the southwest arête (2012), is near the right skyline. *Benjamin Wollant*

THE IDEA OF a free ascent of Mystery Dome had been lodged in the back of my mind since seeing the trip report from the first and only known technical ascent (*AAJ 2014*). This bold and committing 13-pitch route on the southwest arête, clocking in at 5.10 A3, hardly invited thoughts of a free ascent. Nevertheless, with such an inspiring wall in one's own backyard, my thoughts echoed those of first ascensionist Steve Porcella—what if?

From June 20 to 22, friends Brendan Campbell, Ryan Garnsey, Elissa Taylor, and I made a scouting trip up White Cap Creek Trail from the end of the Magruder Corridor Road. We reached the base of Mystery Dome after a nearly 20-mile approach. Among a trio of potential free lines, a long, curved dihedral on the west face appeared most promising.

I returned to the area from July 20–24 with Ben Holmgren. My father, Doug Wollant, accompanied us and fished. Unfortunately, poor weather permitted only a single attempt that was cut short by rain after just 500' feet of climbing. Despite the bitterness of logging nearly 80 miles hiking up White Cap Creek coming to naught, I decided to roll the dice one final time. I was able to recruit Liam Brown for my final attempt.

We hiked in August 24, and after a rest day we set off on the west face at 7 a.m. on August 26. After reaching the lower-angle base of the main dihedral, we regained the previous high point and set off on new terrain. The dihedral pitches were characterized by long runouts between small, often marginal placements. Other than the crux (pitch six), all pitches were freed ground up, on lead. The crux was first aided to clean the pitch before freeing it. After pitch six, we chose to bypass the last 250' of the dihedral by way of a crack system out left in hopes of moving fast to avoid a storm on the horizon. (The unclimbed top of the dihedral remains an aesthetic potential addition to the line.) We reached the summit 11 hours after tying in. The ascent was entirely clean, with no pins or bolts placed, in respect of the current bolting ban in Bitterroot National Forest.

To my knowledge, ours is the second technical ascent of Mystery Dome, the first ascent of the west face, and the first free ascent of the feature. Our route, Bitter Fruit, covers 1,650' over 10 pitches with difficulties up to 5.11- and several R-rated sections. 📷

– BENJAMIN WOLLANT

SAWTOOTH MOUNTAINS, HORSTMANN PEAK, PATH OF MOST RESISTANCE; PEAK 10,050', WHITE LINE FEVER

IN MAY, Ky Hart and I climbed a probable new route on the north face of Horstmann Peak (10,475'). This huge, striking face can be seen from Stanley. After hiking in, 750' of gradually steepening snow brought us to the face. Temps were warm, and we chose a line up the middle of what we called the Central Pillar, hoping it would be protected from the near-constant avalanches and rockfall on either side.

We climbed the first pitch with ice tools and crampons due to very wet conditions, then switched to rock shoes and enjoyed nine pitches of varied rock climbing. Nearly every pitch had sections of unprotected, loose 5.9 climbing, and there were at least two pitches of 5.10. There were occasional glorious cracks and sometimes even fun climbing! We pulled on gear a few times when the rock was too wet to climb or when a fall would have been too dangerous. At the top of the pillar, we switched back to tools and crampons and climbed an easy mixed pitch to the northwest ridge. Two more pitches of easy snow and rock brought us to the summit. We bivied on top of the fourth pitch (not recommended) and again at the summit (all-time).

Several technical routes have been climbed on Horstmann Peak, but details are sparse. Our route, Path of Most Resistance (1,900', 13 pitches, V 5.10 A1), showed no evidence of being traveled.

Later in the month, Ky and I returned to the Sawtooths and climbed a probable new mixed route on the north face of an unnamed peak (10,050', 44.1402, -114.9996), the easternmost point on the ridge leading east from Thompson Peak (10,751'), the highest summit in the range.

Four pitches of mixed up to M5 brought us to a false summit, where we were shocked to discover a beautiful ice pillar tucked into a gully on the north face. I've been dreaming of finding something like this since the day I swung my first ice tools! Above the wild pillar, more pitches of steep snow and easy rock brought us to the top. We named the route White Line Fever (1,100', 9 pitches, M5 WI6). Peak 10,050' is a spectacular summit that doesn't appear to have any nontechnical routes to the top, though I couldn't find any information on previous climbing activity. 📷

— MATT WARD

[Top] Hortsmann Peak, showing Path of Most Resistance (1,900', 13 pitches, V 5.10 A1). The Northwest Buttress (IV 5.9, Bachman-Young, 1979) follows part of the right skyline. [Bottom] Peak 10,050', a subpeak of Thompson Peak, showing White Line Fever (1,100', 9 pitches, M5 WI6) on the north face. A WI6 ice pillar was discovered above the initial buttress. *Matt Ward (both)*

MONTANA

CABINET MOUNTAINS, A PEAK, CASTOR SALLY

OVER TWO DAYS in September, Alex Marine and I climbed a line up the pillar that forms the lower northeast ridge of the east subsummit of A Peak (8,634') in the Cabinet Mountains Wilderness. We'd been intrigued by recent impressive ice and mixed ascents in the basin (*see AAJ 2019*), by our own summer reconnaissance years earlier, and by a relatively easy approach.

The eastern aspect of A Peak is a complicated collection of radiating ridges, gendarmes, pillars, and faces, with about 2,400' of fifth-class rock leading to the main summit. The rock consists of

A Peak seen from above Granite Lake, with the line of Castor Sally (1,900' climbing distance, 13 pitches, 5.11) shown above. The summit of A Peak is far to the right of the top of the pillar. *Spencer Gray*

bands of quartzite, argillite, and siltite, splotched with lichen in shades of white, pumpkin, and chartreuse. Dan Doody and William Echo were the first to climb a technical line to the main summit, in 1962, and we would be surprised if others haven't traced rock routes up the mountain.

Our route traced a line up the center of the obvious large pillar below the east subsummit. We followed lower-angle entry pitches for about 600' (5.6–5.8), then a 300' chimney-corner system on the left side of a red pillar (5.10+), including a neat keyhole slot that required the leader to take off both rack and pack to squeeze through. Another few pitches of fun corners and faces brought us to 300' of tricky route-finding, with cruxes pulling through overhung arêtes (5.11) to avoid large roofs that capped each corner. Two more pitches of pleasant corners (5.9) penetrated the final roof system to the flat top of the pillar (7,740').

We named our route Castor Sally (1,900' climbing distance, 13 pitches, 5.11). We chose not to attempt the upper ridge to the summit, given a snowstorm forecast for the next day. A dozen different lines could converge at the top of this pillar, and the character of the climbing changes above here, with a series of gendarmes on the upper ridge that are not obvious from the ground.

What stands out about the mountain are dozens of dihedrals on the north and especially south aspects of the various ridges and pillars. Our rappel line down the pillar's south side passed over largely clean rock, with good face holds adjacent to dihedral cracks for protection. That said, any long route is likely to encounter stretches of choss. Roofs are generally too loose to pull through directly, arêtes are often blank or unstable, and sheer faces are climbable but lack cracks even for knifeblades. Choose carefully.

Is the rock on A Peak "A-plus"? No. B-minus? Sure. Pass or fail? Yes. If A Peak were in parts of the Canadian Rockies, would it be a local semi-classic? Fair question.

– SPENCER GRAY

ANACONDA RANGE, PEAK 10,259', NORTH FACE, COWBOY KILLERS

On September 29, in early winter conditions, Matias Francis and I climbed what we believe to be a new route on the north face of Peak 10,259' in the Anaconda-Pintler Wilderness, approached by Maloney Basin. To our knowledge, the only previously recorded ascent of the face was by Dylan Hertz and Matt Klug in fall 2008—they christened it the Beaver Wall (IV 5.9).

We began by soloing up a left-trending snow ramp and roped up at the base of a dihedral/chimney feature. From there we climbed five more pitches, trending generally up and left, and encountered sustained mixed climbing and winter conditions. Once we hit the summit snow slope, we soloed to the ridgeline and then traversed to the summit of Peak 10,259', which lies directly east of Warren Peak. We named the route Cowboy Killers (400m, 5.8 AI2 R M6). 📷

– OWEN SILITCH

BEARTOOTH MOUNTAINS, GLACIER LAKE AREA, EEDICA

ON DECEMBER 11, I left my home in Red Lodge at noon and took my snow machine to just before the Glacier Lake trailhead in the Main Fork of Rock Creek. I was intent on scoping an ice line previously climbed by Aaron Mulkey (Splitsville, 1,100', M6), a prominent weakness in the center of a northeast-facing buttress directly above the road. As I looked through binoculars, I noticed what appeared to be a small drip in a left-facing corner, 300' to the right of the existing route. Having looked at this wall for years and never seen much ice, I decided to explore it. Two hours later, I found myself on top, being blasted by beautiful sunlight and watching the clouds move in and out of the valley below me.

The first half of the route was steeper than it looked from below and featured a mix of dry-tooling and frozen moss, up to 90° in some sections. I then traversed left around a corner and found a 60' ribbon of ice in a chimney. This led to some very exposed mixed climbing and eventually a large ledge. I climbed up and right to what I hoped would be a simple exit, but it proved to be very loose rock with down-sloping ledges, so I traversed again to the left and found a steep chimney that led to the top. I was not roped for any portion of the climb and I regret that. I named the route Eedica (650', AI5 M5), which is the Crow word for "far away".

– JUSTIN WILLIS

BEARTOOTH MOUNTAINS, SILVER RUN PEAK, QUANTUM ENTANGLEMENT

ON OCTOBER 3, Ben Hoiness, Dustin Kisner, and I climbed a long new route on the west face of Silver Run Peak (12,542'), about four miles up the West Fork Trail along Rock Creek. Ben and I had attempted the line four years prior and bailed after finding difficult mixed terrain. Ben returned the following year and found the route to be completely out of shape, with little to no ice.

On this attempt, the three of us found a beautiful ribbon of blue ice reaching to the ground, which we followed for 500' to a series of small hanging daggers. Both Ben and I attempted to climb directly up this steep pitch, but backed off due to difficult climbing and poor gear. Instead, we climbed around the ice on the right, up moderate mixed terrain, to a spacious ledge, from which we climbed a large chimney to reach a snowfield and then the base of the ice headwall. Three wonderful pitches of blue ice up to WI5 led to a low-angle chimney that took us to the plateau on top, which we reached five hours after leaving the ground.

We named the route Quantum Entanglement (2,100', WI5 M4). We walked to the north and found an easy descent gully that led us straight back to the car, 11 hours after leaving. [*Editor's Note: Aaron Mulkey and partners attempted this line twice, retreating due to lack of ice connecting to the upper headwall. In 2016 and 2018, they climbed the two prominent lines to the left; see photo caption below.*] 📷

– JUSTIN WILLIS

The three big ice lines on the west face of Silver Run Peak are (left to right) Light Before Wisdom (WI4 M6, 2018), Last Call (WI4 M6, 2016), and Quantum Entanglement (Hoiness-Kisner-Willis, 2020); the latter moves right and then back left to avoid the thin middle section. All routes are about 2,000'. *Aaron Mulkey*

MT. OWEN, NORTHWEST FACE, RENNY TAKE THE WHEEL

ON JULY 25, Michael Gardner and I set out from the Exum Mountain Guides office to take a look at the northwest face of Mt. Owen (12,928'). We departed around 6 a.m. and briskly hiked up Cascade Canyon, wallowed across the creek, and bushwhacked our way up Valhalla Canyon to the alpine meadow below Mt. Owen and the Grand Teton. Once there, we took some time to establish our intentions on the wall above.

To this point, we simply had a vague notion of clean rock and proud position somewhere up on the west face, based on an encouraging tip from our friend and Teton legend Renny Jackson. We had only decided to head up in this direction at midnight the night before—both of us had the day off from guiding. We gazed upward and traced an independent line up a very prominent, clean-looking golden face to a crack splitting an upper headwall. We took a low traverse to access the start of the line, which began about 1,000' lower and quite a bit left of Serendipity Arête, Mt. Owen's west ridge.

The lower portion of the climb went well and we were constantly able to sniff out weaknesses. When we reached the headwall, a major thunderstorm rolled over the top of the Grand Teton and unleashed its fury as we hung in our harnesses below the crux pitches. During a brief lapse in the storm, we quested up steep and wet climbing. The final two pitches went through vertical to overhanging black rock and into a beautiful golden splitter, ranging from offwidth to fingers. We arrived at the summit in time to catch an incredible sunset through squalls. The climbing was high quality and completed all free, with a single 60m rope and a double rack.

[Top] Michael Hutchins low on Renny Take the Wheel (1,500', 8 pitches, IV 5.11) on the northwest face of Mt. Owen. The route continued up the overhanging rock and golden splitter above. *Michael Gardner* [Bottom] A view of the upper headwall pitches of Renny Take the Wheel on the northwest face of Mt. Owen, taken from the north ridge of the peak. *Vic Zeilman*

We named the route Reilly Take the Wheel (1,500', 8 pitches, IV 5.11) in honor of our friend, who had tipped us to this zone and kept tabs on our whereabouts throughout the day. We descended the West Ledges route back into Valhalla Canyon. After wading through Cascade Creek and making it back onto the trail, we stripped off our wet clothes and walked back to the trailhead in our undies through the dark forest. In total, our round-trip time was around 16 hours. 📷

– MICHAEL HUTCHINS

MT. OWEN, SKI DESCENTS

MT. OWEN (12,928') is the second-highest peak in the Teton Range, but it sees minimal ski mountaineering action due to its relatively remote location in the winter and extremely technical nature. The north aspect—specifically the Northeast Snowfields route—has been among the range's testpieces since it was first skied in 1980. The standard ski route involves a 60m rappel to escape the snowfields. In 2017, Beau Fredlund and I were able to ski a new variation and avoid the use of a rappel on the lower choke by trending skier's right into some rocky terrain—we called this the Freddy-Fab variation. On that descent, we only did one short 10m rappel from the summit block and skied the rest of the East Ridge into the Northeast Snowfields, the most complete descent known to date.

On March 25, 2019, I returned to Owen with Brian Johnson and Brendan O'Neill. We climbed up the Koven Route on the southeast side to roughly 200' below the summit and then skied down the bulk of the upper Northeast Snowfields. We then put our crampons back on and climbed about 500' to the North Ridge at roughly 12,100'. Here, we began our ski descent into the Run Don't Walk Couloir (ca 2,000', WI4 M4). Nearly 50 years after the route's first ascent, it was one of the few remaining couloirs in the range left unattempted by skiers. [Editor's Note: The Run Don't Walk was first climbed in 1972 in difficult summer conditions, requiring a

[Top] Beau Fredlund making turns on the upper east ridge of Mt. Owen during the 2017 descent. [Bottom] Mt. Owen from Cascade Canyon showing the upper portions of two ski descents: (1) East Ridge to Northeast Snowfields via the Freddy-Fab variation (2017) and (2) Run Don't Walk Couloir (2019). To reach the latter, the skiers first descended the Northeast Snowfields, then booted up to the ridge line. *Adam Fabrikant (both)*

pitch of A3. Now done most often earlier in the season as a pure alpine ice route, the climb features two pitches of WI4. See AAJ 1973.] We found it imperative to click into our skis as high on the mountain as possible to make our descent. Without style in the mountains, what do we really have?

The upper couloir provided sustained 50° jump turns in an incredible position, and we were able to ski a few hundred feet more than we thought based on scouting photos. Three 40m rappels got us through the ice pitches, where we were once again rewarded with scenic hop turns in the bowels of Mt. Owen. Another rock band guarded the lower couloir, forcing us to do one more 10m rappel. The final crux was another short rock band where dry skiing techniques allowed us to descend without the use of a rope. The lower couloir was first descended in 2010 and is more of a classic freeride tube feature. After safely negotiating the hazards of the upper mountain, we enjoyed sunlit and carefree powder turns before the 10-plus miles of touring back to the Taggart Lakes trailhead.

Like many first ski descents of this era, this descent was built on the foundation of an ice climb from a previous generation. Making turns down the alpine ice routes of the '70s and '80s has become something of a rite of passage for the modern ski mountaineer.

— ADAM FABRIKANT

GRAND TETON, NORTH BUTTRESS DIRECT

COVID CANCELED OUR foreign expedition plans in 2020, so Justin Bowen lassoed me into one of his dream projects: a new route on the north face of the Grand Teton. A Jackson Hole local, Bowen had been researching the Grand for a number of years and had identified a 2,000' unclimbed line left of Simpleton's Pillar and right of Grand North Couloir.

The north face of the Grand Teton, showing the line of North Buttress Direct (ca 2,000', 14 pitches, 5.10+ R). Justin Bowen and Mark Jenkins climbed this new line on August 16. *Justin Bowen*

On the morning of August 16, after a bivy on the Teton Glacier, we surmounted the bergschrund at the base of the Northeast Couloir. (A friend ran in later that day to collect our bivy gear.) We swapped our approach shoes and crampons for rock shoes, then scrambled about five pitches of fourth- and easy fifth-class rock, diagonaling right to reach the beginning of the North Buttress. We roped up here. The best pitches were in the beginning of the technical climbing: fingers and fists in clean rock, finishing with a protectionless, balls-shrinking crux through a blank section that Justin led with equanimity. These fun pitches were followed by a dozen rope lengths of 5.7 to 5.9 to reach the East Ridge, then some cramponing up sun-cupped snow to the summit.

We topped out at 6:30 p.m., 13 hours after leaving our camp, completing the North Buttress Direct (ca 2,000', 5.10+ R). It was a gorgeous line with a good friend—doesn't get any better than that. (Minus the interminably long stumble in the dark back to the car.) 🔲 🔍

— MARK JENKINS

Aaron Livingston on pitch 10 (5.12) during the team's free ascent of The Optimist on the northeast face of Mt. Hooker. *Drew Smith*

THE OPTIMIST
NEW ROUTE ON MT. HOOKER IS TRIBUTE TO A LOST FRIEND

BY AARON LIVINGSTON

THE PLAN TO do a new route on the northeast face of Mt. Hooker first formed in August 2019. That month, my closest friend, Nolan Smythe, and I hiked out from Hooker, having done the second free ascent of Original Sin (Birdwell-Huey, 2017; *see AAJ 2018*). We realized the potential for quality free climbing through the face's blank sections, and we agreed to return in 2020 to attempt a new line.

Sadly, Nolan would never return to Hooker. On March 6, 2020, he passed away while we were climbing together on El Gigante in Basaseachic Falls National Park in Chihuahua, Mexico. A large chunk of rock came out from under his feet while he was on lead, severing his rope. The world lost an incredible human and the best man I knew.

I was determined to follow through with our vision to put up a new route on one of the finest alpine walls in the country. I rounded up Jackson Marvell as a partner and, since I didn't want to be out on a remote wall again without a third, we called up Drew Smith. On August 5, Nolan's birthday, the three of us hiked into the Wind River Range.

After a day of scouting, we decided that a route on the left side looked promising. There were some obvious cracks, with the only real question marks being a blank shield of granite in the middle of the wall and a large roof a little lower.

Our route, The Optimist, starts on the same right-trending ramp as Cache Pirates (Kimbrough-Mestre, 2019; *see AAJ 2020*), but continues up the ramp where Cache Pirates breaks left. We utilized two anchors on that route's rappel line and added a belay atop our third pitch. The fourth pitch, a feature we dubbed the Razor Roof, met up with the end of the pitch-five traverse on Cache Pirates and shared that belay. We began by climbing Cache Pirates to the top of its fifth pitch and fixing to the ground to make sure the roof would go free, and to clean a truckload of loose

Livingston airs it out on pitch four—the Razor Roof (5.11)—of The Optimist. *Drew Smith*

rock from the third pitch. Above, we continued ground-up, climbing about 15' up the sixth pitch of Cache Pirates before breaking left on independent terrain for good.

The big question mark was the sixth pitch, dubbed the Optimist Slab, which offered incredible stone but few options to hook or aid, and it seemed like we might get shut down there. We didn't want to drill a bolt ladder or use bat-hook holes if it wouldn't go free. Jackson had tried, Drew had tried. Now I was up. I had to harness every bit of the optimism for which Nolan was so well known. I free climbed the 5.12 slab, stopping at stances and equalizing hooks that I could drill from. After several hours on lead, I was at the next belay and the most intimidating obstacle of the route was behind us.

Atop pitch six and out of rope for fixing, we would need to climb to the summit in a push. We all agreed we wanted a direct finish as opposed to the long walk up Der Major Ledge, where many Hooker routes finish. Mostly moderate climbing took us three pitches above Der Major, but another question mark—a steep wall with no obvious crack systems—loomed above and weather was coming in. We made a hasty retreat.

Drew and I took two rest days lounging around camp. Jackson's version of "resting" was to run 16 miles to the trailhead and drive to Lander so he could buy bacon, quesadilla supplies, a new belay device, and fresh rope. Legendary.

On August 13, Drew's birthday, we made a push for the summit. Jackson was able to aid through the steep terrain on pitch 10 that had perplexed us a few days earlier. We added two bolts to this pitch on top-rope after verifying it would go free. Then Drew took us up through the birthday corner and Jackson led the final 5.10 terrain to the summit. Our route was ready for a free attempt.

After another rest day, we came back on August 15 to free the full route in perfect weather. We swapped leads throughout the day. I managed to free every pitch, leading both crux pitches, with preplaced gear on the pitch 10 crux. Jackson and Drew came a few moves short on the full send, but we had a complete free climb.

I miss Nolan with all of my heart. We carried him on the wall with us every day. I used his hammer, Grigri, and his Mini Traxion. Throughout the trip we dug deep to summon his infectious optimism. He had a special way of believing in people, even if they didn't believe in themselves.

The Optimist is the proudest accomplishment of my career. I'm so grateful to Drew and Jackson for being incredible partners, and I'm beyond thankful that we could dedicate a route to Nolan that he would have been psyched to have climbed. 🖼 🔍

SUMMARY: *First ascent of The Optimist , a.k.a. The Nolan Smythe Memorial Route (1,500', 12 pitches, 5.12) on the northeast face of Mt. Hooker in the Wind River Range, Wyoming, by Aaron Livingston, Jackson Marvell, and Drew Smith. The all-free ascent was August 15, 2020.*

SUNDANCE PINNACLE, NORTH FACE, FREE ASCENT

IN JULY I spent 10 days (including hiking, rest days, and resupplies) attempting to rope-solo the first free ascent of the north face of Sundance Pinnacle, just south of the Cirque of the Towers. Four days were spent top-down brushing lichen, working cruxes, and figuring out the small and funky protection before sending the route on lead, rope-solo, from the ground. My route mostly followed a 2012 as-free-as-can-be line by Matt Hartman and Jake Tipton (5.11- C1 PG-13; *AAJ 2013*), with a significant variation on pitch three (5.12-) up a technical, smeary slab corner over small but decent gear.

The pitch five crux (5.12+) is characterized by an overhanging, flaring corner with twin cracks to a body-length horizontal undercling/jam roof, before a no-hands rest and then thin and powerful laybacking. On my send, I was unable to reach a crucial gear placement under the roof and went for it with my last piece back in the corner. Jamming out the roof, I found myself incredibly pumped from the climbing and rope work, and without the energy to set my feet properly, I dynoed for the rest ledge, shrieking like a demon as I caught it and manteled up, my chest pounding nearly hard enough

The north/northeast face of Sundance Pinnacle, showing the line of Oso Scary (6 pitches, III 5.12+), a free version of a 2012 route. *Kevin Heinrich*

to knock me off the six-inch ledge. I felt guilty for not sharing the experience with a friend.

While scrambling down the descent to my mosquito-infested swamp camp, I heard a rock rolling behind me. As I turned to look, a bear's snout shot out of a bush not five feet away. I jumped into the talus below and ran for my life, the bear keeping chase long enough for me to ponder my death. Upon reaching my bear spray in camp, I ripped the safety off while spinning around to face the very brown black bear. Thankfully, before I was forced to discharge the spray, he lost interest and sauntered off, while I tripped on adrenaline. The free line is Oso Scary (6 pitches, III 5.12+).

— KEVIN HEINRICH

CIRQUE OF THE SUN, NEW ROUTES

THE CIRQUE OF the Sun is a small hanging valley south of the Monolith cirque and just north of the Cirque of the Moon. In recent years, several new routes have been done on a large west- and north-facing formation, dubbed Resolute Buttress by the first documented party to climb it, via the route Thunder Child (7 pitches, 5.11; *see AAJ 2014*). In 2018, Jonathan Awerbuch and Jeff Woodward climbed Icarus (950', 9 pitches, 5.11+), a sustained route on what they called "among the best alpine rock we've ever found." They found an old piton on pitch eight, but believe most of the route is new. Awerbuch and Woodward returned in July 2020 to free the complete route.

In 2020, two new routes were climbed on the buttress. In early August, Steph Williams and Drew Lovell completed Campion Cracks (1,400' climbing distance, 10 pitches, 5.10a), which follows an obvious sweeping ramp to the right of Icarus. In September, Andy Constantino and Michael Goodhue climbed Solar Winds (500', 4 pitches, 5.9+) on the buttress' north face, a quarter mile to the left of Icarus. 📷

— ANDY ANDERSON, *WITH INFORMATION FROM MOUNTAIN PROJECT AND STEPH WILLIAMS*

CIRQUE OF THE MOON, SUMAC POINT, VARIOUS ACTIVITY

RELATIVE TO OTHER areas in the Winds, the Cirque of the Moon has seen few climbing parties. We were drawn to the promise of seclusion and an opportunity to attempt the first free ascent of one of the newer routes, Space Ghost (5.10+ C1, Ferro-Hughes, 2016; *see AAJ 2017*).

On July 25, Lane Mathis, Rob Pizem, and I hiked in from Dickinson Park. The next day we climbed Space Ghost, with the follower trundling some leftover loose rock. I aided through the crux, brushing a bit as I went. Rob freed it on the follow at around 5.12-, and we topped out to enjoy a shiver bivy on the rim. The next morning Rob hiked out, leaving us with his extra food.

After a couple of days of rain, Lane and I shifted our focus to the unnamed, low-angle wall looker's left of the Sunset Buttress. We began referring to this as Sumac Point. Our first route, Chicken Talk (1,100', 8 pitches, 5.10+), followed obvious dihedrals up the right side of the wall. Although the first 200' were wet and loose, the rest of the line followed wonderful rock. Most of the day was spent bouncing from corner to corner, laybacking above great protection.

The next route, Forest Creatures (900', 6 pitches, 5.9 R) began about 100 yards up and left of Chicken Talk, aiming for what looked like splitter thin-hand cracks. Unfortunately, they all turned out to be flaring seams; however, the low angle and great rock quality allowed for an awesome 82m pitch of run-out face climbing. Cracks then led to a major ledge just below the summit—we took the best-protected exit and found a rusted fixed nut 40' below the summit. Given the nature of the wall, it's impossible to say how much our line shared with this previous, unknown ascent.

After hiking down to treeline, Lane returned to camp and I went back for a final line on Sumac Point. On the far north end of the west face, I soloed a less than aesthetic line: Bo Mambo (500', 5.9). A grueling 4th-class hike led back to the summit and the final descent of the trip. 📷

— DAKOTA WALZ

MOUNTAIN CRITTERS ON SUMAC POINT: *On August 27, with no knowledge of Mathis and Walz's Forest Creatures route, Dave Nettle and Glen Poulsen climbed a similar line on Sumac Point, which they later named Mountain Critters (6 pitches, 5.9). They too began just left of the large eyebrow feature at the base of the wall, then made several face climbing variations (adding some bolt protection to mitigate runouts) before climbing an independent finish on a long, right-facing flake. Nettle and Poulsen equipped the line with bolted rappel anchors, likely providing the best descent from the top of the wall.* 🔍

Sumac Point, showing (1) Forest Creatures (Mathis-Walz, 5.9 R), (2) Mountain Critters (Nettle-Poulsen, 5.9), and (3) Chicken Talk (5.10+, Mathis-Walz). All routes were climbed in 2020, but evidence of an earlier ascent of the face was found. *Dave Nettle*

Jamey Sellew mid-crux on the 5.12 second pitch. [Inset] The line of Californian Dreamin' (1,000', 5.12 A2+) on Little El Capitan. The original Southeast Face line (1991) is at far right. *Ben Spannuth*

LITTLE EL CAPITAN, SOUTHWEST FACE, CALIFORNIA DREAMIN'

ON AUGUST 3, Jamey Sellew, Ben Spannuth, and I set off from Big Sandy trailhead to take a look at the southwest face of Little El Capitan (12,825'), which appears from Steeple Peak to the west to be one of the biggest, steepest walls in the area. Little El Capitan is a half-mile northwest of Wind River Peak (13,197'), separated by the very dramatic notch referred to in the old version of Joe Kelsey's guide as "the V." Kelsey claimed the formation looks like Yosemite's El Cap, and from the south it kind of does. The approach is about 12 miles from Big Sandy, via Black Joe Lake.

Jamey is a talented 20-year-old competition climber from Georgia, and Ben is one of America's top sport climbers. Neither had much trad climbing experience, but they both had toughness, work ethic, and skill. I was excited to share the experience of climbing a backcountry wall with them, and possibly learn some new tricks myself.

Camped below the east face of Haystack, we noticed an obvious buttress to the right of the remote and rarely climbed East Pillar (IV 5.9). The next day we went ground-up for seven pitches on the buttress, much of it up a clean dihedral: Dihedral in a Haystack (1,200', IV 5.10). After that we moved our camp up to Lake 11,400', immediately below Little El Capitan.

Only one previous ascent had been reported on the formation: the Southeast Face (Alzner-McGown, 1991). The report in AAJ 1992 was a bit ambiguous but mentioned offwidth cracks and a triple-tiered roof below the summit. The most obvious new line to us was a right-angling dihedral that ran up the center of the face. The scale was very hard to determine from the base—we weren't sure if the wall was 500' or 1,500' tall. One thing was certain: Being that close to the biggest peak in the area and on the Continental Divide meant lots of wind and weather.

During our first two days on the wall, the rain came early. We climbed and fixed 500', including difficult aid and free climbing up to 5.12; the harder sections required cleaning, and the going was slow. On the third day the wind blew so hard that as I climbed the rack of big cams was flying above my head, only to come slamming down on me as the gusts abated. On the fourth day, Jamey sent the super-clean 5.12 dihedral of pitch two, and I aided through the final 300' of 5.12+ corner to top out the wall.

Afternoon clouds snuck up on us as we enjoyed the views on top, and soon we watched in horror as lightning struck nearby formations. We boogied down about 150' from the summit, found the most sheltered spot we could, and waited. Lightning struck very nearby, and we all experienced a substantial jolt. When the storm passed and the adrenaline wore off, we made our way back to camp, humbled by Mother Nature yet again.

Our close call was too close for Ben, and he understandably made plans to return to the cragging near Lander. Jamey and I spent two more days working on freeing the route, but the full send escaped us for now. Several sections up high will be in the 5.12+ range and require more cleaning. As it stands, California Dreamin' (1,000', 5.12b A2+) is a beautiful, all-natural line with no fixed protection, a rare gift in a world where sport climbing is finding its way into the mountains. We cleaned every single piece of gear, leaving nothing but chalk and a few blood stains. 🖹 ⊡

— MATT FANNING

COLORADO

SOUTH PLATTE, BIG ROCK CANDY MOUNTAIN, BULLEIT TRAIN

BIG ROCK CANDY Mountain is the largest formation in Colorado's South Platte region, rising more than 1,000' above the South Platte River. Early climbers were drawn to the lower-angle slabs of its west face. In 1979, Pete Gallagher and Pete Williams made the first ascent of Fields of Dreams Growing Wild (5.11+ R)—not the first route up the formation but still a bold testpiece. It wasn't until the early '90s that the steeper north face was climbed. This face isn't as tall, but the rock is considerably more vertical and characterized by cracks and dihedrals. In 1991, Kevin McLaughlin and Glenn Schuler topped out a route on the left side: Shock Treatment (700', 5.12+), named for a lightning encounter when they first started working the route.

I discovered a potential new line up the north face while looking through Jason Haas' South Platte guidebook; the mysterious "Big Aid Route A2" and a technicolor 200' dihedral drew my attention. I drove out there on a solo mission to search the wall. Once back into service, I immediately texted my friend Nick Schlichtman that we had found our next project.

Nick and I established the route ground-up, bolting from stances and hooks, taking roughly eight days over three years. The lower cracks took a lot of gardening but yielded promising climbing. Once we reached the upper slabs, the stone needed little cleaning. The climbing varies with each pitch and requires the leader to be well versed in all techniques. One pitch you are heel hooking right off the anchor and then the next you are dancing up super-technical slab. After a tag-team effort to establish the final pitch, Nick sent this slab crux (proposed 12b/c) third go.

Bulleit Train (700', 8 pitches, 5.12) is named in honor of the fuel source needed to climb the route. Previous evidence of unknown aid climbing attempts were found up to pitch three. After eight pitches, the route joins Rotten Teeth (5.10) and climbs three and half more pitches to the summit. We both feel honored to have added a big new climb in Colorado. 🖹 ⊡

Bulleit Train (8 pitches, 5.12) is shown in red. The route joins Rotten Teeth (yellow, 5.10) to the top. Fields of Dreams Growing Wild takes the 1,000-foot buttress at right. *Wade Morris*

— WADE MORRIS

ROCKY MOUNTAIN NATIONAL PARK, LONGS PEAK, GAMBLER'S FALLACY

THE GAMBLER'S FALLACY is the mistaken belief that a certain outcome is more or less likely to occur, given a previous series of outcomes. For example, if you flip a coin and get four tails in a row, the gambler's fallacy would suggest a greater chance of heads on your fifth flip. In reality, the odds remain 50-50.

And so it went for Bruce Miller and me on our four-year Diamond project, when, day after day, season after season, we expected a different outcome than the usual: getting schooled. Whether by rain, cold, or lightning, cryptic cruxes, altitude or exhaustion from the four-hour "approach" to the summit of Longs Peak, we got the beat-down more often than we made any tangible progress.

Chris Weidner (leading) and Bruce Miller on pitch eight (5.13a) of Gambler's Fallacy. *Jon Glassberg / Louder Than Eleven*

Alas, the chance of failure remained just as likely, even after 50-plus days of effort.

Gambler's Fallacy follows the first three pitches (5.6, 5.9, 10a) of Hearts and Arrows (also shared with Enos Mills Wall), then takes an 11a crack to the base of a huge, shaded, right-facing corner. From the base of this Winter Wall Dihedral (first freed by Jeff Achey and Leonard Coyne in 1980—the hardest Diamond free pitch back then), the next 300 feet are overhanging, with pitches of 11d, 13b, 12b, and 13a. This is now the steepest Diamond free route. A final, vertical pitch follows a razor-thin 12d traverse into a sequential finger crack to the top. It wasn't until three years into it, during the summer of 2019, that we finally deciphered the crux pitches enough to know, at the very least, the route was possible.

I felt ready to redpoint before Bruce did, so on August 9 he supported my effort by belaying and jumaring while I led. Neither of us had led the hardest pitches before, but countless solo toprope attempts had prepared me well. As nervous as I was—concerned that having to repeat any pitch would substantially diminish my chance of sending—I somehow managed a no-falls ascent.

But if the Diamond was the protagonist in our four-year journey, Bruce was the real hero. On August 22 he sent through pitch seven (including pitches of 13b and 12b), which, even at a roadside crag would have been one of his best climbing days ever. The 13a "Roof Pitch" above spit him off three times, but that only seemed to sharpen his determination.

We aided to the top, bivied below Chasm View, hiked to the top of the wall the next morning, and rapped in. Bruce made quick work of the Roof Pitch on August 23, and he sent the 12d final pitch in a couple of tries.

His free ascent over two days, though not ideal, was truly heroic. Did I mention that eight days later he would turn 57 years old? I've seen Bruce dig deep on many occasions, but this route required of him a long-term level of effort and commitment several magnitudes greater than anything else has. I know this because the same is true for me.

In the end, the pitfall of the Gambler's Fallacy is also its upshot: Our dozens of previous failures had zero effect on our eventual chance of success. How about that? 📷 ▶

— CHRIS WEIDNER

THE CUTTING EDGE: *Chris Weidner tells this story in episode 33 of the AAJ's monthly podcast.*

Tommy Caldwell and Alex Honnold's 35-mile traverse included 12 classic technical routes and 17 summits: (1) Mt. Meeker, (2) Longs Peak, (3) Pagoda Peak, (4) Spearhead, (5) Chiefshead, (6) Mt. Alice, (7) Arrowhead, (8) McHenrys Peak, (9) Powell Peak, (10) Taylor Peak, (11) Petit Grepon, (12) The Saber, (13) Sharkstooth, (14) Mt. Otis, (15) Hallett Peak, (16) Flattop Mountain, and (17) Notchtop Mountain. They finished at Bear Lake.

THE CDUL TRAVERSE
A MASSIVE LINKUP IN ROCKY MOUNTAIN NATIONAL PARK

BY ALEX HONNOLD

LAST SUMMER TOMMY Caldwell invited me to Colorado to attempt an enormous linkup along the Continental Divide. We'd each been locked down in our respective homes all season—he in Estes Park and me in Las Vegas—and joining up for a big climbing adventure seemed like a welcome change of pace. My wife, Sanni, and I drove out in our van and spent the month of July living in the Caldwells' driveway, podded up with them and a few of their local friends.

Tommy's vision was to traverse much of Rocky Mountain National Park, climbing as many classic routes as possible, while summiting all the major peaks. A big source of inspiration was that much of the traverse was visible from his back deck.

We prepared by climbing almost all of the various sections, which helped me to acclimatize, as the traverse is almost entirely between 11,000' and 14,000'. On our first forays I was noticeably slower and more winded than Tommy, who'd recently run up and down Longs Peak in under three hours. There were a several big question marks, like how to get over to Mt. Alice and back [*the 13,310' peak is well south of the main ridgeline in the Park*], or how to negotiate the terrain around the Petit Grepon, Sharkstooth, and the Saber, each of which is a free-standing spire usually rappelled with two ropes. Or even simple things, like whether to summit Pagoda, which is a cool summit but wasn't really on the way.

Two weeks after I arrived, we'd finished all of our basic route-finding. There were some sections we hadn't climbed—we'd just improvise on the go. We got a good forecast for July 17 and 18. Our friends Adam Stack and Maury Birdwell planned to meet us at various places with food and supplies, allowing us to climb with minimal weight. We used a 6mm static line (an Edelrid cord with some dynamic properties, which Tommy swore was OK for a lead fall—I never weighted it) and took a bare-bones rack. We each had ultralight harnesses and carried everything in small running backpacks. We were also in running shorts, which would come back to bite us later.

We got a normal alpine start and cruised up the Flying Buttress (5.9) on Mt. Meeker, then traversed over to Broadway and the Casual Route (5.10a) on the Diamond. We hiked over the summit of Longs (14,259') and along the ridge to Pagoda, backtracked a little to access a gully, and descended to the base of Spearhead. Next up was the Barb (5.10), then across the top to the base of Chiefshead. We hesitated there because clouds were building and it looked like it might storm. The next route was Birds of Fire (5.11a slab), one of the longer and harder routes of the day. Thankfully it didn't rain more than a few drops. We traversed the summit plateau to Mt. Alice, the most far-flung peak on the traverse, where we got lucky with snow conditions in a couloir and slid to the base, then climbed back up the Central Ramp (5.8) and crossed back to the main ridge.

Arrowhead was next, and that's where things went a little sideways. We had planned to meet another friend at the base who'd have our pants, jackets, and headlamps for the long night of climbing to come. Unfortunately, he got sick and bailed. We managed to top out Arrowplane (5.11a) right as it got dark, then clawed our way to the top of McHenrys and through the notch to Powell, using our iPhone lights to help with route-finding. Needless to say, down-soloing 5.6 in the dark, at 13,000', with a cold wind and only running shorts and light raincoats, was character-building. Thankfully, Adam Stack had backtracked along the Divide and showed up near Powell with snacks and real headlamps, which greatly improved our speed and morale.

We traversed over Taylor Peak and dropped into a feature we'd dubbed the Sending Hole, an airy perch tucked above the west face of the Sharkstooth, where we scarfed all the food that Adam had brought us (including a still-warm burrito from Chipotle—what a mensch!) and prepared for a long night. This is where Tommy's name for the traverse (the Continental Divide Ultimate Linkup, or CDUL, pronounced "cuddle") came into play—Adam had brought us a light sleeping bag liner, so Tommy and I squeezed our legs together and huddled for warmth. Sadly, we just got colder and colder and ultimately had to start climbing again.

We pioneered a new descent to the Petit Gepon and simuled the South Face (5.8) in our tennies, desperately trying to maintain warmth. We then rappelled into the notch by the Saber and managed to find our way right onto the start of the Southwest Corner (5.10c, but pretty hard!). Tommy led the whole route in a single pitch, a heroic effort in the cold and dark. After a romp up the Northeast Ridge of the Sharkstooth (5.6), we rappelled the west face via a rap line that Tommy had previously pioneered and met Adam again. The sun had come up on top of Sharkstooth, and we were now about 26 hours into our outing. The rest of the traverse seemed to move in slow motion, even though it was now technically much easier. It took us several hours to reach the base of Hallett Peak, with Tommy stopping to vomit a few times.

Near the base of Hallett, Maury met us with fresh cookies, breathing new life into our weary bodies. We simuled the Culp-Bossier (nails hard 5.8+) in a pitch, with Maury hiking around to meet us on top, and then carried on over Flattop to Notchtop, where we down-soloed the Spiral Route (5.4) to reach the Direct Southwest Ridge (5.9), our final route. Both of our wives and some friends met us at the lake below Notchtop, and we spent some time eating and relaxing before trudging down the trail to the car.

The CDUL: It's an incredible outing and an efficient way to climb most of the classic rock routes in the Park in a push. But it sure is tough. All in all, the traverse took us about 36 hours and entailed, by our best estimate, about 20,000' of vertical and 35 miles of hiking over 17 peaks. The numbers belie the difficulty of the terrain and the overall strain. And since GPS struggles with vertical travel, our numbers varied wildly anyway, which serves as a good reminder that some things are better left unquantified. [*Editor's Note: Honnold and Caldwell described this traverse in depth in episode 37 of the Cutting Edge podcast.*]

ALASKA

THE STRAW HAT RIDGE
THE FIRST ASCENT OF 'MT. GANNON' IN DENALI NATIONAL PARK

BY MARK WESTMAN

On May 6, Paul Roderick, Charlie Sassara, and I made what we believe to be the first ascent of Peak 8,900'+, a pyramidal mountain in the Dall Glacier area, approximately 5.5 miles to the southwest of Mt. Russell in Denali National Park. Paul is the longtime glacier pilot and owner of Talkeetna Air Taxi and is also my brother-in-law. Paul had been looking at this peak for years, and we had loose plans to try it someday. COVID-19 had shuttered his business and altered my own plans for the spring, so we finally had some free time to check it out. Being family, Paul and I were in the same COVID pod and well quarantined. Charlie is a longtime Alaskan local (and climbing legend), and he needed no air travel or subsequent quarantine to join us.

After landing on a small arm of the Dall Glacier at 6,000', about a mile east of the mountain, we skied for an hour up through an easy icefall, passing crevasses on the right. We reached the steeper face below the col north of the mountain, put on crampons, and climbed several hundred feet of snow and ice (up to 45°) to reach the col. From here we ascended the north ridge. Some large crevasses and ice formations midway up the ridge were easily passed to the left, which involved simul-climbing some ice up to 50°. After a short knife-edge section, the angle eased. Paul and I reached the summit only three hours after leaving the landing site, as Charlie waited

[Left] A rare view of Mt. Dall, the prominent summit on the left, and the Kichatna Mountains (at back), looking southwest from the summit of Peak 8,900' ("Mt. Gannon") in the Dall Glacier area. Most of the peaks in the Dall area have never been climbed. Unfortunately, both the rock and the weather in this area of the Alaska Range are typically poor. [Above] The east face of Peak 8,900', named Mt. Gannon by the first ascensionists. The team skied through a gentle icefall (off-picture to the right) to reach steep slopes below the col to the north (right) of the summit. From the col, they followed the north ridge to the top. *Mark Westman (both)*

some distance below. With clear skies in all directions, the view to the southwest encompassed nearby Mt. Dall and the Kichatnas, standing out among a sea of unnamed and unknown mountains. (Mt. Dall likely has been climbed only once, back in 1970, and most other peaks in the area remain unclimbed.) To the northwest, the lakes and rivers of the tundra shimmered below us.

We downclimbed the ridge, making two short rappels off V-threads (leaving no slings behind), then endured classic survival skiing through the now-shaded icefall, the snow surface a frozen sun crust overlaying mashed potato snow. We reached the plane five hours after starting up the mountain. After a quick hot drink and snack, Paul fired up the airplane and we returned to Talkeetna, following a scenic, twisting course past Russell and Foraker in beautiful evening light.

We have informally dubbed the peak Mt. Gannon, after our longtime friend Ted Gannon, who passed away at age 84 in 2019. Ted was an eccentric and influential character in our lives. He joined the Peace Corps in 1963 and spent a significant part of his life living in remote villages in Nepal, becoming fluent in Nepali and deeply connected to their culture. An avid climber himself—he had summited Denali and climbed extensively in Washington's North Cascades—Ted in his later years was a fixture at Talkeetna Air Taxi. He often could be found helping out around the airport, eating cinnamon rolls at the Roadhouse, or talking to anyone who would listen about eastern philosophy, relationships, ending violence, and the inner workings of the human mind, always wearing his characteristic pastel-colored sweats and a large straw hat.

We're calling the north ridge of "Mt. Gannon" the Straw Hat Ridge. Ted would have enjoyed both the climb and the conversation. We'll miss you, Ted. 📷

Jay Rowe leading a clean golden dihedral on Mocha Direct (1,000', 5.9) on Mocha Spire. *Dan Barton*

COFFEE GLACIER, NEW ROUTES

ON JUNE 6, Dan Barton and I landed on the northwest fork of the Coffee Glacier, and over the course of a week established new routes on both Coffee and Mocha spires. I originally came across these spires in 1993 during a ski tour from the lower Coffee Glacier after a failed attempt on Broken Tooth. My subsequent first ascents of the spires by their south faces, in 2008 and 2009, both were done after additional unsuccessful attempts on Broken Tooth.

After setting up camp, Dan and I skied 45 minutes to Coffee Spire. Under a cloudless, calm sky, we climbed six pitches of well-protected cracks to the right of the 2008 line, following a golden ramp-corner system capped by a large roof. At pitch four, we were able to exit the corner and then climb a black face crack; this pitch involved pulling on gear in a few spots, but would probably go free at 5.11. From the top of the face, our climb joined the 2008 route for six more pitches to the summit, with snow climbing, 4th-class scrambling, and a summit pitch of loose 5.8. To descend, we made 10 rappels down the 2008 route, installing new webbing at all the stations. We named the route Cappuccino Corners (2,000', 12 pitches, 5.10 A1).

Back at camp, we enjoyed two sunny days of rest, continually entertained by avalanches that emptied the massive summit dish of Broken Tooth, pouring its contents down the 3,000' south face. We then turned our attention to Coffee Spire's smaller neighbor. During the first ascent of Mocha Spire in 2009, Peter Haeussler and I had peered over the summit edge into a large right-facing corner—this corner was to be our new objective.

Dan and I started with the first pitch of the 2009 route, then continued up the right-hand of two corners: This pitch had some of the nicest rock I have seen in the Alaska Range, and had us both grinning ear to ear. Two moderate pitches on the original route led to a belay below a large right-facing corner. From here, three new pitches of varied crack and face climbing led to the summit: Mocha Direct (1,000', 7 pitches, 5.9). At the top we joked about the perfect weather, only to get soaked on our last rappel by a rogue rainstorm. 📄📷

— JAY ROWE

NENANA MOUNTAIN, SOUTHEAST BUTTRESS, BROWN PANTS

TOWARD THE END of a long summer of perpetually attempting to align busy schedules, weather, and transportation, on August 8, Jonathan Koenig, Tristan O'Donoghue, and I flew with Temsco Helicopters to what's known as the Hotel Glacier, south of Nenana Mountain (7,881'), near the western tip of the Hayes Range. The north side of this valley is home to some impressive walls.

On our first morning of climbing, we began up a nice corner on Nenana's south face; Jed

Brown and Kevin Wright had cragged on this line 16 years prior but were rained off. Glacial recession had graciously provided an additional 10m of climbing beneath where Jed started up the rock. Before long we were on pitch four, far above the previous high point. Lured by perfect hands above the belay, Jonathan started up a 50m splitter, which slowly got wider until he whipped off a strenuous section of number 4s. Lacking large cams to push higher, we bailed.

Taking in the expansive southern aspect of Nenana Mountain. The south buttress (1) starts in the center, and the southeast buttress (2), climbed by Brown Pants (2020), is partially visible at far right. *Jonathan Koenig*

After a day of rain, we attempted the route again in a light mist. The third pitch (5.11) had gone without a hitch on our first attempt, but this time wet rock ejected me from the corner, pulling two pieces and landing on the rope without a scratch. Jonathan, on the other hand, took the brunt of my fall on his chest. Again, we bailed. Pursuing redemption, we established Consolation Crack (5.10b), a stellar two-pitch hand crack on the southwest aspect of Nenana.

The next day brought more rain but also brought our friends Tait Chandler, Andy Sterns, and Grant Wilson into the valley; they had come to repeat the only previously established route on the peak, the South Buttress (1,500', IV 5.8; *see AAJ 2005*), a plumb line up the center of the south face, just to the west of the route we had been attempting.

Waking the next morning to perfect weather, we started our third attempt. We managed to find high-quality variations to the third and fourth pitches that had stifled us previously, and after that, easier terrain allowed quick passage. We simul-climbed and soloed the last 400' to the top of a pinnacle we labeled the southeast buttress: Brown Pants (1,100', IV 5.11a). We did not continue to the summit of Nenana as it would have required multiple rappels and a loose 4th-class scramble.

We spent our final morning sunbathing and watching our friends complete the South Buttress on their second attempt. Our trip was partially funded by an AAC Mountaineering Fellowship Grant. 🖸

PEAK 9,630', DEWILDE STYLE; MT. MOFFIT, LONGING FOR LIGHT

ON A RECONNAISSANCE flight into the Hayes Range in early September, Ben Lieber and I previewed a handful of promising objectives. Less than 48 hours later, we were making the seven-mile approach from a dry landing strip near the tongue of the Gillam Glacier up to a dry lake near the southeast face of Peak 9,630'. [*Editor's Note: This peak lies about four miles north-northwest of Mt.*

The southeast face of Peak 9,630' showing the line of DeWilde Style (700m, AI4+). The first ascensionists descended from the ridgeline without going to the summit (left) due to unstable snow. *Alex Hansen*

Alex Hansen on Longing for Light (800m, AI5 R) on the northeast shoulder of Mt. Moffit (13,020'). The 2,300-meter north face of Moffit and the upper Entropy Wall (Brown-Haley, 2006) are in the background. *Austin Schmitz*

Deborah (12,339')]. During the autumn season, a heavily cracked glacier and highly featured moraine system make landing in this area extremely difficult. Instead of carrying heavy rucksacks for the entire approach, we opted to push three bags out the side of the plane near where we intended to place our advanced camp.

On September 14, the morning after arriving at our camp, we set off toward the 700m southeast face. A beautiful, snaking couloir split the face and was seemingly choked with alpine ice. Moderate terrain led to two distinct crux sections up to AI4+. The ice conditions were sufficient for climbing, but left something to be desired for placing protection. Each section of ice was broken up by long snow ramps that we encountered in good condition. We simul-climbed the entire route, but if pitched out we estimate that it would take 12 pitches.

Our route ended at the summit ridge, forgoing the avalanche-prone traverse west to the true summit (9,630'). Long stretches of corniced ridge would be encountered on this traverse. We opted to descend our route via a combination of rappelling and downclimbing. We named our route DeWilde Style (700m, AI4+) after our good friend and life-mentor Ray DeWilde.

A few weeks later, Ben and I flew back into the Hayes Range, along with Austin Schmitz, this time to the north side of Mt. Moffit (13,020'). The landing strip for this part of the mountain sits 10 miles to the north at the toe of the Trident Glacier. Again, we opted to drop bags from the plane to conserve energy on the approach.

On October 13, we climbed a new route on Moffit's northeast shoulder, after a first attempt two days prior. The climb consisted of moderate snow gullies interlaced with engaging alpine ice and steeper snow climbing near the ridge crest, with a handful of five-star pitches. We simul-climbed a good portion of the route, belaying the crux sections. The route climbs roughly 800m from the valley floor and ends at approximately 8,400' on the northeast ridge. [*Editor's Note: This route lies on a rocky shoulder to the left of the huge north face of Moffit, home to the Entropy Wall (Brown-Haley, 2006) and the Miller-Teale (1989).*] Seventeen rappels back to the base lasted deep into the cold autumn night. The late-season temperatures and the strenuous approach from the landing strip created a bit of difficulty, but overall the autumn presented an incredible time to be in these mountains. We named our route Longing for Light (800m, AI5 R) after not seeing the sun or feeling its warmth for nearly a week.

An extended thank you is in order to our talented pilot and fourth team member, Jesse Cummings. Without his knowledge of the terrain and ability to confidently fly into the mouths of these giants, we'd have had limited chance of success. 📷

— ALEX HANSEN

COAST MOUNTAINS / BOUNDARY RANGES

STIKINE ICE CAP, MT. BURKETT, COYOTE CALLS, AND OTHER ASCENTS

ON SEPTEMBER 11, Simon Frez-Albrecht and I flew into the Witches Cauldron below the Stikine Icecap. A day and a half of carrying backbreaking loads up 4,000' through the Witches Cauldron icefall had us at the base of the Devils Thumb. We climbed the classic east ridge (Beckey-Craig-Schmidtke, 1946) in a 12-hour round trip from camp.

With the Devils Thumb complete only a couple of days into the trip, we began searching for new lines. Across from our camp was an unnamed symmetrical pyramid (7,600'), and the morning after summiting Devils Thumb, Simon and I trekked across the glacier to its north face. We climbed steep snow and névé to 85° to a short section of moderate mixed climbing, finally depositing us on the west ridge. There we unroped and blitzed to the summit. This peak has been climbed before via its east ridge by Dieter Klose (and probably others), as it's within close proximity to base camp for Devils Thumb. The line we climbed was likely a first ascent.

A high-pressure system was forecasted for another week—almost unheard of in these mountains. Simon and I shouldered packs and marched into the heart of the Stikine Icefield toward Mt. Burkett (9,730'), another fabled mountain with very few ascents. We crossed into British Columbia on a perfect crust, moving efficiently, but soon reached another sinister icefall. Simon and I rappelled through icy blocks, listening to seracs topple and ice snap. A stressful day brought us through the icefall with our lives intact, and we made camp along a lateral moraine across from Mt. Burkett.

The Golden Gully (5.8, Bearzi-Klose, 1980), a couloir on Burkett's southwest face, was on the itinerary, but the glacial access to this classic line has disintegrated into a dangerous, exfoliating rock band with hanging seracs looming above. We shifted

[Top] This wasn't in the brochure.... Moving to a new camp below Mt. Burkett with huge packs. [Middle] Mt. Burkett (center left) from the south, with the southeast face falling to the right. The 2020 route crossed over the east ridge to finish on the far side. Burkett Needle is the pointy summit to the left. [Bottom] Traversing toward the summit of Burkett along the upper northeast face. *August Franzen (three photos)* attention to the southeast face, identifying several distinct couloirs braiding up to the east ridge.

The following morning, we navigated another icefall by headlamp, traversing onto a hanging glacier and arriving at the base of the first distinct couloir as the sun rose. We tied in and simul-climbed perfect snow and névé to 80°. At each fork in the couloir systems, we headed left to stay on the face and avoid the ridge. At a choke point we found 80° water ice and solid granite that went at 5.7. We gained a prominent notch on the ridge and wrapped around to the northeast face. Sustained steep snow, moderate mixed climbing, and sparse rock protection continued for another 1,500' to the rarely trodden summit.

We named the route in loving memory of Kalley Rittman, my girlfriend who had recently died in an ice climbing accident on the Valdez Glacier: Coyote Calls (5,700' climbing distance, IV 5.7 and steep snow). [*Editor's Note: The southeast face of Burkett was climbed directly in 1994 by Dan Cauthorn and Greg Collum (see AAJ 1995). The peak's first ascent in 1965 was by the east ridge (described as the southeast ridge in AAJ 1966), and the 2020 team likely climbed some of the same terrain on the upper northeast face.*] 🔘

— AUGUST FRANZEN

MENDENHALL GLACIER, SUICIDE BASIN, NEW ROUTES

BETWEEN 2012 AND 2020, I teamed up with several partners, including the late Ryan Johnson, to complete three long ice routes on the committing Suicide Wall, comprising the eastern wall of the Suicide Basin, a tributary of the lower Mendenhall Glacier. Utilizing foot, ski, and helicopter access, we were able to make the most of limited weather windows to climb Bathtime with Toaster (400m, WI5), Path of the Fallen (330m, WI5), and Infinite Jester (350m, WI6 M6+).

Ryan Johnson at base camp below the Suicide Wall in 2018, two months before his passing. (1) Path of the Fallen (330m, WI5, 2018); (2) Infinite Jester (350m, WI6 M6+, 2020); (3) Bathtime with Toaster (400m, WI5, 2012). *Samuel Johnson*

Alaska is entering its third generation of ice and mixed development, with motivated locals slowly working out access, strategy, and conditions to complete large, high-quality objectives. The Suicide Wall is one such location, with the complexity of backcountry access presenting a major homefield advantage.

Bathtime with Toaster was completed in 2012 by myself, Tim Banfield, and the winter climbing visionary Ryan Johnson, following Ryan's first ascent of Tide Line (420m, WI6) in Tracy Arm, southeast of Juneau, with Tommy Lanagan and Jason Nelson. Path of the Fallen, completed with Johnson in January 2018 and named in homage to fallen climbers Scott Adamson, Kyle Dempster, Hayden Kennedy, and Inge Perkins, is accessed by a sprint under the Suicide icefall, followed by a moderate free solo to a snowfield and four excellent pitches of thin and/or steep water ice. It was Ryan's second-to-last first ascent prior to his death in the Mendenhall Towers in March 2018.

Finally, in March 2020, following a backyard warmup making the second ascent of my route Blood Moon (240m, WI4 M7) and the first ascent of Varcolaci (240m, WI4+ M6+ R), both near Seward, Ryan Sims and I returned to the Suicide Basin to climb Infinite Jester (named in honor of Johnson), which takes the wall's line of strength through thin ice and rime to access the final pitch: a steep pillar and mixed roof that finishes with a mantel over a classic broken-pillar eyebrow to access the top of the wall. In my mind, this was the last major independent route on the wall. There are smaller independent routes (still large by continental USA standards) and variations to be completed by a motivated party. ▣

– SAMUEL JOHNSON

SHARK'S TOOTH, SOUTH RIB

ON SEPTEMBER 5, Evan Hartung, Mike Miller, Ben Still, and I helicoptered to the base of the Shark's Tooth, an appealing peak north of Juneau that Matt Callahan and I had climbed for its first ascent in 2018 (see AAJ 2019). While Mike and Ben did the second ascent of the southeast ridge, Evan and I climbed the south rib, a steep, obvious line that arced from the base to the summit.

After about 100' of scrambling, we began up heavily lichened 5.7 cracks, but as the buttress steepened the cracks became cleaner, and after six glorious 60m pitches of mostly 5.9, with some 5.10 moves, we crested the top of the rib and walked a short distance to the top. We descended the southeast ridge and were back in camp that evening. The next day, Mike and Ben flew out while Evan and I hiked the 10 miles of trail-less terrain back to the road.

– DYLAN MILLER

The Shark's Tooth, north of Juneau. Matt Callahan and Dylan Miller made the first ascent by the right skyline in 2018. Miller returned in 2020 with Evan Hartung to climb the South Rib (5.10), the aesthetic sun/shade line. *Dylan Miller*

JUNEAU ICEFIELD, MENDENHALL TOWERS SPEED ASCENTS

ON JULY 4, Gabe Hayden and I made a speed ascent on the Mendenhall Towers classic Solva Buttress (1,250', 5.8). We started at the West Glacier trailhead, north of Juneau, and took off for the 15-mile glacier hike to the base of the towers. We climbed the route in one long simul pitch, hung out on top and enjoyed the view for an hour, then made the return trek home, arriving back at the trailhead 16 hours and 57 minutes after departing. In all, we covered around 30 miles and 7,000' of gain, and dubbed the journey the Mendenhall Marathon.

A few weeks later, Gabe Wechter and I repeated the hike into the towers, this time climbing the Mountaineer's Route (1,400', 5.7) on Main Tower in 18 hours and 34 minutes round-trip. These are the fastest known car-to-car times for these mountains.

– DYLAN MILLER

CANADA

Hélias Millerioux and Thomas Delfino on the east ridge of Mt. Logan. The 3,500-meter descent took two and a half days and is the most continuous known ski descent of the east ridge. *Alex Marchesseau*

UNE GRANDE AVENTURE
A 48-DAY TOUR OF MT. LOGAN, WITH A SKI DESCENT OF THE EAST RIDGE

BY DOUGALD MACDONALD, *WITH INFO FROM ALEXANDRE MARCHESSEAU AND HÉLIAS MILLERIOUX, FRANCE*

FROM APRIL 29 to June 10, 2019, a team of French climbers and skiers traveled more than 650km by foot, skis, and boat through the wilderness of Wrangell–St. Elias and Kluane national parks, scribing a great semicircle around Mt. Logan (5,959m), Canada's highest peak, from east to west. In the middle of this journey, they climbed the east ridge of Logan and descended nearly all of the route on skis, snowboard, and monoski.

Thomas Delfino, Grégory Douillard, Alexandre Marchesseau, and Hélias Millerioux were dropped off by a fishing boat from the village of Yakutat, Alaska, on the beach by the outlet from Malaspina Lake. At the start of the trip, they had 80kg (176lbs) of gear and food per person. With no snow on the ground after a dry winter, the quartet began an arduous trek up a "moraine from hell," making three 5km round-trips per day for three days to haul all their gear to the glacier. Once on the ice, they were able to pull sleds, but they endured five days of rain as they skied across the Malaspina Glacier. Eventually they entered the Yukon Territory, crossed the vast icefield of the Seward Glacier, and reached the upper Hubbard Glacier. They established base camp for the east ridge of Logan after 16 days—about twice the time they had planned.

An old back injury had flared up for Douillard, and he remained in camp while Delfino, Marchesseau, and Millerioux started up the east ridge of Logan, which rises more than 3,500m from the glacier to the summit. The trio spent six and a half days climbing the ridge, two of them stuck in snow caves because of bad weather. They summited the main peak in poor visibility on

Crossing the vast Seward Glacier to Mt. Logan, with the east ridge on the right skyline. *Thomas Delfino*

May 23 and began their descent: Delfino on a snowboard, Marchesseau on a monoski, and Millerioux on skis. During the two-and-a-half-day descent, they stopped riding only for two sections of knife-edged ridge and for a rappel at the bottom of a gully off the south side of the east ridge. They were back in base camp in the morning of May 25.

The next day, as the team began its trek out of the mountains, Douillard realized he could not continue. He was evacuated by ski plane. The rest of the team continued down to the west, along the Hubbard and Logan glaciers, first on snow, then bare ice, and eventually 30km of moraine, carrying packs of more than 35kg (77lbs) each. On June 2 they reached the Chitina River and the airstrip at Hubert's Landing. Here, a small plane dropped off a resupply of food and a cataraft and picked up Delfino to return home, as Marchesseau and Millerioux prepared for the final leg of the journey: a 300km raft trip down the Chitina and Copper rivers, through the Chugach Mountains, to reach the Gulf of Alaska.

"We totally understood Thomas' decision," Marchesseau wrote in an email. "We were already on our 40th day in the trip, and after crossing the moraines of the Logan, Walsh, and Chitina glaciers, we were far from the human condition, looking like shit with dust on it."

Marchesseau and Millerioux relaxed and recovered along the flat-water stretches of their river run, enjoying fresh vegetables and long days in the sun. Eight days after leaving Hubert's Landing, on June 10, the two beached the raft for the final time at Flag Point, near Cordova, Alaska, 48 days after starting their epic journey.

The expedition, Marchesseau said, had been Millerioux's idea, motivated by "the irrepressible desire to 'get lost' in order to better find yourself internally." The trip "was not led by anyone, there was no hierarchy in our group of friends, because it is a combination of four personalities with their own experiences and practices, who found in this project a common goal."

Day 38: Marchesseau and Delfino rest their 35kg loads amid endless moraine. *Hélias Millerioux*

EARLIER SKIING ON LOGAN'S EAST RIDGE: *In May 2004, Stephen Canning, Sparky Steeves (both from Canada), and Duncan Maisels (U.K.) climbed the east ridge of Mt. Logan to the east peak (5,898m). During their ascent, as they ferried loads, the trio skied most of the ridge in stages. They were able to ski the upper of two knife-edge ridge crests that form cruxes of the route; Canning and Maisels skied the upper knife-edge on belay and then solo, and Steeves was lowered for the first 60m and then continued on skis. Tragically, after summiting the east peak, Canning was killed in a fall at around 5,500m. — Information from Sparky Steeves, Canada*

(1) Stokeman Pillar (250m, 5.11a) and (2) south face of Stoltmann Tower (350m, 5.11a). The first route up Stoltmann Tower, the Lillarete (Brayshaw-Buda, 1999), generally followed the left skyline over both towers. *Paul McSorley*

MT. ATHELSTAN, NEW ROUTES

IF YOU'VE EVER felt deep reverence in a stand of coastal old growth, you are a friend of Randy Stoltmann. An avid mountaineer and conservationist, Randy was the first to document British Columbia's dwindling ancient forests, creating what became the BC Big Tree Registry. At 32 he was killed in a crevasse fall. In 1999, Drew Brayshaw and Mike Buda climbed and christened a beautiful granite tower on the flanks of Mt. Athelstan (2,800m) in honor of this inspirational human.

With the smacking irony of logging road access, Paul Cordy, Tony Richardson, and I left the truck on August 9 at a clear-cut west of the mountain and surfed up a steep stand of old-growth fir and cedar to reach a scenic bivy beneath Stoltmann Tower. Our itinerary was a compelling golden pillar on the south (right) side of the Gnomon Tower, a prominent subsummit that Brayshaw and Buda had traversed on their climb. [*Their full route is called Lillarete (ca 2,500', 5.8 and snow.*] After avoiding a couple of slabby pitches by scrambling up the Sinnes Couloir, we climbed 200m of very featured but sometimes unprotectable stone. (We placed three bolts on the route, two on the lead and one at a belay.) The line culminated in a long dihedral that led to a subpeak just below Gnomon Tower, and then easier scrambling brought us to the top.

We rappelled to the north, beefing up the existing stations with a few bolts, and hit the toe of the rockfall-strewn glacier that descends from the Athelstan plateau. Good vibes with an amped crew made the route naming easy: The Stokeman Pillar (250m, 5.11a). Previous routes on the Gnomon Tower are well to the left of our line.

After spying several appealing options on the south face of the main tower, I returned with Josh Lavigne in October. We opted for a day trip from a ditch bivy in the clear-cut and blasted quickly up the easier lower wall of the south face, just right of the Stokeman Pillar. Once we gained the upper headwall, we were greeted with spectacular face and crack climbing up golden stone. Again, we added just a few bolts to protect some crackless sections and several more to rap the wall: the south face of Stoltmann Tower (350m, 5.11a). 📷

– PAUL MCSORLEY, *CANADA*

ELDRED VALLEY, AMON RÛDH, THE SLABS OF NIM

IN 2018, WILL Stanhope and I took a trip into the Eldred Valley in search of unclimbed stone and solace after the loss of a friend. After a multi-hour hike through one of the last stands of old-growth forest in this once pristine valley, we settled in for a sleepless, insect-molested bivy below the Amon Rûdh wall. Morning found us scrambling up to the left of The Mormegil (11 pitches, 5.10 C1, Cawley-Guilbault-Hodgson-Richards) on the left side of the wall. We got started with a mix of trickery and bolts and made it a few pitches before running out of bolts and motivation on the baking south-facing wall.

In late July 2020, I returned to the area to attend a grassroots climbers' festival. With Kieran Brownie, Max Fisher, and Emilie Pellerin, along with a crew of friendly locals (who helped us porter gear to the wall!), we cruised through the now-threatened stand of ancient fir and cedar trees back to a more comfortable bivy, complete with mosquito netting. The next morning, our foursome quickly regained the 2018 high point. A total of eight long pitches plus some scrambling brought us to the summit of the formation, where we skinny-dipped in a natural infinity pool carved into the granite. We called our route The Slabs of Nim (385m, 5.11a). 📷

– PAUL MCSORLEY, *CANADA*

SQUAMISH, TANTALUS WALL, CALL OF THE SIRENS: A PLAY IN THREE ACTS, WITH A SURPRISE ENDING

I MET MARC-ANDRÉ Leclerc around a campfire in the Yosemite high country. Sitting across from him in the thin, crisp evening air, I could feel his energy. He'd just come from a solo winter-climbing trip to Patagonia, and his eyes burned with the fresh experiences. He and Brette Harrington were beautiful to watch together—so clearly in love, sitting quietly and holding hands, looking into the fire. Here was a unique man, living with a vision and intensity that most only dream about.

A year and a half later, in January 2017, Bronwyn Hodgins and I packed our lives into our van in Ottawa and drove 4,000km across the Canadian winter-scape to Squamish. Granite pilgrims from the East. Marc visited for a couple of days and enthusiastically showed us his favorite slabs

in the Smoke Bluffs. He kindly suggested I try one of his projects, and I ended up making the FA a few weeks later: The Magician (5.13d), by far the hardest slab climb I had done. It was then that I fell in love with this unpopular style. I think what drew both Marc and me to hard slab climbing is the mental focus required. To succeed you have to be present with the uncertainty of an unknown outcome—keep weighting the feet and hoping, even though you know they will slip.

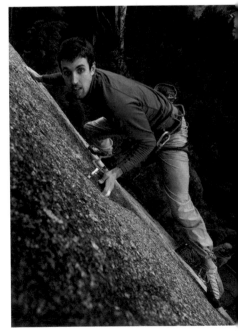

That winter, Marc mentioned his project, a five-pitch free version of the aid route Wrist Twister on Stawamus Chief's Tantalus Wall. The first three pitches would be independent free pitches, and the final two shared with his and Luke Neufeld's ground-up slab testpiece Labyrinth (5.12c). The way he spoke made it clear it was a step above any other slab climbing he'd done, and therefore, probably very hard indeed! Tellingly, despite talking about the route a lot, Marc never mentioned exactly how far he had progressed on it.

Marc's purity of vision and obvious, infectious love for what he was doing meant even small interactions with him left a lasting impression. His death in March 2018 saddened me deeply. I decided to try to finish his Wrist Twister project as a lasting testament to his unique vision.

Jacob Cook eyeing the first ascent—or was it the second?—of pitch two (5.13d) on Call of the Sirens. *Bradford McArthur*

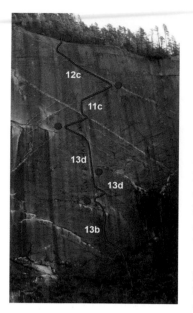

Call of the Sirens (5 pitches, 5.13d) on the Tantalus Wall. *Jacob Cook*

I first went to try it with two of Marc's good friends— Kieran Brownie and Will Stanhope—a couple of months after Marc's death. Kieran knew that Marc had sent the first pitch, but didn't think he'd done any of the others. We were dismayed at how hard it felt; there were multiple sections that were deeply ambitious and potentially impossible. Defeated, we sat on the portaledge and poured the first sip of our beers over the side in honor of our friend.

Had I scoped this line myself, I would have written it off and moved on to other things. But the fact that Marc had bolted it and clearly believed it was climbable kept me coming back to beat my head against the wall. That fall of 2018, I managed to send the first pitch. It was sustained 5.13b slab with many low-percentage moves, but still by far the easiest of the three pitches Marc had left behind.

A year later and another fall slab season: I was deep in project mode on the third pitch, a long, beautiful 5.12 splitter into a desperate V10-ish slab boulder, with a final 5.12 dike-walk. Eventually I extended the bolt after the crux with a long sling so I could clip earlier. I'm sure Marc would have done this pitch the bold way, and the challenge is still there for someone else. I was burning through belayers at almost the same rate as the edges on my climbing shoes, but I succeeded in getting Mathew Waring up there one last time.

Part of the mystery of hard slabs is that they feel borderline impossible and then feel easy when they go. I danced the dance and arrived at the anchor, leaving only the deeply questionable second pitch standing in the way of a completely free route. Or so I thought.

I decided to commit the fall 2020 season to the second pitch. Unfortunately, it seemed on the impossible side of the spectrum. Many extremely low-percentage moves stacked one on top of the other. A *Tomb Raider*–style tunnel of lasers. The pitch required absolute precision and a wonderful combination of focus, try-hard, and acceptance. Even if I tracked perfectly, to send would still require a subtle mixture of conditions, sticky rubber, and luck. I had to be right there. Floating. On the foothold, light, moving. Not thinking about the moment before or the one after.

On Sunday, October 4, I fell on the last hard move. On Tuesday I fell on the move *after* the last hard move, rocking onto the first good foothold after a long string of time-bomb smears. I couldn't believe it! I very rarely get frustrated with climbing, but this time I let out a real yell. On Wednesday afternoon I looked at the forecast in dismay. Weather was rolling in that night. Rain forever. Frantic texts ensued. Duncan O'Regan rallied to support a last-ditch headlamp attempt that same night.

We got up there and it all felt pretty hopeless: very humid, my arms were tired, my skin was a train wreck. But I gave it one more go and hit that magical flow state that makes climbing so special. I lowered down to the portaledge quietly, hardly daring to believe it had happened. We sat on the ledge and watched the mist roll into Squamish below us. Within 20 minutes we were in a thick cloud of moisture. I had sent the pitch in the last possible moments before the storm.

My suggested grades for the first three pitches of Marc-André's Call of the Sirens project were 13b, 14a, and 13c/d. I believed Marc had made the first free ascent of pitches one, four, and five and I of pitches two and three.

Several months later, though, I was talking about the route with Brette, Marc's longtime partner. After looking through some of her old Instagram messages, it became clear that Marc had not only sent the first pitch but also freed pitch two, in November 2015. Not only that, he had graded that pitch 5.13c, believing the *third* pitch to be the 5.14 crux. Marc had managed to send and downgrade my project from the grave! It was funny, and I'm sure he'd find it funny, too.

Nothing about this new information changes my experience on the route. I feel lucky to have shared the subtle dance required to climb pitch two with Marc. This also goes to show how much guesswork goes into grading hard slabs. Based on our two independent data points, I'll revise my grade suggestions to 5.13d for both pitches two and three.

I had sent one pitch a year on this route for three consecutive years. A continuous ascent of Call of the Sirens would be a true masterpiece of slab wizardry. I'm thrilled to leave a challenge for future slab pilgrims to try, and maybe improve on my style.

– JACOB COOK, *CANADA*

NORTH SHORE MOUNTAINS, GOAT MOUNTAIN, SUGAR MUMMY

ON FEBRUARY 9, Matteo Agnoloni, Tom Schindfessel, and Antony Wood completed the first known winter ascent of the north face of Goat Mountain via Sugar Mummy (600m, AI4 R). Goat Mountain (1,401m) is just north of the Grouse Mountain ski resort. The north face had been attempted once prior in winter, to my knowledge, by Steve Harng and Jordan Peters (date unknown). There was at least one ascent via an obscure summer rock route in the late 1950s.

We approached by hiking up the Grouse Grind trail, along Goat Ridge, and dropping in to Hanes Valley. With Antony and Tom being Squamish locals, the idea of not using a gondola to access the route was a bit foreign, but they were still able to get a cappuccino from a ski resort coffee shop after slogging it up the Grouse Grind.

We reached the base of the route after four hours and climbed nine rope-stretching pitches to top out the face. The cruxes were on the second, fourth, and seventh pitches, involving difficulties up to AI4 and 90° snow. As the previous party to attempt this face found, it largely consisted of vertical sn'ice. Future parties should expect large runouts and non-ACMG-certified belays. 📷

– MATTEO ANGOLONI, *CANADA*

VANCOUVER ISLAND, SUTTON PEAK, NEW WINTER ROUTES

DURING A SPELL of excellent climbing conditions in December, Ryan Van Horne and I completed routes on three separate days on Sutton Peak (1,874m) on Vancouver Island. The first was Blackbird Ragging (350m, AI3) on the far right side of the east face. Liam Gilchrist joined us on the next two windows, when we found excellent névé in gully and chimney features and climbed Sutton's Seasonal Ale (350m, AI4+), to the right of East Rake (Van Horne–Piché, 2015), and then Talisman (350m, AI5), taking a direct line up the left side of the face. Sutton's Seasonal Ale has the crux during the first pitch and is quite run-out on thin ice. Talisman is a classic in the making, with spectacular, techy, run-out climbing, great belays, beautiful steep ice with good pro, and some snow slogging to give a well-rounded island alpine experience.

Also in December, Van Horne and Marie-Lou Piché put up line called Twas the Night Before Xmas (350m, AI 3+/4) at the north end of the face, following a cool gully feature into the easy upper section of Blackbird Ragging. 📷

– MAX FISHER, *CANADA*

MT. MACDONALD, THE LITTLE FACE, WATER OF LIFE

IN AUGUST 2019, Tony McLane and I ventured out to one of Canada's greatest roadside attractions: The Little Face of Mt. Macdonald. The goal was to climb an entirely free route through the meat of this north-facing wall right above the Trans-Canada Highway, linking as much clean, steep, dry terrain as possible. By early afternoon on our second day, our plans had been foiled by a blank slab. We tried an adjacent corner system, but it was soaking wet. We decided to bail. On the hike out, we spotted an encouraging line closer to the center of the face. It seemed that a rising traverse led into the upper part of the wall's original climb, the Waterman Route.

In 1974, cousins John and Dane Waterman came from the eastern United States to western Canada on an epic road trip. In July, they made the first ascent of the 600m Little Face. "The steep route took four days and three bivouacs, two in the rain and one without water," John Waterman wrote for the AAJ, his description of the impressive ascent not exceeding a paragraph. "We used many pitons, with difficulties up to A3 (including one "waterfall" pitch) and F8."

Various guidebooks have placed the Waterman Route more or less in the center of the face. Will Stanhope has twice attempted to free the climb (once with Andrew Boyd, once with Kiff Alocer). He didn't get far either time, nor did they find any sign of previous passage. The lower route also is soaking wet, even after long dry spells. Even dry, it would be much more difficult than the start of Tony and Jason Ammerlaan's 2016 route Position of Comfort (*AAJ 2017*).

Tony and I met up again to try the Waterman Route in September 2020. We packed a double rack, hammer, pins, 14 slings, and a 60m rope and tag line. We planned for two nights out, bringing two ultralight sleeping bags and a double siltarp to share. We also packed a power drill and eight bolts, reasoning that if we needed any bolts to link crack systems or to bail, a hammer drill would be a good idea.

We approached the wall in late afternoon on September 21 with a good forecast for two days, and slept just below the treeline. That night, rain sprinkled the tarp consistently, but when we woke at 5 a.m., the sky was clear. With relief, we brewed a couple of strong coffees before setting off.

Tony won the first lead block in a rock-paper-scissors game. The apparent start of the Waterman Route was again soaking wet, so Tony started on Position of Comfort and efficiently dispatched the first four pitches. I led three more corner and chimney pitches of Tony and Jason's route, and then ventured left into unclimbed terrain, finding a nice rising handrail traverse that led to a small ledge.

Next up was a big arching undercling feature, which Tony led: slabby feet with a crack for hands and gear. The crack was at times stuffed with loose flakes, which Tony tiptoed around and I trundled while seconding. Manteling onto a thin rail, his last gear well below him in the overlap, Tony yelled, "Drill!" I clipped the drill to the tagline and then watched as he expertly placed a bolt from a precarious stance. He followed the bolt with a couple of body lengths of run-out 5.10d terrain, finally finding a good crack and then a ledge. It might have been the most impressive onsight lead I have ever seen. Above here, we thought we'd join the Waterman route, but we saw no signs of it.

Tony started the next pitch with another bolt and a tricky slab downclimb/traverse, and when I followed I had to lower out from the bolt to avoid a terrible fall if I blew the downclimb. I then led up a steep and mostly solid left-facing corner. When Tony arrived at the belay, I cheerfully suggested that we spend the night there. With 11 lengthy pitches and the steepest parts of the wall below us, we happily refueled and nodded off to sleep, figuring we had it in the bag.

That night rain pattered steadily on our tarp. We were only mildly concerned, because of the good forecast, but at dawn the rain had intensified and a thick fog had moved in, obscuring the mountain above us. We sat and brewed coffee under the tarp, munched on a few hundred calories each, and discussed options. We were 400m or so up, the hardest climbing was likely behind us, and we still had a good margin of safety. So, without further talk, Tony started up the next pitch.

Nothing wanted to go on the plumb line that day, and we were still free climbing, so we followed zigzagging weaknesses; a few were dead-ends, and we had to downclimb. The day went by quickly. It was pouring rain, and we were soaked. The wet, friction-less quartzite felt dicey even on moderate slab moves. Finally, after ten shorter pitches above the bivy, we reached the west ridge.

We didn't feel like the summit scramble

Tony McLane leading the crux pitch—a techy undercling traverse—of Water of Life (600m, 5.10d R), before the weather deteriorated. *Niall Hamill*

would add any value to the line, so we headed down the ridge to the top of Position of Comfort and began to rappel the face around sunset. On the third rappel, our rope got badly stuck, and the tagline suffered a core shot. On the following rappel, Tony ended up over a huge roof in space and discovered the lead rope was horribly core shot. After he jugged back up, we chopped our rope down to 50m. A couple of rappels later, another core shot. Again, we shortened our rope, forcing us to build intermediate anchors between Tony and Jason's fixed stations. For the last two rappels, we fixed our pathetically mangled ropes as single strands to reach the ground. Finally we took off our harnesses. Slashing rain pounded our tarp as we sat underneath, rehydrating with hot soup and coffee before the steep hike down to the road.

Just below a waterfall in the descent gully, I noticed small rocks whizzing overhead. The sound of tumbling blocks reached our ears only milliseconds before they crashed over us. Tony dove for cover in the bushes. I was in the guts of the gully and had to duck under a tiny bulge in a turtle position. It felt like we were in the jaws of the mountain, dodging its gnashing teeth. Needless to say, we bushwhacked the rest of the way down to avoid the gully.

Crossing back over Connaught Creek, now swollen with rain, Tony slipped on a jagged tree snag and tore his pants nearly clean off, from crotch to ankle. I couldn't stop laughing for the sight of us, totally spent, tufts of insulation poking out of our coats, and soaked, as we bushwhacked toward the harsh glare of the highway lights and into our cars for warmth, snacks, and a shared moment of reflection on this outing. It was the water of life, and our cups were overflowing. 📷

— NIALL HAMILL, *CANADA*

EDITOR'S NOTE: *Hamill and McLane climbed about 200m of Position of Comfort before adding 180m of terrain to link into what they believed to be the line of the Waterman Route; they then climbed another 220m to the top. All pitches were led free. "Whether we were ever on the Waterman I'm still not sure," Hamill said. "We were looking for signs that they had been there, but we didn't see anything. If the Watermans did go straight up the middle of the face, that certainly would have been impressive."*

The west face ski descent on Mt. Macdonald. The skiers continued down and left for a total descent of 1,600 meters. The rocky Little Face (see previous page) is partly visible in left center. *Lee Lau*

MT. MACDONALD, WEST FACE, SKI DESCENT

THE TRANS-CANADA HIGHWAY passes directly underneath Mt. Macdonald (2,883m), just east of Rogers Pass, and my neck is always cranked from looking up as I drive past, hitting the rumble strips as my truck and mind swerve off the beaten path. I can't recall a time I haven't been in total awe of this area.

My first-ever ski mountaineering experience was in Rogers Pass, in 2008, with Andrew McNab. We toured up an area called NRC, the impressive lines on the west shoulder of Mt. Macdonald, then up and down Avalanche Peak (2,861m), then back around to climb up the south shoulder of Mt. Macdonald. We finished the day by skiing right underneath Macdonald's west face. Tired and oblivious, I kept my head down and linked turns to the valley. I doubt I would have noticed the west face as a potential ski line at that point in my career.

I was 26, and it had been about a year since I left the Canadian alpine ski team. Although I had skied my whole life, something about that day opened my eyes. It was my first year in the TRU (Thompson Rivers University) Adventure Guide program, and I was hungry to become an ACMG ski guide. As my mountain skills evolved, from skiing around red and blue gates to learning about snow crystals and rope handling, so did my vision for new lines. Much of my time was spent skiing around Rogers Pass, where it's hard to ignore Mt. Macdonald—it's prominent from all over Glacier National Park.

Winters rolled around. Intrigued and curious, I started flirting with the idea of attempting the west face. Could it be skied? What conditions would be favorable? What style? Partners? Gear? Year after year, I would study the mountain and take photos from different positions on the pass. Each season, that line always seemed to escape from reality.

On February 20, at about 5:30 p.m., I texted Andrew McNab about plans for the following day. Retired from ski mountaineering racing, he has become an established ACMG ski guide and good friend. I had just finished three days of guiding in the pass, and I finally felt like conditions were lined up. He responded quickly: "Sure, that could be fun. Bring some ropes."

A large cliff band midway down the west face splits this line into two skiing pitches. It was hard to judge the relief, but we knew it would likely involve multiple rappels. We decided on two 70-meter 7.7mm half ropes, a rack of nuts, pins, and one axe each. I picked up Andrew at 6:30 the next morning. It was the fourth day of high pressure, and there were tracks all over Rogers Pass.

We drafted up a track that took us to the col below NRC. Here, we transitioned to downhill skiing, took a few good turns, and traversed over to the bottom of Macdonald's south face (a route that has been skied from the summit before). We managed to skin up the lower face before it choked up and forced us into climbing. An easy boot pack and short sections of rock scrambles led to the top, where we harnessed up and transitioned to ski mode.

Skiing right off the summit and rolling into the unknown was pretty exciting: A small section of rocky ski steps led us into the snow-covered guts of the line, steepening to around 45° for 200m. Approaching the first rappel, we took calculated turns to a good stance and found a fridge-size rock horn to sling for an anchor, then confidently rappelled into the unknown. At this point, we were only going down. After a second rappel, we reached a shelf above the steepest part of the cliff, where we quested a bit and found a solid nut and pin anchor. Directing the rope off the fall line, we were able to rappel all the way onto the next snow slope.

At this point, we coiled the ropes and dropped into great skiing on a beautifully slanted ramp. Taking it to the valley bottom with few stops, we arrived at the creek crossing for high fives and quick texts to friends, telling them we were safe. Our descent had been around 1,600m. Much like that first day in Rogers Pass with Andrew, I felt fully satisfied and dreaming of what's next. ◙

— CHRISTINA "LUSTI" LUSTENBERGER, *CANADA*

BRITISH COLUMBIA / PURCELL MOUNTAINS – BUGABOOS

NORTH HOWSER TOWER, WEST FACE, VOODOO CHILE

ON AUGUST 3, the day before Alik Berg and I climbed All Along the Watchtower (900m, 5.12-) on North Howser Tower, we spent some time scoping the west face. Traditionally, to reach the start of all routes on the west face, you have to do several abseils. However, Alik had spotted a line a few years earlier that began on the ridge where these abseils start. Not only would the new line avoid the committing rappels to the very bottom of the face, it would be about 400m shorter as a result. The splitters on golden granite high on the buttress seemed to be worth a look.

Less than a week after hiking out of the Bugaboos, on Saturday, August 15, at 5 p.m., I phoned Alik from Hope, B.C., two hours east of Vancouver. There was another weather window on the way, and I had a bit of free time. We decided that if I packed and left in an hour, I could do most of the eight-hour drive that night, meet Alik and walk in the next day, and climb on the last day of the good weather.

Tired from the previous night's drive, we needed a lot of rest breaks during the six-hour walk to East Creek in blistering heat. We packed our bags and set alarms for 5 a.m. on the 17th, wishing we could take a rest day. Fortunately, the cracks we were aiming for turned out to be mega. Our line is the rightmost on North Howser's west face, and the buttress we climbed has no other

routes. We did 11 pitches, with the 5.11+ crux on the top headwall. In total, it took 19 hours (East Creek to East Creek), but that included a few bits of time-consuming route-finding.

Our route, Voodoo Chile (500m, 5.11+) led directly to North Howser's summit. With a few points of aid, it would go at 5.10, making it a great option for climbers who want to climb North Howser Tower but don't quite feel up to the longer routes. The next day, as the weather began to turn, I packed up camp while Alik, who had lost at rock-paper-scissors, went back to get the axes and crampons we had left at the base of our route. ▤◙🔍

— UISDEAN HAWTHORN, *SCOTLAND*

Voodoo Chile (500m, 5.11+) on the right edge of North Howser's west face. *Uisdean Hawthorn*

CANADIAN ROCKIES

The Berg-Roberts route on the east face of Mt. Forbes. *John Scurlock*

MT. FORBES, EAST FACE

"Hey Q! Time to do this!" Alik Berg was still in his sleeping bag, propped up against the wheel of his Pontiac Vibe, stove roaring and coffee in hand. It was October 1 and Alik and I were on the gravel of the Saskatchewan River Crossing parking lot in Banff National Park. We were riding the tail end of a huge system of good weather. It was a warm window, but we hoped that Mt. Forbes (3,612m) was high enough that the ice hadn't fallen apart. I took the coffee Alik handed me and swallowed my reservations about the 27km approach to a face that might well be out of condition.

We made our way southwest toward Glacier Lake and on through the river flats before turning south toward the Mons Glacier, interrupting a grizzly feasting on the last wildflowers of the season. At the tongue of the Mons Glacier, we wrapped back east toward the glacier below the north face of Mt. Forbes. We pitched our tent on a rock outcrop above the glacier's tarn. Our objective, the unclimbed east face, was still out of sight.

Alik had climbed a new route on Mt. Outram (2,461m) with Maarten van Haeren on October 1 the previous year, and they had seen various possibilities on the east face of Forbes. We knew it was warmer this year, but as we fell asleep with our sleeping bags wide open, we kept our fingers crossed for decent ice conditions.

The next morning, we crunched up the north glacier, over the northeast shoulder, and down to the base of the east face, gaining around 800m and losing around 200m in the process. Moon-shadows danced on the ice as we worked our way up the glacier. The east face was already running with water, and the rising force of the sun would only make this worse. We traversed the wall in search of climbable ice and eventually found an easy snow ramp that took us to an ice gully tucked out of the sun. We couldn't see where it went, but we hoped it would get us high enough to find usable ice.

We never really found that ice, but it didn't matter. The climbing was technical throughout but never overly difficult (700m, M4 WI3), and we climbed the route in short simul pitches between sheltered spots. The conditions were perfect in every way aside from the temperature. I'll always carry a memory of Alik tearing through the steep, unfrozen summit shale, wearing gloves for excavation and a T-shirt for comfort in the baking sun.

We descended the northwest side of the mountain to our camp as the sun sank behind the Columbia Icefield. In the morning, blowing sleet pushed us back to the road. 📄📷

— QUENTIN LINDFIELD ROBERTS, *CANADA*

CANADIAN ROCKIES ANNUAL HIGHLIGHTS

There is a renaissance in new route activity in the Canadian Rockies, with a wide cast of characters establishing routes in all climbing genres. Three of the most interesting alpine ascents from 2020 are reported elsewhere in this edition: a new route up the Emperor Face of Yexyexéscen (Mt. Robson), see page 34; the east face of Mt. Forbes (above), and, most audacious of all, Brette Harrington and Tony McLane's perilous 5.11 X route up Neptuak's sheer northeast face (see page 113).

In the Bow Valley, with various partners, Alik Berg continued a spree of new routes up obvious rock faces: the northeast buttress of Miner's Peak (250m, 5.10b); The Georgetown Wall on the third buttress of Mt. Rundle (450m, 5.10a); Plantaris Pillar on Noseeum Mountain (250m, 5.10, plus 350m of scrambling); and the east spur of Panorama Ridge's south peak (300m, 5.9). Truly inspiring was a two-day ascent of iconic Mt. Rundle with Kevin Rohn on August 12–13. The Perseid Ridge (1,000m, 5.10+) ripples above the Bow Valley and climbs all three tiers of the eighth buttress of Rundle. Berg also climbed Corner Story (450m, 5.11-) with Dave Peabody, ascending the west face of Mt. Robertson's south tower and continuing to the main summit.

Other climbers were not idle in the summer. Peabody and Angela Tse climbed the West Face, Right Corner of Elpoca Tower (200m, 5.9) in the Elbow Lake area. On August 5, Maarten van Haeren and Christian Schlumpf snagged the obvious Siksika Buttress of Crowfoot Mountain (600m, 5.9), which seems destined to become a classic.

Around Jasper, Francois Laplante and Sam Wall climbed Gut Feeling (335m, 5.10) on Roche Miette, far to the left of the route they had intended to climb, New Orleans is Sinking. In the Slate Range, the prolific Rob Schnell added a moderate finish to the left of the north ridge on Mt. Lychnis with Dr. Mark Heard (an orthopedic surgeon to whom half the valley owes thanks.) And in the Pedley Pass area near Windermere, Steve Tersmette and Matt Honeyman added A Firm Specimen (375m, 5.8) on Mt. Aeneas, following an obvious crack that splits the lower east face. This and earlier routes will be in Tersmette's new guidebook *East Kootenay Rock*.

Many locals wait for Rockies choss to freeze together before venturing onto new ground—once a good weather window hits in the fall, it is game on. At the same time as the Robson and Forbes routes mentioned above were done, Dylan Cunningham and the Rockies legend Jim Elzinga added The Anna Smith Memorial (11 pitches, M5 AI3) to Cirrus Mountain, sharing a few pitches at the top of the northwest buttress with Elzinga's original 1983 route up the face.

[Top] **Kevin Rohn on Perseid Ridge (1,000m, 5.10+), Mt. Rundle.** [Bottom] **Maarten van Haeren on the Plantaris Pillar, Noseeum Mountain.** *Alik Berg (both)*

By the end of October, the mixed and ice action was in full gear, but first we'll mention a few ice ascents from the previous season. In February 2020, Sarah Hueniken completed her dream of linking the three big routes in the Hydrophobia basin of the North Ghost area, amounting to one of the most impressive days of climbing ever seen in the range. Hueniken led every pitch of Cryophobia (6 pitches, M8 WI5+), Nophobia (5 pitches, M10-, WI3), and Hydrophobia (4 pitches, WI5+), though she wisely decided not to top out on Hydrophobia after an ice dam broke at the top of the climb. In early 2021, in a safer venue, she climbed every route in the Haffner Upper Cave in a day.

In the Waiparous Valley, between Caroline and Marion falls, Seth Keena, Maia Schumacher, and Raphael Slawinski put up Little Fluffy Clouds (155m, WI4 M7). Over three days, they climbed five pitches, several of them consisting of dry-tooling with a midway blob of ice, and topping out on a dagger. In late winter, Jon Jugenheimer and Dave Rone established six new multi-pitch routes in the Icefall Brook area. Dropped off by helicopter before the North American outbreak of COVID-19, they had a surreal return to civilization.

First ascents at multi-pitch mixed venues come in waves, depending on which seasons and locations form the most ice. In the fall of 2020, the Storm Headwall was surely the hot spot. Sebastian Taborszky and partners nabbed four new lines. Niall Hamill and Patrick Maguire climbed Fancy Feast (130m, WI6 M4), an all-icy version of his route from last year called The Sphynx. Takeshi Tani and Toshiyuki Yamada climbed a bold smear clearly visible to all from the usual approach to the headwall: Ichinen (130m, 3 pitches, WI5 R M4).

At the end of October, Berg, along with Cunningham and Peter Hoang, attempted a very striking ice line (410m, WI4 M5+) on Goat Mountain, just left of Mt. Yamnuska. Berg backed off after encountering running water just a few body lengths from the top and therefore insists it not be counted as an FA. Less exacting in their conventions, Cunningham, Rohn, and John Price climbed a gully on the east face of Boom Mountain to half height and named it Red Beard (420m, WI5 M5). In previous years, they climbed two more of the main gullies on this major face without continuing to the summit—these lines undoubtedly do await complete ascents.

At the start of official winter, images emerged from Katana (245m, WI6+ X, by Stas Beskin, Cunningham, and Taborszky), clearly demonstrating the mastery of the medium by Beskin, a frequent visitor to the range, who led the crux pillar. On an east face above Margaret Lake, next to Hector Lake, the pure ice line of Katana featured two freestanding pillars and is a contender for most audacious ice route ever climbed in the range.

Further up the Icefields Parkway, Mt. Murchison was a center of activity. One hundred meters left of Cosmic Messenger, Slawinski and Juan Henriquez memorialized the passing of an icon from a much more popular sport than climbing with Hand of God (135m, M7 WI5), which is four pitches overall with bolted dry-tooling leading to an obvious dagger. On a lower band, Taborszky and James Walter climbed Ferrethawk (160m, WI3+ M6), which had been the site of a 20m whipper onto a micro-cam by a previous suitor. About 200m to the left of Murchison Falls, beginning on the ice climb Aboriginal Genocide, Continuum (230m, WI4+ M5+, by Jacob Dans, Rob Owens, and Mike Stuart) took a rightward slanting rock corner in three pitches.

The extraordinary pillars of Katana (245m, WI6+ X). *Sebastian Taborszky*

At last year's favorite ice and mixed venue, the Protection Valley, Rory O'Donnell and Ryan Daniel Patterson climbed High Hanging Fruit (305m, M6+ R WI4), which intersects Grab the Cupcakes midway and then climbs left to a waterfall pitch before finishing on bold face climbing. In Kicking Horse Canyon, Slawinski and Hamill climbed Gasoline Alley (160m, M5+ WI4), ascending the buttress to the left of Asylum and topping out on a flow of ice that appears most years.

As this was written in mid-March, big new routes already had been done in 2021—there will be plenty more to report in next year's journal. [*More details on many of these routes, as well as additional new routes from the Rockies, are included with this report at the AAJ website.*] 📄 📷

— IAN WELSTED, *CANADA*

The northeast face of Neptuak Mountain. (1) Psychological Effect (700m, M7 WI5+, Leclerc-Lindič, April 2016). (2) The Hammer and the Dance (750m, 5.11c, Harrington-McLane, August 2020). *Brette Harrington*

THE HAMMER AND THE DANCE
A STIFF CLIMB UP NEPTUAK MOUNTAIN IN THE CANADIAN ROCKIES

BY BRETTE HARRINGTON, *CANADA*

AUGUST 3, 2020: The world is in shambles. The global pandemic is riding rampant, borders are closed, countries are in lockdown. I am an American expat temporarily residing in Canada. Amid a seemingly endless stream of doom-scrolling, I read an article by Tomas Pueyo—The Hammer and the Dance—which paints a grim picture of the world, describing the fluctuations to which society would ebb and flow according to epidemiology.

Lying on a lakeshore outside of Regina, Saskatchewan, I check the weather for the Canadian Rockies on my phone. The little yellow sun icon has finally replaced the sad cloud that has resided there for months. I dial up my friend Tony McLane, over in Squamish. "Tony, can you meet me in Golden tomorrow evening? Weather looks good." I know this will be our best shot at getting the right conditions to try Neptuak's northeast face.

I first scouted the face during the summer of 2016 with Marc-André Leclerc. He had noticed the striking rock quality (by chossy Rockies standards, anyway) while climbing in the Valley of the Ten Peaks that spring with Luka Lindič (*see AAJ 2017*). [*Neptuak Mountain (3,241m) is part of the steep wall at the west end of the Valley of the Ten Peaks, rising just to the northwest of Deltaform Mountain, the highest peak in the group.*] The northeast face on Neptuak is large and imposing. Four years after we scoped it, the face still has never been climbed. Tony is game, and a day later we are preparing for what will turn out to be the most engaging alpine rock route either of us has ever climbed.

At five in the morning on August 5, at the Moraine Lake car park, we do not find the usual quietude and stillness of the mountains one might expect. Throngs of tourists are bustling around with cameras at hand, hurrying to catch the iconic photo of Moraine Lake at sunrise. Tony and I sneak through all the chaos unnoticed and head up the dark forest path toward Wenkchemna Pass.

We make our way over to the prominent pillar just left of the central face on Neptuak, and separated from it by a large gully. The rock on the pillar appears to be better quality than on the main face, and is steeper and less threatened by overhead hazard.

Tony takes the first lead block, meandering through chimneys and choss, while I battle with the haulbag, helping to push it up while following the pitch. The next block is mid-5.10 up a steep face

Tony McLane follows the upper crux of The Hammer and the Dance. See another photo from this route on p.5. *Brette Harrington*

of bulletproof black quartzite speckled with tiny edges. I tack my way upward carefully. With nothing for gear but the occasional birdbeak placement, it feels more like free soloing than roped climbing.

Around 4 p.m. we arrive at a ledge big enough to bivy. We fix our lead line 60m above to get a head start in the morning, then begin unpacking our "bivy kit essentials" from the haulbag: my ultralight G7 hanging pod and Tony's *How the Grinch Stole Christmas* fleece pajama pants. We are set to sleep like angels, but a bit of rockfall in the night keeps me awake. The gully to the right sees quite a lot of action from the melting snow up high, and I am glad we aren't over there.

The next day we awake with vibrant energy and begin picking our way through the maze of flakes and roofs. Around midday, from a belay behind a giant tower, I begin the first crux of the route. Tricky moves across a pegmatite band lead into a shallow groove. Tony is around the corner and out of sight. Jaws of choss point down at me from under a small roof. I find sparse gear and gingerly start up. Out to my left is a single white rock sticking out amid the orange; it looks to be connected to the mountain better than the rest. I gently swing my left foot from under the roof and dig my heel into the white rock. I slowly transition my weight, matching my left hand onto the hold, then gradually pull up and over, breathing a sigh of relief when I am clear of the dangerous choss.

Tony leads through an offwidth and then onto some of the worst rock on the entire mountain—the red bands before the rock transitions to limestone. The red material is so decrepit, I hesitate to even call it rock. But Tony keeps a clear head and guides us safely through.

We are making decent time and at this point are high on the wall, but our options are narrowing. To the left, a blue limestone wall with dark fissures hangs above the deep gray basin. The wall drops steeply below as I traverse a thin flake. A limestone tooth the size of a microwave hangs down, and with one gentle touch it nearly detaches. To keep it from slicing my rope, I give it a powerful shove and it sails off the wall and into the sea of gray below.

Feeling somewhat relieved, but now jittery from my lack of confidence in the rock, I tech my way up delicate 5.11c climbing. It isn't till dusk that we find ourselves on the summit, completely exhilarated and exhausted. We snap some summit pictures, set up our bivy, and go to sleep.

We wake at 5 a.m. to beat the rainstorm that is forecasted to hit midmorning. We descend the ridgeline to the north—downclimbing and rappelling—and make it back to the base just as a torrential storm hits. Soaked to the bone but completely satisfied, we slosh our way down the trail and back to the car.

Our climb, as harrowing as it was at times, feels like a reprieve from a shattered world. Returning to the endless news cycle is a rude awakening. "What should we call it?" Tony asks. "How about The Hammer and the Dance?" I reply. Tony nods his head, smiling. "Sounds appropriate."

EDITOR'S NOTE: *The Hammer and the Dance (750m, 5.11c) is the second route up the northeast face of Neptuak and the first completed as a summer rock climb. Harrington and McLane team-freed the climb, onsight, taking no falls on lead.* 🄾

ANIJAAQ FJORD, VARIOUS ROUTES

WITH TRAVEL RESTRICTIONS across the globe, Sarah McNair-Landry and I focused our attention on backyard adventures. Luckily, our backyard is Baffin Island. Auyuittuq National Park (where most climbers go) was closed, so we spent months poring over satellite images and scouting for granite walls accessible from Sarah's hometown, Iqaluit on southern Baffin Island. I finally found a hidden fjord with granite cliffs that rise 1,500' out of the Arctic Ocean. The fjord is on the east side of Frobisher Bay, 200km-plus from Iqaluit and only accessible by boat.

It took three days to navigate the ice and fog and wait for winds to calm before we boated into Anijaaq Fjord and set eyes on the cliffs we had only seen via satellite images. It was our little paradise. After a day, our friends boated back to Iqaluit and promised to pick us up, eventually. With a month of food, climbing gear, and kayaks, we set up base camp and settled in, surrounding our tent with a solar-powered electric fence to keep away polar bears (we saw 12 on the trip).Over the next 25 days we put up five moderate routes (5.7 to 5.10), each with between 1,000 and 1,500 feet of climbing.

On July 22, we climbed an obvious line we could see from camp: a fun west-facing route following a wide crack on flawless and featured granite. We named it The Line (1,200', 6 pitches, 5.7).

A week later, we established two routes on a wall we named Sedna, a reference to the Inuit goddess of the sea and marine mammals—we often saw beluga whales and seals from our climbs. To access the base, we kayaked 2km southwest from camp and hauled our boats up onto the wall to secure them from the tides. This south-facing wall rose 1,500'

[Top] The west-facing wall across from base camp, showing (1) Ijiraaq (8 pitches, 5.10) and (2) The Line (6 pitches, 5.7). The climbers' solar-powered electric bear fence can be seen in the foreground. [Bottom] Sarah McNair-Landry on pitch two of Ijiraaq. *Erik Boomer (both)*

from the ocean and required long days. The first route, Sedna (1,500', 10 pitches, 5.10) had some memorable climbing, including pitch four, a full 70m of 5.10 cracks with a scary slab finish. We also completed a 10-pitch 5.8 we named Beluga. From the top of the wall, we could walk back to camp and then retrieve our kayaks the next day with an inflatable packraft.

For our final route we went back to the west-facing cliff across from camp and found our favorite climb of the trip, north (left) of The Line. Ijiraaq, a.k.a. Shapeshifter (1,000', 8 pitches, 5.10) had outstanding rock, two 5.10 cruxes, and numerous fun 5.8 and 5.9 crack pitches. 📷 🔍

— ERIK BOOMER, *CANADA*

ECUADOR

The general line of Razuyaku on Illiniza Sur (5,263 meters) as viewed from the west. *Nicolas Davalos*

ILLINIZA SUR, SOUTHWEST FACE, RAZUYAKU

ON SEPTEMBER 19–20, Nicolas Davalos and I climbed what may be a new route on the rarely visited southwest face of Illiniza Sur (5,263m) in Ecuador's Cordillera Occidental. This face, according to our local sources, was first climbed by Jorge Anhalzer and companions in 1977 and repeated in 1998. A second route was climbed by Thomas Hunt, Jorge Montopoli, and Delia Montopoli in 1983 (*AAJ 1984*). These routes likely ascend the rock features, ramps, and couloirs to the right of our line; it's possible our routes share terrain at the start and near the finish.

I first tried to access the southwest face from the refugio on the north side some years ago; however, this is difficult to do and requires a lot of descending. This time, we approached from the plains above the town of Planchaloma and hiked for a full day to a high camp at the base of the southwest face. (The description of the climbers' approach in *AAJ 1984* is similar to ours.)

The next day, we ascended a short couloir above camp and then traversed left to reach a series of steep snow ramps and steps of ice and mixed terrain. The climb took about seven hours to the summit. It is totally condition dependent, and we were lucky to find exceptionally good water ice from a prior melt-freeze cycle. We called the route Razuyaku (400m, TD WI5 M5), which means "ice water" in Quechua.

On our descent down the opposite side of the mountain, we encountered a major problem: The Ecuadorian Ministry of Environment accused us of trespassing. As of this writing, commercially guided climbing or recreational climbing are formally permitted only on established routes, though enforcement of this rule varies. We do not agree with these measures, but we recommend future travelers stay informed of current regulations. 📷

— FELIPE PROAÑO, *ECUADOR*

EDITOR'S NOTE: *The normal route up Illiniza Sur ascends snow and ice ramps on the north-northwest face just left of an area of seracs. A more difficult route, La Rampa, ascends the north face; however, glacial recession has made ascents of this once popular route exceedingly rare. To the right of the normal route is La Araña, which ascends the west flank of the mountain (AAJ 1997).*

Wrapping to the right, the routes on the southwest face include the 2020 route Razuyaku, the 1977 route, and the 1983 route. Further right, the south ridge and southeast flank form a shorter but steep and rocky wall. The south ridge was first ascended in 1973 by Joseph Berge and Marco Cruz (AAJ 1974). There are at least four routes on the 200m southeast wall climbed by Nicolas Corti, Andres Herrera, and various partners, with difficulties to TD+ 6b+. The route known as Celso Zuquillo (PD+) climbs the east ridge. In addition, Santiago Quintero climbed a solo new route on the east face (date unknown). Photos showing many of these routes are at the AAJ website.

CHIMBORAZO, SOUTHEAST FACE TO SOUTHEAST SUMMIT, PARAPHERNALIA

OVER OCTOBER 9–10, Nicolas Davalos and I targeted the very rarely visited southeast face of Chimborazo (6,268m) and its attractive southeast summit, which is commonly known as Pico (or Cumbre) Nicolás Martínez (5,719m). After a relatively short approach to a high camp at 5,000m, we observed a possible line following a series of icefalls and funnels.

Departing early, we opened nine new pitches up unequivocally great ice (85–90°)—conditions I have never seen before in tropical Ecuador. The morning was very clear, with intense views of

Pico Nicolás Martínez, showing Paraphernalia (700m, TD AI4) on the southeast face. Chimborazo's central summit (a.k.a. Politénica) is at left; the main summit is off-picture left. *Nicolas Davalos*

the volcano Sangay (5,300m) erupting. However, due to early morning sun exposure, we were bombarded with debris from the hanging cornices above. Below the upper headwall, our line deviated left toward the col between Cumbre Politécnica (5,900m) and the southeast summit.

We descended untraveled terrain on the same face (climber's right of the ascent route), following a complex series of ramps and funnels exposed to falling debris. The ascent took around six hours and the descent about five hours to base camp, followed by three more hours to our vehicle.

We named the route Paraphernalia (700m, TD AI4) for all the tools one needs amid the currently complex political environment in Ecuador, which has led to various climbing restrictions. [*Editor's Note: Previous routes on the eastern flank of Nicolás Martínez include a 1983 route from the Boussingault Glacier (left of the 2020 route) and a route up the northeast ridge (AAJ 1984).*] 📷 🔍 ▶

— FELIPE PROAÑO, *ECUADOR*

ANTISANA ESTE, SOUTH FACE, SÍ HAY MERENGUE

ON DECEMBER 13–14, Juliana García, Francisco Pulluquitin, and I completed the first route up Antisana Este (5,580m) from its base, via the south face. This face is located between the central (main) and south summit in a southeast-facing cirque rarely explored due to its remoteness. In the past, the few unsuccessful attempts on this side of Antisana were approached by hiking around the southern summit. This time, we used the normal route on the west face to reach the saddle

Juliana García on the south face of Antisana Este (5,580m), with Antisana Sur on the right and Cotopaxi on the far horizon. [Inset] The line of Sí Hay Merengue on the south face of Antisana Este. *Joshua Jarrin (both)*

between the south summit and the central summit; from there, we descended east and northeast into the cirque until reaching a camp at the base of the south face (5,000m).

On the second day, we started navigating the lower glacier at 2:30 a.m. and eventually gained elevation up the right side of an obvious debris funnel. After passing a rock band above the bergschrund, we climbed straight up snow ramps to a second rock band at two-thirds height, which we traversed left. At the western edge of the outcrop, we used a steep gully to access the final serac barrier. This was the most challenging part of the route, presenting short sections of vertical alpine ice and hollow rime. We navigated this section by climbing up and right to a spur dividing the south and east faces of this peak, eventually finishing up a snow ramp on the south face.

We reached the summit ridge at noon and then continued west along the ridge to reach the east summit. To descend, we continued west toward the central summit to join the normal route. Merengue is one of the words used in Spanish for rime; that's why we named the route Sí Hay Merengue (500m, TD AI4 M3 50° snow), which means "Yes, there's rime." 📖 📷 🔍

– JOSHUA JARRIN, *ECUADOR*

PREVIOUSLY UNREPORTED ROUTES IN THE ANTISANA GROUP: *The summit of Antisana Este (5,580m) in the Cordillera Oriental was first reached by Chilean climbers Miguel Andrade and Hugo Torres in 1974 by walking east along the ridge from the main summit. The adjacent peak Antisana Noreste was first climbed in 1972 by Leonardo Meneses and Hugo Torres, likely also from the main summit via the connecting ridge; this attractive summit may hold opportunities for new routes. Numerous routes and variations from MD to ED- were established on neighboring peak Antisana Sur (5,570m) in the early 2000s, all of which were unreported in the AAJ. This sought-after peak was once referred to by South American climbing historian Evelio Echevarría as "one of the finest peaks in Ecuador." The ten known routes on Antisana Sur are described with this report at the AAJ website, with a link to additional information. — Erik Rieger*

PERU

CORDILLERA BLANCA

HUAMASHRAJU, WEST FACE, BUEN DÍA, DÍA

IN EARLY JUNE 2019, Juan Pablo Cano, Ian Schwer, and I (all from Argentina) climbed a new route up the good granite on the west face of Huamashraju (5,434m). This mountain is part of a group that is "not so high" and "not so far" from Huaraz, and thus it has been climbed numerous times. However, the exact location of some routes is vague. [*Editor's Note: The west face of Huamashraju has approximately 10 reported routes on its 200–300m face.*]

We repeated two routes and climbed one new line over three consecutive days. Starting just right of the Sims-Hanning Route (1998), we passed a small roof and then climbed into a corner system that is a bit dirty. After that, we passed another roof and a scary flake to reach good slabs with little protection. Our route, Buen Día, Día (280m, 6a+), went all-free with no fixed gear. We descended after reaching the summit ridge by rappelling the Sims-Hanning.

In early July, sadly, Juan Pablo and Ian fell to their deaths on the south face of Caráz I. Loving memories remain. 📷

— MATI KORTEN, *ARGENTINA*

HUAMASHRAJU, EL CHUMITA; HUAMASHRAJU ESTE, EAST FACE

ON JUNE 25, 2019, James Baragwanath (Chile) and I climbed a new route up the west face of Huamashraju (5,434m), following a clean panel to the right of Buen Día, Día, established earlier in the same month (*see report above*). Our route had 300m of high-quality granite, which we climbed free to 6a+, with only one move of A1, stepping high onto a birdbeak to connect crack systems. We finished on 100m of easy snow to the summit. The route is El Chumita (6a+ A1).

In August 2019, I revisited this area with Ignacio Vasquez (Chile), and we climbed the east face of Huamashraju Este (5,350m), a satellite of the better-known Huamashraju. After hiking into the Rajucolta Valley, we established camp in a scenic meadow at the foot of the rocky east face, which is approximately 250m high. At first light we headed up vegetated crack systems and intermittent ledges, eventually reaching cleaner rock in the upper reaches. Cool chimney and crack features led to a final overhanging pitch that allowed us to pull onto the summit. We made four rappels toward the northeast ridge, leaving all anchors in place, and descended a final rocky gully to the talus field above our camp. We named the route Vitamina Huancaina (6b). 📷

— SEB PELLETTI, *AUSTRALIA*

CASHAN OESTE, NORTHEAST FACE, EL PÁJARO Y EL POTRILLO

IN JULY 2019, Nicolas Secul (Chile) and I headed into the Rajucolta Valley in the Cordillera Blanca. The Pou brothers from Spain had tipped us about their first ascent of the big granite northeast face of Cashan Oeste (5,686m) earlier in the same summer (*see AAJ 2020*), and said we could likely find another line up the face.

The northeast face of Cashan Oeste, showing (1) Richey-Rugo, 1993. (2) Andean Kingdom, 2019. (3) Pelletti-Secul, 2019. (4) Cabaza-Fernández, 2011. *Seb Pelletti*

After a rattly ride in a beat-up taxi, we approached Cashan Oeste and established a base camp in the moraine below the northeast face. We hiked our gear up to the base of the wall and climbed two pitches that same day out of pure excitement and curiosity.

Before sunrise the next day, we reclimbed the two pitches and quickly reached a crack system. This brought us to the Gray Dihedral, a huge, 50m corner that we had seen from the base of the wall; it seemed to lead into a series of cracks that would keep us on the right-most edge of the vertical northeast face instead of spitting us onto the longer-angled ridge to the right. From the dihedral, we climbed a series of bouldering-style pitches, including a crux overhanging crack that ranged in all sizes from fingers to fists; this was too difficult for onsight free climbing in the oxygen-deprived air. A few easier pitches brought us to the upper ridge, where the leader used a piton hammer as a makeshift ice axe while kicking steps into the corniced snow and ice leading to a foresummit on the ridge.

This tower was completely caked in verglas and snow, and we jammed icy cracks with our mittens and climbing shoes up two mixed pitches to its top. This was not the true summit of Cashan Oeste; there is another summit tower approximately 10–15m higher and 300m south-east along the ridge. The main summit seemed too dangerous for us to bother climbing, a castle of rotten granite blocks all stuck together with rime ice and old glacial snow, rapidly melting at this altitude in the Cordillera Blanca. [*Editor's Note: This foresummit is the same one reached by the 2019 Spanish route Andean Kingdom, which is entirely to the left of this climb. In 2011, Carlos Cabaza and Diego Fernández completed a route up the northern ridge, stopping below this foresummit (see AAJ 2012). The difficulties of reaching the main summit are highlighted by Barry Rugo in AAJ 1994 in a report on the route he climbed with Mark Richey that finished up the northeast ridge and may have been the second and last successful climb to the summit of Cashan Oeste.*]

We descended directly from the western foresummit to our base camp, using a rappel route left by the 2019 team; our round-trip had taken 15 hours. We named the route El Pájaro y el Potrillo (700m climbing distance, 6b M3 C1) after two friends of ours who unfortunately lost their lives in a nearby valley in the weeks prior to our climb. This long route has just one section of easy clean aid to overcome the crux crack—highly recommended! 📷

– SEB PELLETTI, *AUSTRALIA*

CORDILLERA VILCABAMBA

NEVADO PALQAY, WEST FACE

IN LATE AUGUST 2019, IFMGA guide Henry Moya (Ecuador) and I guided Ted Mueser and Mark Yoder (both USA) up a new route on the west face of Nevado Palqay (5,422m). This peak lies along the far end of the ridge extending east and then north from Salkantay. I made Palqay's first ascent in May 2015 (*AAJ 2016*) via the mountain's west buttress.

Nevado Palqay with (1) first-ascent route up the west buttress (2015) and (2) west face route (2019). *Nathan Heald*

Our ascent required a long day from a camp at 4,700m below the west glacier. After ascending the heavily crevassed glacier, we climbed moderate snow slopes up the center of the west face. We finished at the highest point directly above this face (500m, AD), about 150m from the summit. We decided to descend from there since the snow on the summit ridge had melted to expose unstable rock. 📷

— NATHAN HEALD, *PERU*

CORDILLERA VILCANOTA

NEVADO MARIPOSA, SOUTHEAST RIDGE

IN LATE JULY, Luis Crispin and Thomas Schilter (both Peru) planned to try the unclimbed south face of Nevado Mariposa (5,842m) from the base camp used to access the normal route on Ausangate. However, because of COVID-19 restrictions, the communities on the southern side of the mountain were not letting in any outsiders. The two adapted their plan to the southeast ridge, accessing it from the north side, where Pacchanta (Luis' village) was open to visitors.

On June 28, they left from Luis' house with horses. Luis' brother Macario helped to porter gear to a high camp at 5,500m at the foot of the ridge. On the 29th, Macario returned after traversing the ridge to Peak 5,680m (a.k.a. Huekeriti or Huequeiriti), where previous teams have turned around (*see AAJ 1970, 1978, 1981*). Meanwhile, Luis and Thomas continued over mixed terrain along the knife-edged southeast ridge, making a 15m rappel at one section. They reached the top of Nevado Mariposa by 8 a.m. (700m from the valley, D). They descended the north face (Mariposa's normal route) by downclimbing and rappelling. At 4:30 p.m. they arrived back at base camp. 📄📷

— NATHAN HEALD, *PERU, FROM CORRESPONDENCE WITH* LUIS CRISPIN *AND* THOMAS SCHILTER, *PERU*

Nevado Mariposa (5,842m)'s southeast ridge is the left skyline, crossing over Peak 5,680m. The descent was by the north face, down glacial slopes to the right of the sharp peak. *Thomas Schilter Collection*

MACHU RITI, WEST RIDGE AND OTHER EXPLORATION; NEVADO KISHUARNIYOQ, WEST FACE, NIGHT OF THE MUKIS

I HAVE BEEN exploring the Cordillera Vilcanota in southeastern Peru for 10 years, climbing all of its 6,000m peaks and many 5,000m peaks. At the northeastern edge of the range, beyond Yayamari (6,049m) and the Ritipampa de Quelcaya, are many peaks that have had only one ascent, and there are a few unclimbed summits. Here, rivers drop abruptly for 3,600m—northeast to the Amazon and southeast to the San Gabán River (which divides the Vilcanota from the Cordillera Carabaya in Puno). Researching past ascents of peaks in this area is quite difficult. The only recorded ascents date back to the 1950s–1970s, though they include notable climbers such as Piero Ghiglione, Olaf Hartmann, Faye Kerr, and John Ricker.

As I pieced together reports and maps, the principal mountains of the area revealed themselves. East of Yayamari and north of the Quelcaya Icecap, there are several groups of glaciated peaks: Alccachaya (5,780m), San Braullo (5,674m), Sombreruni (5,645m), Imata (5,475m), Chimboya (5,550m), Kishuarniyoq (5,665m), Kiscalaya (5,645m, a.k.a. Taltoquere), Taipicala (5,485m), Kellurata (5,500m, a.k.a. Chilimoco), Huinccocha (5,315m); the Huallanhuañusca group, including Ocororopata (5,031m) and Yanaruna I and II (5,302m); the Ayachincana group (a.k.a. Llushcarite or Chuquichanca), which includes Quiruyoq (5,250m) and Huayacauri (5,240m); and the Pomachanca group with Huamanlipani Grande (5,305m). I made note of one peak further east, Machu Riti (5,310m), which appeared untouched. This is the final glaciated peak before the San Gabán River, located a few kilometers north of the mining town of Corani. [*A helpful labeled panorama is at the AAJ website.*]

In October 2018, Thomas Schilter and I attempted to reach Machu Riti, taking a 4WD truck over Chimboya Pass to Corani. From there, we turned north into a valley with a couple of large lagoons southeast of Machu Riti. We reached 5,000m on the peak but retreated due to snow and thick clouds.

Two years later, Thomas, Maximiliano Taylor, and I decided to give Machu Riti another try and explore other peaks in the area. After studying satellite images, we decided to go to the western side of the peak. From Urubamba, we followed dirt roads to the town of Quichu and herder community of Alto Chia (4,800m), located between the Pomachanca and Machu Riti.

There was little visible snow or ice on Machu Riti, so we took just one ice axe each and some rock gear. On October 10, we traversed the west ridge (staying on its northern side) over a few false summits and the last remnants of glacier close to the summit. There are a few rocky tops, and we

Kellurata (5,500m, left) and Kishuarniyoq (5,665m; estimated at 5,720m with GPS) from the west. Both peaks had only one prior ascent, from the east side; the west faces shown here unclimbed before November 2020, when Kishuarniyoq was climbed by Night of the Mukis (600m, D+ WI4). In back on the left are Quiruyoq and Huayacauri in the Ayachincana group. *Nathan Heald*

tagged the two highest, obtaining a GPS elevation of 5,310m. The way up was relatively easy, with no technical, roped climbing but great scrambling and a few exposed moves on the summit.

The next day, we moved camp to Chimboya Pass (5,150m). On October 12, we climbed the peak Imata (5,475m), just north of the pass; it is a southern outlier of San Braullo. Thomas brought his unicycle to the top and completed the highest descent on record in Peru!

That same day, we packed up camp and descended with the truck toward the town of Phinaya. From there, we turned north on the road below the east flank of Alccachaya (5,780m); this impressive dirt road runs to the Abra Laccopata Pass (5,200m) and through sandy dunes to a gap in the Suyuparina Glacier to reach one head of the Marcapata River. We were blessed with savage views to the north side of Yayamari (6,049m) and our final objective, extending north along the ridgeline from Yayamari: the west face of Kishuarniyoq (5,665m) and impressive tooth-like Kellurata (5,500m).

We found a family pasturing their alpacas at 4,800m. Though wary at first, they soon offered their warm, Andean hospitality and a spot to park near their earthen home. The next day, we hired Luis Alberto to help us portage our gear to the base of Kishuarniyoq (also spelled Kishuarnioq). Our hopes were high, but it snowed all night and we decided that we would not climb. Kellurata (5,500m) and Kishuarniyoq (5,665m) each have had one known ascent from the other side (east side); the west faces are unclimbed. It took only an hour to return to Luis Alberto's house, where we gifted food and some carabiners to his kids.

One month later, Luis Crispin, Thomas, and I returned to Kishuarniyoq. After studying the Barrys-Hartmann (1969) ascent, along with Google Earth imagery, we'd become convinced that the central summit of three was highest. On November 24, we drove toward Marcapata and up the valley we had descended a month earlier. We parked the truck with the same family and rested through the afternoon, then left the truck at 11 p.m. that same day.

Once on the glacial ice below the west face, we navigated several large crevasses and had to jump a gap to reach the steep wall. Luis and Thomas took turns leading 350m of ice runnels (60°). The final pitch steepened to a consistent 80° and included one 5m vertical step. As Luis set out on the crux lead, I saw his boot soles bending a bit. I asked him why he hadn't brought his technical boots, and he replied, "It didn't look this difficult from the photo!"

As we topped out on the ridge, the summit came into view only 50m away. Supposedly November is the "off season," but this day was crystal clear, and we had spectacular views of the remote peaks of the northern Vilcanota, many of them having been explored only once. We descended on V-threads and made it back to the truck at dusk, 19 hours after leaving. We called our route Night of the Mukis (600m, D+ WI4) and estimate the central (main) summit to be 5,720m (GPS). 📷

– NATHAN HEALD, *PERU*

BOLIVIA

Approaching Chachacomani base camp in 1996, looking back at the northwest face of Jankho Laya (5,545m). It's not clear whether this face has been climbed, but an ascent of the skyline spur above the 5,200-meter col on the right was made in 1979 by French climbers. *Angela Goodacre Donini*

CORDILLERA REAL

CHACHACOMANI, SOUTHEAST RIDGE, HISTORICAL NOTES

AAJ 2020 CONTAINED an account of several climbs on and near Chachacomani (6,074m). In a photo of Chachacomani's south face, one line is labeled "first ascent unknown." In 1996, I was part of the party that probably did the first ascent of this route.

In late May, Cesar Humberto (Tito) Carrasco, the guides Gregorio and Eduardo Mamani Quispe, and I drove from Peñas to Paso Mullu Apacheta and from there hiked northwest 4km to below the southern flanks of Jankho Laya (5,545m). Next day, moving from moraine to glacier, we climbed to a 5,200m col to the west of Jankho Laya's northern top. On the far side, we roped to descend the glacier snout into the Huarca Juahiri Valley, where we established base camp.

On the 30th we hiked 4km to a camp on the col between Chachacomani and Himaciña (5,458m). We set off before dawn the following day for the left flank of the southeast ridge. After crossing the bergschrund, we climbed a 300m, 60–70° ice slope. We continued up the corniced crest to reach a snowfield and a steep 20m step that led to the summit ridge and finally the east (and highest) top of Chachacomani. We reversed our route to descend.

Tito and I had met the Mamani brothers in 1992 through the Club Andino Boliviano. They grew up in Zongo village, and their affinity for the mountains was spurred by encounters with foreign climbers. In 1993, Tito returned to Bolivia and persuaded the two guides to diverge from their "day jobs" and try the west face of Huayna Potosí. They were the first Bolivians to complete this challenging ice route and went on to achieve international accreditation as mountain guides.

Tito was killed by rockfall in El Potrero Chico, Mexico, almost exactly one year after our ascent of Chachacomani. A short time ago, when I reached out to Eduardo to talk about our ascent of the southeast ridge, I found him disheartened by the death in July 2020 of his older brother, Gregorio, from COVID-19. In his grief, he finds himself instinctively calling his brother from the mountains whenever he has a cell signal. ◙

— ANGELA GOODACRE DONINI, *USA*

PICO ITALIA, EAST FACE, DÍA LIBRE

WHILE COMPLETING PART of our IFMGA guide course in September 2019, Aldo Coral (Ecuador) and I spotted an unclimbed line on the east face of Pico Italia (ca 5,750m), right of the existing routes. At the time, the face was quite snowy and we anticipated a good mixed line. When we returned four days later, on September 23, the face had shed almost all its snow and ice, leaving just rock, some of it verglased, which we would now have to climb in our bulky mountain boots.

The east face of Pico Italia. (1) East face buttress (TD+ 6c, Beisly-Monasterio, 2012). (2) Al Fondo Hay Sitio (6a+, Lobo-Rauch, 2016). (3) Arthritis (TD+ 6a, Beisly-Monasterio, 2013). (4) Día Libre (6c, Coral-Pelletti, 2019). *Erik Monasterio*

Getting onto the route was tricky; we had to dodge ice-covered sections on the first two pitches of slabby rock. Once we reached the left-slanting groove line that runs up this section of the wall, we climbed two hard pitches: Aldo led a bouldery 6b section, and I led an overhanging 6c pitch to get us onto the crest of the ridge on the right. Two airy pitches took us to the summit ridge, which we followed to the top of the mountain. Protection was scarce on the first few pitches but good in the upper section; I'd recommend a single rack up to Camalot 3.

Three rappels in a snow chute below the summit led us down to the Glacier Viejo in between existing routes. We named our route Día Libre (360m, 6c), as it was our only "day off" during the month of our guides' course. ◙

— SEB PELLETTI, *AUSTRALIA*

CHARQUINI AND MILLUNI, VARIOUS ASCENTS

DURING A MONTH in the Zongo Pass area in August and September, Rodrigo Lobo and Robert Rauch climbed the northeast faces of two short but attractive rock towers along the west ridge of Charquini (5,392m), with a crux crack pitch of 6c/7a on the First Tower. The two traversed along all the towers of the west ridge for a full alpine day. On another day, Rauch soloed the east ridge (5c) of the First Tower. Lobo and Rauch later climbed another rock tower on a ridge leading to the main summit of Pico Milluni (5,500m), with a crux of 6b. Rauch's report is at the AAJ website. ▤ ◙

— *INFORMATION FROM* ROBERT RAUCH, *BOLIVIAN TOURS*

PICACHO KASIRI, WEST RIDGE

IN 2018, JUAN Gabriel Estellano and I made the first known ascent of Picacho Kasiri's south face (*AAJ 2019*). We returned on March 12, 2020, to attempt the complete traverse of the Kasiri massif

Juan Gabriel Estellano following a pitch close to the main summit of Picacho Kasiri. The climb was completed in thick mist, and at the summit they were caught in a heavy hailstorm. *Alex von Ungern*

from west to east, starting with the west ridge, which was likely unclimbed.

We parked Juan Gabriel's minibus at 4,170m, then hiked up to the col between Picacho Pucusani and Kasiri, where there is a little lagoon and mesmerizing views onto the Amazon Basin. We started up the west ridge, at first with difficult hiking, then scrambling, and eventually real rock climbing that we pitched. The climbing was never harder than F5, but we were using mountaineering boots, a single rope, and little protection. Plus, Juan Gabriel had forgotten his harness, so he improvised with a long Dyneema sling. All this made the damp and less than solid rock rather interesting.

Two pitches before the summit, we joined the route we'd opened in 2018. We'd hoped to break through the mist into sunshine, but as we reached the main summit we were hit by a heavy hailstorm. We decided to retreat without completing our planned traverse over Kasiri East, following the descent to the north that we had taken in 2018. 📚 📷

— ALEXANDER VON UNGERN, *ANDEAN ASCENTS, BOLIVIA*

HAMPATURI REGION, PEAK 5,540M, SOUTH TO NORTHWEST TRAVERSE

PEAK 5,540M IS between Serkhe Kollu and Hathi Kollu, and only 20km in a straight line from La Paz. It is unnamed on IGM Map 6044-IV and other sources. I had heard that locals refer to it as Khasiri, which is a little confusing because a peak on the opposite side of the Unduavi Valley is named Picacho Kasiri. I had previously climbed Peak 5,540m via the north face during a three-peaks traverse above the Serkhe Valley (*see AAJ 2018*). This time I wanted to try a different approach.

On March 7, Alice Huon and I drove to an altitude of 4,250m, above the village of Palcoma. A 4x4 is recommended for the last 30 minutes. We then walked up the valley that descends west and then southwest from Peak 5,540m. After three and a half hours we reached a good bivouac spot close to 4,800m.

In the morning, we reached the west-facing glacier below Peak 5,540m in one hour. We gained the south ridge of the peak at sunrise and simul-climbed hard-frozen snow slopes up to 50–55° before reaching the first rock section. A pitch of mixed climbing and one last short snowfield brought us to the upper south ridge, which was now more like a broader face. From there, four pitches on dry, sometimes loose rock got us above the steepest section. The last of these pitches was very demanding, and I resorted to a move of A2 to get through. At the belay below this pitch we saw two sunbleached slings wrapped around a boulder. Had previous parties turned around from this point?

We continued up the ridge to the summit. To descend, we followed the northwest ridge for about three-quarters of a kilometer (climbing over three subsidiary tops) to reach the glacier. We then headed south, traversing along the base of the west face to regain the point where we had accessed the glacier earlier. We returned to the road approximately 12 hours after leaving our bivouac that morning. Overall, the route was about D, with several sections that were overhanging or had small roofs and went at 5c/6a. 📷 🔍

— ALEXANDER VON UNGERN, *ANDEAN ASCENTS, BOLIVIA*

CORDILLERA OCCIDENTAL

ACOTANGO, NORTHWEST FACE AND NORTH-NORTHEAST RIDGE

In September 2016, Libor Forst, Jeff Sandifort (the head guide from Climbing South America), and I spent a week around Sajama National Park. We intended to climb Cerro Acotango (6,052m), a dormant volcano likely first ascended by Incas. It is probably one of the easiest 6,000ers in the world when climbed by the standard routes, including the north-northeast ridge. We decided to attempt the northwest face to the upper north-northeast ridge.

We reached the bottom of the face via a miners' road and a trek up a narrow valley. Given Acotango's easy reputation, we hadn't even taken a rope, but the face, which is covered by a receding glacier, turned out to be challenging. The lower half was a 45–55° slope full of sharp, icy penitentes, each about one meter high. Above, we followed a 2m-wide snow terrace toward the ridge before meeting overhanging rock, which we skirted by returning to the face and climbing a 50° slope covered by hard-packed snow. Above this, easy climbing up the north-northeast ridge brought us to the summit. The face was approximately 400m high, and the ascent took three hours. 📷

— ROMAN SIEGL, *CZECH REPUBLIC*

BRAZIL

MINAS GERAIS / SERRA DE MANTIQUEIRA

PEDRA DO SERTÃO, NORTHWEST FACE, SOLO COM COLIBRI

Pedra do Sertão is located in Marmelópolis in the Serra da Mantiqueira, approximately halfway between São Paulo and Rio de Janerio. Despite this formation having an official name, it has no trail to its summit and the cliff is unlikely to have been climbed. On October 21, I began a four-day ascent by rope-soloing the northwest face. I placed 47 bolts on my five-pitch route, including two-bolt anchors equipped for rappelling. Solo Com Colibri (215m, 5.11a) may be the first climbing route in this area. 📷

— LEONARDO JULIANO MANGANO, *BRAZIL*

ARGENTINA/CHILE

VOLCÁN LLULLAILLACO, SOUTH FACE

Volcán Llullaillaco (6,739m) is on the border between Chile and Argentina and was a sacred mountain to the Inca, who climbed it more than 500 years ago. In February 2021, the archaeologist and climber Christian Vitry, along with Adrián Gandino, Gerardo Casaldi, and Federico Sánchez (all from Argentina), reached the summit by what is likely a new route up the south face, following an icy couloir with some easy mixed terrain, starting from a high camp at the foot of the couloir. They called the 800m route Huamán, which means "hawk" in Quechua. On January 30, 72-year-old Sergio Ceruti from the same expedition ascended a minor volcano, thought to be unclimbed, to the south of Llullaillaco; he named it Chungara (5,200m). 📷

— **MARCELO SCANU**, *ARGENTINA*

ANSILTA 7, AGUJAS DEL GLACIAR FRÍA, NEW ROUTES

Gabriel Fava reports that he and other Argentine climbers have established many new routes at the Agujas Del Glaciar Fría (31°45'41"S, 69°51'34"W), an area of remote, high-elevation granite needles along the eastern ramparts of Ansilta 7 (5,780m), the tallest and only glaciated peak in the Cordillera de Ansilta.

The needles are reached by a two-day approach from the town of Barreal, which lies to the east. Along the way are some nice bouldering areas at a camp in the grassy tundra (3,100m) and at base camp (4,100m). Fava established the first technical rock climb in the zone, Alegría (230m, 6c), in 2014 on the Aguja Nico Made (ca 4,700m; *see AAJ 2015*). The area now hosts more than a dozen routes across six major rock groupings, mostly climbed in January 2021. A summary and links to additional information are at the AAJ website. 📷

Looking west toward Glaciar Fría and Aguja Nico Made. *Daniela Avellaneda*

— **ERIK RIEGER**, *WITH INFORMATION FROM* **GABRIEL FAVA**, *ARGENTINA*

CERRO MONO VERDE, NORTHEAST COULOIR

Undoubtedly one of the strangest names in the toponymy of Chile's Central Andes is Cerro Mono Verde (4,524m), which means "green monkey." The peak is about 70km northeast of Santiago and 40km south of Aconcagua in the Monos de Agua valley (named by local people for the extensive penitentes found here). The first ascent was by Wolf gang Förster, Fernando Montenegro, and Sergio Montenegro in 1964 (aspect unknown). There are no other known ascents, though there have been unsuccessful attempts.

On November 16, 2017, a team of six approached the northeast side of the mountain with mules. The next day, four of us departed camp at 4 a.m. We chose the narrow, left-most couloir of three, thinking it would reach the summit directly. Three members of the team continued to within 150m of the top before turning back in worsening weather and poor snow.

The following week, Rodrigo Benavides and Bruce Swain returned to the mountain, armed with the knowledge from the first attempt, along with Dario Alfaro. They slept for a while at the old Asava refuge, then left at 3:45 a.m. on November 26.

The northeast face of Cerro Mono Verde (4,524m). *Álvaro Vivanca*

They climbed the central couloir (right of their previous attempt), which was mostly nontechnical, and arrived on the summit by 11:15 a.m., happy to have achieved the second known ascent of Mono Verde by a probable new route (800m, 30–50°). Their GPS showed a height of 4,551m. 🔍

– EDUARDO RIVERA ZAPATA, *CHILE*

CERRO ALTO MARDONES AND CERRO PUNTA GALLARDO, FIRST ASCENTS

IN LATE OCTOBER, Yorly Batlle, Juan Pablo Cabbada, Adrián Gambetta, Alejandra Morales, and Álvaro Zerené drove to the Parque Andino Juncal and approached up the Quebrada de Lagunillas, heading north to a camp at 3,400m near some springs. On November 1, they departed at 5:30 a.m. to reach the end of the valley. From there, they ascended Cerro Cabeza del Inca Este (4,105m) by its east face, reaching the summit at 10 a.m. This peak had only one known previous ascent, in 2019. They then continued eastward toward Cerro Alto Mardones (4,098m), following the ridge that connects Cabeza del Inca Este to the more technical Cerro Navarro Norte (4,640m). Rounding some rock spires on the west slopes, they followed the upper northwest ridge to the previously unclimbed Cerro Alto Mardones, after ascending 30m of exposed, loose rock.

On a separate expedition, two of the same climbers made the first ascent of a 4,271m peak located 100km to the south. On November 20, Juan Pablo Cabbada, Paz Pillancari, Edison Sanhueza, and Álvaro Zerené traveled to the springs at Colina, in the Cajón del Maipo. They then approached southwest up the Cajón del Estero Carreño, making camp at 3,500m. On the 21st, they departed at 8:30 a.m., and climbed a snowfield up the west side and then the upper northwest ridge to the top, which they reached at 3 p.m. The summit comprises two towers (east and west) of the same altitude. They reached the west one and called the previously unnamed summit Cerro Punta Gallardo (4,271m) after a friend who died in an avalanche in 2019. 📷

– MARCELO SCANU, *ARGENTINA*

CERRO NEGRO PABELLÓN, SOUTHEAST FACE (NOT TO SUMMIT)

MANY YEARS AGO, a friend pointed out a mountain along the horizon: "That's Negro Pabellón. It's had few ascents. It's hard and far away—a real climb, but close to home." For 15 years, its image stayed imprinted upon my brain. Finally, in late November, Luco Badino, Chicho Fracchia, and I (all from Argentina) organized an expedition to try a new route up the unclimbed southeast face. [*Editor's*

Cerro Negro Pabellón (6,157m) from the southeast, showing: (A) west (main) summit; (1) southwest ridge (Argentine, 1984); (2) south glacier (Japanese, 1969); (B) east summit; (3) southeast ridge (Argentine, 1953); (4) southeast face to plateau (Argentine, 2020); (C) Cerro San Pablo (5,679m). *Google Earth*

Note: Cerro Negro Pabellón (6,157m) is located in the Cordón de las Delicias and is the highest peak of the Cordillera Frontal, near Mendoza. The 1953 route up the southeast ridge reached the east summit, which is just slightly lower than the west (main) summit. In 1969, a Japanese expedition reached the west summit via the south glacier. Lastly, in 1984, climbers from Club Andinista Mendoza made an unsuccessful attempt on the Japanese route and instead completed the first ascent of the southwest ridge, which is now considered the "normal route" up this seldom-climbed peak.]

After three days approaching from Tupungato and crossing the Río Las Tunas many times, we reached the base of the southeast face and made camp. The snow and ice conditions on this tall, glaciated face did not look very good. Regardless, at 4 a.m. the next morning, we started to climb. The first 300m were easy (up to 60°), with some crevasses. Above a bergschrund, the snow turned to very good but hard ice (70°), and we roped up for the next 700m. After 12 hours of climbing, the angle relented, and we climbed hard snow to the top of the wall (60°).

Climbing the face had been our main goal, so when we reached the eastern summit plateau (ca 6,025m), we decided not to continue 1km west to the true summit and instead looked for a way down with our remaining light. We traversed to the southwest ridge and descended it, which was a good decision, given that it took another 14 hours to reach our camp. We had climbed a dream face (1,200m, D+) on a dream mountain, so we were very happy. 📷

— MATIAS HIDALGO NICOSIA, *ARGENTINA, WITH ADDITIONAL INFORMATION FROM* PABLO GONZÁLEZ, *ARGENTINA*

ULISES VITALE PEAK, NORTHEAST FACE

EVEN IN THE 21st century, the Central Andes of Mendoza Province are believed to hold approximately 50 unclimbed summits above 5,000m with at least 200m of prominence. One of them was a 5,194m peak in the Portillo Range. Meiji Peak (5,215m) is the nearest higher peak, and the col between them is approximately 4,900m. The unnamed peak was first attempted in 1955 by local climbers Jesus Casanova, Alfredo Flury, Richard Gallop, and Ulises Vitale, via the southeast face. They retreated just 100m from the summit. Since then, the southeast face has changed considerably due to glacial retreat.

After restrictions eased from COVID-19, Gerardo Castillo, Ulises Corvalán, Claudio Fredes, Adrian Miranda, Heber Orona, Lito Sánchez, and I decided to climb this mountain, 65 years after that first attempt. We started the approach on December 1 from the little village of Manzano Histórico, in Tunuyán Department, and walked 10km south and west along the Pircas Creek Valley to a camp at 3,100m. The second day, we continued west-southwest for 11km more to reach the base of the mountain at 4,200m.

On December 3, we started our climb at 6 a.m. From our campsite to the east, we first had to traverse a large, steep moraine to reach the foot of the northeast face. After a dry winter, the large snow couloir we planned to climb was completely covered in penitente snow formations. After seven hours on this snow slope, all members of the group reached the summit (550m, 40–50°). We agreed to name this mountain in honor of our friend Ulises Vitale, a tireless mountaineer and the last living member of the 1955 expedition. We descended by the same route. ▣ 🔍

– PABLO DAVID GONZÁLEZ, *ARGENTINA*

PICOS DEL BARROSO, SOUTH FACE TO CHILEAN SUMMIT

IN MID-SEPTEMBER, DAMIR Mandakovic, José Vial, and I, members of Club Andino Universitario, opened what may be the first route up the southern side of the southernmost 5,000m peak in Chile, the Picos del Barroso (34°17'17.2"S, 70°1'52.4"W).

This large massif is in the O'Higgins Region, southwest of the well-known Volcán Maipo (5,264m), and has four distinct tops: the west summit (5,113m), Chilean summit (5,135m), central or main summit (5,174), and Argentinean summit (5,165m). More than 5km separate the west summit from the Argentinean (eastern) summit, while the central summit is binational. The Chilean summit (center-west) is approximately 2km from the central top. The central summit was first climbed from the north (Foerster-Meier-Niehaus, 1948), and all subsequent ascents are believed to have been from the north, starting either from the Maipo or Paredones rivers (*see AAJ 1963 and AndesHandbook.org*).

We started our nine-day trip on September 14. Prior to leaving, the Club Andino Rancagua and other local climbers had informed us of one prior but unsuccessful attempt on our goal, the south face of Picos del Barroso. Our three-day approach began from Puma Lodge (1,300m). We trekked east along the Cachapoal River (at first with mules) and eventually north for 30km to reach our base camp (3,200m). From our camp in the southwest cirque, we could look up the nearly 2,000m slope of rock, snow, and glacial ice.

Over September 18–19, José and I chose a path of snow and ice ramps up the south face between west and Chilean summits, while Damir stayed at base camp. We spent a night at 4,800m below the summit ridge, and on day two we reached the Chilean summit. The route was not very technical, with the steepest section around 65°, but exposure was high due to numerous crevasses and seracs hanging from the wall. We descended the same route. ▣ 🔍 ▶

– ROBERTO MAYOL BRIERLEY, *CHILE*

Panoramic view of the southwest cirque of Picos del Barroso, showing the broad glacier (left center) climbed in September 2020 to the Chilean summit (5,135m) of the massif. The rocky west-southwest walls of the central summit (hidden) are believed to be unclimbed. These walls rise over 2,000m from the valley floor. The 2020 party reported the rock looked good from a distance. *Roberto Mayol Brierley*

Though the cliffs rise only 200 meters, the rotten rock of Volcán Campanario required four days to climb. *Tomás Pellizzari*

VOLCÁN CAMPANARIO, FIRST ASCENT VIA SOUTHWEST RIDGE

VOLCÁN CAMPANARIO (4,049m, 35°55'24.15"S, 70°22'2.55"W) is an eroded volcanic skeleton between Chile and Argentina in Mendoza Province. Campanario was first attempted in 1963 by Bión González, Osiel González, Sergio Kuntsmann, and Mario Puig and has seen several other unsuccessful attempts. [*Editor's Note: This is a different peak than Pico Torre del Campanario (5,090m), far to the north.*]

On February 9, Carlos Bravo, Erasmo Gonzaléz, and Tomás Pellizzari approached the peak, making camp on the south side. The next day, they began their route up the southwest ridge. The rotten rock made for slow progress, and the ascent consisted primarily of aid climbing separated by nearly lateral traversing. The team fixed ropes and descended to the ground after each day of climbing. On the 14th, Bravo and Pellizzari reached the summit at 2:30 p.m.

In all, the ascent took four days and required substantial use of pitons for aid. En route, they encountered old knifeblades, carabiners, and anchored steel stakes up to 60cm long abandoned from the 1963 attempt. Though the route's vertical gain is only about 200m, the climbers reported that the "rock breaks in the hands," so they belayed 10 short pitches.

— MARCELO SCANU, *ARGENTINA*

CERRO EL MOÑO, EAST FACE; RISCO PLATEADO, NORTHEAST RIDGE

ON JANUARY 16, 2021, Sebastián Martino and Mauro Schmiedt (both from Argentina) began their approach to Cerro El Moño (4,699m) in Mendoza Province and reached Refugio Soler that day. The next day, they crossed the Río Atuel and entered the Valle de las Lágrimas, close to the site of a 1972 Uruguayan plane crash made famous in the book *Alive*. They crossed the river and, after eight hours, made camp at 2,600m.

On the 18th, they ascended a gully and ridge to a hanging glacial valley below Cerro El Moño, which was believed to be unclimbed. They camped at 3,800m. That night, they heard heavy rock-fall but did not find out until days later that an earthquake in nearby San Juan Province was the cause. On the 19th, they departed camp at 6:30 a.m., ascending a broad apron of snow penitentes on the east slopes to reach a steeper couloir, which provided access to the rocky summit plateau. By 10:30 the pair had reached the southern and higher summit, atop the Argentina-Chile border.

On the 20th they descended to Refugio Soler and rested one day before trekking toward Risco Plateado (4,999m), 25km to the southeast. Alhough there are no recorded ascents of this peak, it may have been climbed in the modern era from the south and likely was climbed in Incan times. From the Río

Cerro El Moño from the east. *Mauro Schmiedt*

Atuel valley, north of Risco Plateado and south of Cerro Sosneado (5,189m), they crossed the Atuel and then hiked southwest 8km to reach a camp at 3,800m below the peak's northeast ridge. On the 23rd, they continued up the ridge, wrapping around a subsummit onto the glaciated saddle and then the summit (about 4km in all). They found a wool doll on the summit, indicating the Inca likely reached this summit. Interesting pre-Columbian discoveries have been made on Cerro Sosneado, and the area may have been one of the southernmost high-mountain sanctuaries for the Inca. 📷

— **MARCELO SCANU,** *ARGENTINA*

NORTHERN PATAGONIA

CERRO LAS PEINETAS AND VOLCÁN QUINQUILIL, NEW ROUTES

CERRO LAS PEINETAS (2,018m) and Volcán Quinquilil (2,052m) are volcanic peaks 15km south of the town of Curarrehue in the Región de la Araucanía. The area is densely vegetated, with somewhat loose rock, but is becoming known for its winter climbing and skiing.

Cerro Las Peinetas (a.k.a. Millallifén or Pocolpén) rises approximately 450m above the vegetation line. Its central tower was first climbed by Pablo López, Claudio Retamal, and Fernando Zemelman (all Chile) in the austral summer of 2002 by the north-northeast face (5 pitches, 5.7). Juan Señoret (Chile) made the first winter ascent of this tower in 2015 by climbing the general line of the López-Retamal-Zemelman (70° M3). He also did the first ascent of a summer rock route on the same face: Japi Verde (5 pitches, 5.8). During the winter of 2020, on July 28, brothers Cristobal and Juan Señoret climbed a new route up the south face (450m, AI5 M5). Their line ascended steep ice and snow on the left side of the face to the rime-encrusted summit ridge, which they traversed east to the top.

The first ascent of Volcán Quinquilil (a.k.a. Colmillo del Diablo) was made by Emilio Frey in 1897 (aspect unknown). Today, the peak is typically approached from the south via Puesco Alto and can be climbed in winter conditions via three pitches of moderate mixed, ice, and snow terrain on the southwest aspect, as well as by other routes. Juan Señoret and Gabriel Navarrete did the first ascent of the peak's striking 400m southeast face in 2014,

The southeast face of Volcán Quinquilil, showing the 2020 ascent. This same general line was first climbed in 2014 and called Psycolmillo (Navarrete-Señoret). The face was skied (with rappels) in 2019. *Victor Astete*

by a route they called Psycolmillo. On September 17, 2019, after climbing the normal route, Juan Señoret and Christophe Henry (France) made a ski descent of the general line of Psycolmillo; Señoret said it involved sections to 70° and five short rappels. In August 2020, Víctor Astete and Uber Quirilao (both from Chile) climbed the Navarrete-Señoret route, with some possible variations, reporting the average angle to be 60–70° with some steeper steps. 📷

— **ERIK RIEGER,** *WITH INFORMATION FROM VICTOR ASTETE AND JUAN SEÑORET, CHILE*

The 2021 team's high camp, about halfway up the northwest face of Cerro Huinay. The area gets about 300 days of wet weather each year. *Francisco "Pancho" Herrera*

THE BIG FATHER
MAKING THE FIRST ASCENT OF CERRO HUINAY

BY HERNÁN RODRÍGUEZ, *CHILE*

CERRO HUINAY (1,430M) holds a beautiful 1,000m granite wall hidden in the Northern Patagonian jungle. The name Huinay means "curved because of the strong winds" in the Mapuche language and refers to the massive alerce trees that grow throughout the area. I learned of Cerro Huinay after Nicolas Gutierrez showed me an article that described Francisco "Pancho" Herrera, Claudio Vicuña, and Erick Vigoroux's attempt to climb it a decade ago. The three made it 750m up the northwest face over five days, stopping because of poor weather 300–400m below the summit.

The place struck me: It was wild and pristine, a valley full of life. Millions of years of evolution with just a few people walking through it. I called Pancho, who was part of the first expedition and is a very talented filmmaker. His words were simple, "The place is amazing. I'm in for another try!" The idea quickly turned to obsession, and Pancho, Nicolas, Sebastian Rojasspent, and I (all from Chile) spent the next three months planning an expedition. Thankfully, the Chilean outdoor clothing brand, Lippi, supported our expedition, with some help from Raimundo Olivos.

Cerro Huinay is in Chile's Región de Los Lagos, a remote labyrinth of fjords and islands. The area was colonized at the beginning of the 20th century by loggers keen to exploit the alerce, trees similar to the giant sequoia than can live for more than 3,000 years. Though they eradicated the trees close to the coast, the seemingly impenetrable upper valleys remained intact.

Today, the area around Cerro Huinay encompasses 34,000 hectares of protected land, administered by the Fundación San Ignacio del Huinay, an organization dedicated to researching and conserving the flora and fauna unique to Fiordo Comau, where the research outpost of Huinay is situated. With no trail to the wall, 30km to the east, one choice was to open a path from Huinay through the jungle—potentially a month of work. After some consideration, we decided to fly in by helicopter and spend all our days devoted to the task of opening a line to the summit.

The climate is a major hurdle in this region, with average annual rainfall of 630cm and 300 wet days per year. Our biggest concern was getting several days of good weather to allow us to climb. We decided to pack food for 30 days and brought two portaledges, 500m of rope, and 80 bolts.

We arrived by boat at the outpost of Huinay on February 9, 2021. Ullrich Pörschmann, the administrator of the Fundación, gave us a very warm reception. (Though, looking at us, he could not believe our group of smelly gypsies could ever climb a mountain.) Early the next morning, a small helicopter took five trips to transport all our food and gear to a tiny snowfield at the base of the wall.

We soon settled upon a long, central line, just left of a large nose that divides the wall. This is well to the right of where the 2010 team began their attempt. Knowing the good weather would only be with us for the first five days, followed by eight days of rain, we tried to make quick progress.

The first 10 pitches required a lot of vertical gardening, climbing through vegetation and searching for protection in mud-filled cracks. The rock quality, though, was amazing—super solid. The middle of the wall became cleaner. We carried all our gear (portaledges, food, and water for five days) to a high point 500m up, the length of our ropes. Then we returned to the foot of the wall to rest and wait for our next weather window. At base camp, we realized the locals' stories were true: It rained hard! Rivers flowed down the wall. It was incredible.

After eight days, the weather finally gave us another chance. We ascended to the portaledges and committed to the summit. We spent the next three days climbing and fixing ropes for 400m above our ledges. In general, the climbing followed a singular crack and corner system for the first 800m, very similar to routes in Cochamó. On pitch 16, we made one 20m traverse to the right to reach a secondary crack system. The fourth day, we jumared to our highest point and headed to the top through an ocean of pure, white granite.

At day's end, the summit was close, but we were dehydrated. We held onto the idea of finding water at the highest point, or at least some snow. As I readied myself for the final 60m separating us from the summit, two small, mammalian heads appeared above us, which made for four loud and frenetic monkeys. We know now that they were black Patagonian vizcachas (rodents that look like rabbits), well north of their predicted range. The intrigue was mutual. This was their habitat, a place unknown to men, and men surely were new to them as well.

Our feelings upon reaching this summit can be described as maximum happiness and eternal gratitude. We embraced the magic scenery and, best of all, lots of water! Under a full moon, we began rappelling. After three to four hours, we were cooking and laughing in the portaledges, admiring the moon: What a gift to encapsulate our 20 days above an impenetrable jungle of larches and manio trees, chilcos (fuchsia), and mosses, where every centimeter of soil is full of life.

Our 25-pitch route, Futa Chao (1,300m climbing distance, 5.12 A2+), is set up for free climbing and has two bolts at each belay (all about 55m apart), along with a few pitons and bolts to protect face climbing sections. In 10 days on the wall, we were able to free every pitch (mostly 5.10–5.11) except for a 10m section of A2+ on pitch four. Standout pitches include the beautiful finger crack on pitch one (5.12) and an enduro corner on pitch eight (5.11+).

Futa Chao means "the big father," god and creator of all living things, to honor the great spirit who rules these wild places. We are truly believers in the perfect synchronicity of nature, and we appreciated that the natural elements allowed us to climb a route of pure quality. 📷🔍

The northwest face of Cerro Huinay (1,430m). (1) 2010 attempt. (2) Futa Chao (1,300m climbing distance, 5.12 A2+). The snow-patch helicopter landing pad can be seen at the foot of the wall at far left. *Francisco "Pancho" Herrera*

MONTE SAN VALENTÍN, SKI DESCENT OF SOUTH FACE

IN LATE NOVEMBER, Raimundo De Andraca, Antonio Eguiguren, Sebastían Rojas, Nicolás Valder-rama, and Galo Viguera climbed Monte San Valentín (4,058m) and then made a ski descent of the steep south face. Their 1,300m descent followed the general line of the Bertoncejl-Lantschner-Pangerc route (1952) and was completed in highly variable conditions, with one 60m rappel on the lower face. The full outing took six days round-trip. 📷

— *INFORMATION FROM* **RAIMUNDO DE ANDRACA**

CERRO NORA, FIRST ASCENT VIA SOUTHEAST FACE

Isidora Llarena scouts the descent route on Cerro Nora (2,460m), with views to the north of Cerro Cachet and Cerro Largo. *Nadine Lehner*

UNCLIMBED CERRO NORA (2,460m) had caught my eye years ago during a scramble behind a remote ranch where I was co-caretaking. Isidora Llarena had hoped to attempt the peak during a NOLS course in March 2020, before the COVID-19 pandemic canceled all plans. With each of us hunting around for a climbing partner we could cajole into "Project Nora," the trip felt like a twist of fate.

On January 8, 2021, Isi arrived in Puerto Guadal in a chilly downpour. Laden with camp-ing, mountaineering, and packrafting gear, plus 13 days of food, our packs weighed 75 pounds each. As we asked for permission to leave our car at Campo Tres Limones in Valle Colonia, don Evaristo plied us up with sopapillas, offered theories about the weather, and asked if we planned to die out there. We tried to assure him to the contrary.

After trekking to Lago Colonia, we napped on the shore and waited for the lake to calm down, then were rewarded with a spectacular evening paddle to the northwest end of the lake, about 7km away. We cached one packraft and hiked northwest toward the Cachet Dos basin, where we used the other packraft to ferry loads (and ourselves) across the river, then continued alongside the Colonia Glacier. On day three, we hiked northwest and established a base camp. Although the forecast for the next day looked ideal, our planned route to the summit looked more arduous than expected. After a lazy morning, I set off to scout out an alternative route. Returning that evening, I proposed a crazy idea: Despite the iffy forecast, we should pack up immediately and move camp into the next valley to the west, opening the faint possibility of summiting the next day. Isi signed on immediately, and at 8 p.m., we started for our new camp.

We awoke at 4:15 a.m. on the 14th to clear skies and no wind. After scrambling up to the Nora Glacier, we moved quickly into the firn zone, then roped up to piece our way through steeper sections of crevasses. After three hours, we reached the expansive summit plateau. From there on, we wished for skis as we trudged 3km across the gradual slope. At the base of the steeper summit cone, we opted for the left (southeast) ridgeline. We gained the ridge (45°), surmounted a bergschrund, and climbed a pitch of alpine ice toward the summit (1,500m from camp, AI2 moderate snow). A small rime-covered boulder was the highest point on top.

From the summit, we descended a chossy gully to the plateau, where the sun burned through the cloud blanket, softening the snow. While checking inReach messages back at camp, we learned we were the first all-female expedition to the Northern Icefield—climbing one of two peaks in the area named for a woman felt fitting.

We packed up and headed toward Cerro Silvia, chosen on the fly as our "stretch goal;" the peak is about 10km west-southwest of Cerro Nora. However, the warm, sunny weather had softened the snow, and the apparent route to the summit, via the east face and north ridge, had many crevassed sections. We made the tough call to turn around.

We left the range by packraft, piling both of us and our gear into one raft to descend the short section of river into Lago Colonia, then taking both rafts down the somewhat spicy Río Colonia to avoid a final 10km hike. On January 19, we returned to Puerto Guadal. 🖹 🖸 🔍 ▶

– NADINE LEHNER, *USA*

SOUTHERN PATAGONIA

CHALTÉN AND TORRES DEL PAINE: 2020–2021 SEASON SUMMARY

DUE TO THE pandemic, Argentina remained closed to most foreign tourists, allowing only those from neighboring countries to enter; Los Glaciares National Park (Chaltén) did not open until early January 2021. Chile opened its borders to tourism in late November, but Torres del Paine National Park remained closed to climbing. With the health care systems of both countries stretched to their limits, travel for tourism's sake seemed best left to calmer times.

It was an unusually warm and dry summer season, with the freezing line above 3,500m (well above the major summits) for a nearly three-week period. Trees lost their leaves three months early. In Paine, this resulted in two massive rockfall events, which affected the routes Riders on the Storm and Magico Este on the east face of Torre Central and Kawesqars on the east face of Torre Norte. In Chaltén, Cerro Torre saw no ascents.

In the Torre Group, there was a lot of activity on the north face of El Mocho, where Seán Villanueva O'Driscoll and partners made three notable ascents over numerous trips. First, in January 2021, he and Lucas Rubiolo freed Grey Yellow Arrow (450m, originally 7a A0) at a grade of 7a+. The crux pitch is a proper offwidth that requires walking a number 6 Camalot and finding other protection every so often. Next, in January 2021, O'Driscoll and Gabriel Rocamora started on the first pitch of Little Big Wall and then continued straight up for nine new pitches to complete Chaltén Sin Clecas ("Chaltén Without Tick Marks"; 450m, 7b). In O'Driscoll's words, the route offers "excellent climbing with a little of everything: mossy wet cracks, blind moves behind arêtes, and a hand jam roof crack with feet cutting loose, followed by a feet-first move—the whole shebang!"

Lastly, in March 2021, O'Driscoll and Matías Korten ascended the same first two pitches of Chaltén Sin Clecas, then completed seven new pitches just to the right, which they christened Chaltén Sin Chapas ("Chaltén Without Bolts"; 450m, 7a+). O'Driscoll had made several attempts on this line with Rocamora and Rubiolo, hitting a dead-end around pitch five that would require bolts; he later bypassed this by climbing into a corner to the right. The route name refers to the unquestioned and widespread use of bolts in the cliffs surrounding Chaltén as the first and only protection option. On all these climbs, O'Driscoll and partners descended via

The north face of El Mocho, showing: (1) Grey Yellow Arrow (450m, originally 7a A0) which Seán Villanueva O'Driscoll and Lucas Rubiolo free climbed at 7a+. (2) Little Big Wall. (3) Chaltén Sin Clecas (450m, 7b), climbed by O'Driscoll and Gabriel Rocamora. (4) Chaltén Sin Chapas (450m, 7a+), climbed by O'Driscoll and Matías Korten. *Rolando Garibotti*

Approach Team Line, which is expedient and highly recommended. At the end of the previous 2020 summer season (during the lockdown) Korten and O'Driscoll climbed a new route on the north face of Aguja Media Luna to the right of Harvest Moon; Cuarentena Clandestina (250m, 7a+) ascends five burly pitches with several wide sections.

In the Fitz Roy Group, in mid-August 2020, Jon Griffin and Lia Peralta climbed a new line on the south face of Cerro Ñire (to the east of Techado Negro). They started via an inviting frozen waterfall on the lower buttress (3 pitches, WI5, originally climbed by Juan Aguada and Tomas Aguilo in July 2019), bivying below the upper face. Next day, they simul-climbed steep snow and two mixed steps (M5 and M6) to a shoulder below the east summit. They climbed one more mixed pitch (M6) to within 30–50m of the top, where 100km/h winds forced them to retreat. Their unfinished line, Rafagas Inolvidables ("Unforgettable Wind," 450m, WI5 M6) is dedicated to Matteo Pasquetto, a young Italian climber who spent the 2020 summer season in Patagonia, doing new routes on Mocho and Standhardt; he died shortly afterward in the Alps.

In early February 2021, O'Driscoll made the solo first ascent of the Moonwalk Traverse, the "reverse" version of the Fitz Traverse (*see story on p.18*). On March 3, O'Driscoll returned to Cerro Chaltén (Fitz Roy) with Jon Griffin to climb La Chaltenense (500m, 7a) on the south face. The new route follows an often-discussed monster offwidth. After two pitches of The Colorado Route, they continued straight up for nine pitches via an extraordinary 350m crack, which is five to six inches wide with a few short chimney sections. This is likely one of the longest and most sustained offwidths in the world, with difficulties consistently in the upper 5.11 range. It was also a cold day, with the freezing line at 2,500m and a total of one hour of sunlight on the face. Both climbers suffered mild frostbite.

Since they only had two number 6 Camalots, O'Driscoll shuffled them, at times leaving no protection between one belay and the next. They reached the summit at 3:40 a.m., sleeping for a few hours (with a single sleeping bag but no tent or stove) before tackling the descent. The route name honors their long stay in Chaltén and is offered as thanks to the local community.

In the FKT (fastest known time) department, in early March 2021, Tomas Aguilo completed the north ridge of Cerro Domo Blanco (600m, 50° 3) in 13 hours 2 minutes, round-trip from the Río Eléctrico bridge, covering 60.8km and 2,500m of vertical gain. Later in March, Santiago Scavolini did the first solo of the Motocross Traverse (750m, 6b+), linking Aguja Guillaumet and Aguja Mermoz in 5 hours 5 minutes.

In an unfortunate development, CONAF, the Chilean park service, placed a big fabric dome at the entrance to Circo de los Altares on the ice cap. This is a disputed border zone, and this action violates the current prohibition on government intervention in the area. High winds broke the dome, it filled with ice, and it's now trash. In recent years, CONAF has installed three controversial Quonset huts to the north, in Paso Marconi and along the margin of Glaciar Chico.

In the Torres del Paine massif, unreported from early 2020, Andrea Zanetti and Antonio Zanetti attempted a new line on the west face of La Mascara, in the French Valley. They climbed 19 pitches, with difficulties to 5.10 and A1, stopping upon reaching the north arête, around four pitches from the top. They placed two bolts at almost every belay and a total of about 20 pitons, 20 bolts, and a couple dozen 6mm rivets for protection. An earlier attempt on the same line had stopped after 14 pitches.

The Torres del Paine National Park Legacy Fund donated and installed two waterless toilets in the park. (They had installed one such toilet in 2018 at Campo Italiano, at the entrance of the French Valley.) This season they placed a toilet at Campo Japonés, the climbers' base camp for the west side of the Torres, and another in the southwest area of the park.

On a sad note, Diego Señoret, a key member of the very strong current contingent of Chilean climbers, passed away in late December in an auto accident. He had climbed exten-sively with Cristobal and Juan Señoret, who, despite being almost the same age, were his nephews. Diego had climbed all three Paine towers, Cerros Torre and Fitz Roy, a new route on Cerro Paine Grande, new routes in Cochamó, and Eternal

Jon Griffin low on the monster wide crack of La Chaltenense (500m, 7a) on the south face of Fitz Roy. *Seán Villanueva O'Driscoll*

Flame on Trango Tower. In August, perhaps sensing what was to come, he wrote, "Here is to many more days in nature appreciating the simple and the essential. To many more days with family and loved ones, warriors of this life. I am grateful for all the experiences and all the beings I have crossed in this path. It has been a magical opportunity to live through it." 📷 🔍

— ROLANDO GARIBOTTI

CLUB ANDINO BARILOCHE DATABASE: *Toward the end of 2019, I approached Club Andino Bariloche (CAB) with a proposal to digitize their publications and create an online archive with free access. The CAB was founded in 1932 and, until recently, published an almost yearly journal, documenting much of the mountaineering history of the Patagonian Andes. To create the digital archive, I enlisted the help of Claudia Posch, Gerhard Rampl, and Milena Peralta from the Institute of Linguistics of the University of Innsbruck, Austria. (They had created similar online archives for the Austrian and New Zealand alpine clubs.) After I scanned the more than 7,000 pages of CAB publications, Milena ran text recognition on the scans and coordinated with close to 30 volunteers to correct errors; this resulted in clean text that optimizes searches. The Digitisation and Digital Preser-vation Group of the University of Innsbruck provided proofing software and created the website and search engine. The archive is hosted by the university's HRSM-Project Digitization and Information Processing for the Digital Humanities. Launched in early 2021, it can be accessed at transkribus. eu/r/clubandino/#/. — Rolando Garibotti*

SIERRA BAGUALES, CERRO REDONDO, SOUTH FACE, PAINAKAN

The south face of Cerro Redondo showing the routes (1) Painakan and (2) Corta Corriente, both climbed in October 2020. *Seb Pelletti*

AROUND THE SAME time that Torres del Paine closed in March 2020 due to COVID-19, we received the unfortunate news that our friend Johan Millacahuin Vivar had died in an accident on the North Tower while descending the Monzino Route. More than 50 people took part in the ensuing body recovery—seven days of hard work in Patagonian conditions. Once back in Puerto Natales, we were required to stay there due to COVID restrictions.

The many monkeys trapped in Puerto Natales were full of motivation, and we explored many new-to-us areas, including Chacabuco, Prat, Señoret, Sierra Contreras, and, later, Sierra Baguales. The conditions for winter activities in this area are impressive, but make sure you bring many layers!

In late September, we decided to explore the Sierra Baguales, a chain of mountains composed of basalt, located to the northeast of Torres del Paine. We based ourselves at the MacLean family's property after asking their permission. We planned to stay 10 days, exploring with our skis as much we could. On the last day of this trip, Eduardo Weber and I skied a steep mountain in front of the property. From the top, we saw the south face of Cerro Redondo for the first time. We knew we would have to come back and climb it.

In the beginning of October, a good weather window arrived. Karla Barria, Gonzalo Vasquez, Eduardo Weber, and I decided to give Cerro Redondo (ca 1,850m, 50°38'47"S, 72°24'7"W) a try. After a three-hour walk to the MacLeans' on October 3, we got some food and slept. Early the next morning, it took us one hour to reach the south face, which rises for 800m.

We followed the left side of the face. The first part ascended ramps of good, hard snow (65–70°). The second part ascended ice and mixed passages with a beautiful 50m section of waterfall ice, with some steps of 80–90° (WI4). This brought us to the final ridge and summit, where there is a view extending from the Torres del Paine all the way to Chaltén. We descended the north face through easy terrain, then traversed back around the base of the mountain. The climb to the top took 12 hours from our camp and was the first on this face and possibly the peak.

The indigenous Aonikenk referred to people from the north as "painakan," and this was also the name of the last Anoikenk chieftain, who lived in this area during the late 19th to early 20th century, before being driven out by colonizers. Thus, we called our route Painakan (800m, MD WI4) to honor the Aonikenk, Johan, and the community of Puerto Natales. ◙

— JOSE "CHACHO" NAVARRO JORQUERA, *CHILE*

CERRO REDONDO, SOUTH FACE, CORTA CORRIENTE

IN OCTOBER, THE Torres del Paine National Park was still closed due to the COVID-19 pandemic. We began to look at climbing objectives in the surrounding ranges. After a tip-off from local climbers who had just climbed the route Painakan (*see report above*) on the approximately south-facing wall of Cerro Redondo (ca 1,850m), Antonia Aldunate, Nicolas Secul, and I set off to make the second ascent of the face.

Cerro Redondo and the Sierra Baguales are made up of volcanic and sedimentary rock—not ideal for climbing in summer but exploding with potential for mixed and ice climbing in the austral winter. We approached from the Baguales River valley, hiking north then northeast, and set up base camp in a gauchos' hut four hours (halfway) into the approach. The next day, we reached the base of the south face at sunrise and got straight into stellar ice climbing, with a 60m pitch of solid vertical ice. After another steep ice pitch, we navigated snow ramps and mixed sections, before traversing slightly east (right) to a runnel we had noticed from the base of the wall. The runnel proved to be quite technical, with ice no more than an inch thick. We alternated between mixed chimney climbing and technical ice hooking to make our way up these two crux pitches.

After pulling through the runnel, we simul-climbed another section of steep snow. A final mixed problem gained the summit ridge, which we followed for 300m west to the top (approximately eight hours from the base).

The view from this range is astounding: Everything from the Torres del Paine massif to Fitz Roy and the Chaltén Massif can be admired amid a full panorama of Southern Patagonia. We descended via the northwest ridge, following the ridgeline until low-angled snow slopes allowed us to loop around to the south (approximately two hours) and exit via the same valley we had hiked in. We named the route Corta Corriente (800m climbing distance, WI5) after a pair of torrent ducks we saw calmly cruising their way up the rapids of the Baguales River. ◙

– SEB PELLETTI, *AUSTRALIA*

PRAT RANGE, CERRO ESMERALDA, SOUTH FACE, CORTINARIUS

ON MAY 28, Aldo Coral (Ecuador), Nicolas Secul (Chile), and I ventured into the valley between Cerro Azucena and Cerro Esmeralda in the Prat Range, which is about 50km south of Torres Del Paine and 35km northwest of Puerto Natales. After battling through the dense Patagonian lenga forest, we established our base camp at the foot of the south face of Cerro Esmeralda (1,460m).

The next morning, we simul-climbed up and left on steep snow until reaching a mixed section that avoids the hanging seracs on the upper west side of this face. After climbing up and right via two mixed pitches, we continued navigating up steep snow ramps. In the middle of the face, we reached a rock band and belayed the two crux mixed pitches. The rock provided scarce protection, and the ice conditions were too poor for screws. After overcoming this vertical band of rock, we simul-climbed for another 100m to, finally, reach good water ice. Two pitches up the ice saw us to the summit ridge, from where we headed west to the true summit. We descended the east ridge back to our vehicle.

We named the route Cortinarius (700m, WI4 M4) after the genus of purple mushrooms we found littering the forest on our way into the valley. [*Editor's Note: According to Andeshandbook.org, Esmeralda was first climbed in 1937 by Germans Gustav Fester and Ricardo Jakob, presumably by the east ridge that rises directly above the road.*] ◙

– SEB PELLETTI, *AUSTRALIA*

The route Cortinarius (700m, WI4 M4) on the south face of Cerro Esmeralda, climbed in May 2020. *Seb Pelletti*

ANTARCTICA

Climbing the northeast ridge of Mt. Gwendolyn. In back is the Shambles Glacier, emptying into Stonehouse Bay in Laubeuf Fjord. In the distance in upper right are the Tyndall Mountains on the Arrowsmith Peninsula, part of the Antarctic mainland (also seen in top photo on the opposite page). *Rob Taylor*

ANTARCTIC PENINSULA / ADELAIDE ISLAND

MT. GWENDOLYN, NORTHEAST RIDGE; THE LEGEND, WEST RIDGE, ATTEMPT

SAM HUNT AND I work as field guides at Rothera research station on Adelaide Island. On November 27, we left the base at 6 a.m., and with two sledges of emergency equipment, traveled by linked snowmobiles to McCallum Pass. We left one sledge and our skis at the base of the standard route (south ridge, normally a ski ascent) on Mt. Gwendolyn (1,230m, 67°24.0'S, 68°20.2'W), an outlying peak to the east-northeast of Mt. Mangin (2,040m), then continued on the snowmobiles with the other sledge, around the east side of the mountain to the bottom of the northeast ridge.

We began climbing on a north-facing snow slope to gain the northeast ridge at a notch above a shattered outcrop. We continued along the crest or the left flank, on rock of variable quality, to mixed ground and eventually a large, north-facing snowfield. (It would be straightforward to escape from this point by descending the snowfield.) We climbed the snowfield past one prominent snow gully to reach the next, which we ascended via a short section of thin Scottish 4 ice (some objective danger). Another gully led to increasingly mixed terrain featuring rimed rock. Above this, a sharp, horizontal snow crest led us back to the main ridge by a large rime mushroom.

We continued on easy ground up and left to shattered mixed terrain that proved difficult to protect. Another narrow ridge and more mixed ground took us to the final cluster of mushrooms/ seracs. The way through these will vary from year to year, but we generally trended right and

eventually reached easy-angled slopes leading to the summit.

The 900m-high route had taken 10 hours; we graded it D- Scottish IV,4. In a further two hours we had descended the south ridge, collected our equipment, and skied back to our snowmobiles.

Previously, on September 26, we attempted the west ridge of The Legend (1,840m, 67°34'S, 68°41'W), about 3.5km southwest of Mt. Gaudry (2,315m), the highest peak on Adelaide. This involved reaching the col between The Myth and The Legend, and to do that we climbed the standard northwest ridge of The Myth (1,235m, a relatively popular route first climbed in April 1968 by Alistair "Bugs" McKeith and Dave Rinning). We then descended The Myth's east ridge, which we believed to be previously unclimbed. [*In September 1972, two climbers (surnames Carrol and Dark) ascended a route on Myth they named Pinnacle Ridge. The east ridge has a prominent rock pinnacle, but the southwest ridge, recorded in the "Rothera guidebook" as being climbed in 1976 by Rob Davies and Trevor Phillips, also sports a large rock gendarme at its base.*] We continued up the west ridge of Legend, reaching the far side of the jagged, relatively-level section conspicuous in photographs. At this point we ran out of time and retreated.

The first known ascent of The Legend was in August 2009 via the south ridge, by Adam Clark and James Wake, but it is likely to have been climbed earlier. The impressive west face understandably remains unclimbed. 📷

— ROB TAYLOR, *U.K., WITH ADDITIONAL INFORMATION FROM* DAMIEN GILDEA

[Top] Sam Hunt on Mt. Gwendolyn. *Rob Taylor* [Middle] The northeast ridge (900m, D) of Mt. Gwendolyn. *Sam Hunt* [Bottom] Looking from The Myth to the west ridge of The Legend. The unclimbed west face is at right. *Rob Taylor*

SCANDINAVIA

Bjartur Týr Ólafsson leading the pitch above the second snowfield on the southeast face of Skarðatindur, moving up tenuous blobs of rime splattered on choss. *Rory Harrison*

END OF THE LINE
A NEW ROUTE UP A DAUNTING ICELANDIC FACE

BY BJARTUR TÝR ÓLAFSSON AND RORY HARRISON, *ICELAND*

THE SOUTHEAST FACE of Skarðatindur (1,381m) is the ultimate goal for many Icelandic alpinists. This peak is near the southern edge of the Vatnajökull ice cap, northwest of Hof, and the southeast face was first climbed in 1988 after several unsuccessful attempts, then again by a new line in 2007 (*AAJ 2008*). These routes have only seen a handful of repeats over the last three decades. I (Bjartur) spent countless hours looking at the face with the thought of climbing a new line, collected photos from different seasons and decades, and even hiked there one fall to see what it looked like when dry, trying to find wet streaks that might turn into climbable ice during the winter.

In February I was guiding in Vatnajökull National Park and conditions appeared good, so I called my friend Rory Harrison. We decided to attempt the face in a single push from the Hafrafell car park. With snow down to the lowlands, we approached up the Skaftafellsjökull (glacier) on skis. We reached a point a few hundred meters from the base of the wall, where we left our skis and gained the foot of the route around dawn.

The first part consisted of a 180m icefall that we thought would be the hardest section of the route. We were so wrong. Four pitches of WI4 and 4+ brought us to the first snowfield, which was easy, so we simul-climbed to the rimed rocks above. A route through these cliffs would hopefully lead us to the second snowfield, but this was where the real difficulties began. After two pitches we were unsure about continuing. The rock towering above looked unclimbable, and with bad weather approaching, we grabbed the opportunity to bail from a solid Abalakov anchor.

For the next couple of weeks we debated on whether this line could be climbed. Then came another weather window.

Rory Harrison continues:

On March 9, familiar with the first half of the route, we climbed quickly to our high point, then elected to traverse to the upper snowfield via a narrow, exposed ledge, with little solid protection. (This might be slower than climbing one more pitch on ice smears and then making a higher traverse.) We crossed the snowfield and arrived at the real difficulties. Bjartur led off with increasingly sparse protection on tenuous blobs of rime, splattered randomly on the chossy rock as if a small child had been let loose with a paintbrush. With a northerly storm forecast to bring winds of more than 100 km/h on the Vatnajökull ice cap that evening, time was of the essence.

Above, a ramp appeared to lead into a chimney/gully between two towers. Accessing this ramp was the technical crux of my pitch. With only psychological protection, I slowly weighted my right foot on an edge of shattered rock and reached high over the bulge above. My axe found something solid, and doubts were replaced by action. Standing on the ramp, I realized I was as committed as I've ever been. Still unable to find a piece of protection that would hold a fall, I was able to move around the corner into the gully and arrange a good belay.

Bjartur grabbed some gear and quested up. From my vantage point, it looked fairly simple, but Bjartur took his time, climbing up and down, sniffing around for safety like a cat in a new home. He got two pieces of protection about 10m above me, but I could see they were as much use as a one-legged man at an arse-kicking contest. Suddenly, he committed out right, feet on shattered rock, reaching past an overhang and swinging into blobs of rime. A whoop loud enough to carry over the now gale-force wind told me he'd made it. We hastily began our descent along the ridge to the north, until we could follow a couloir east to the glacier and regain our skis. By the time we reached the car we had been going for 18.5 hours. We named the route End of the Line (TD+ AI4+ M5). ▤ ▣ ▶

EDITOR'S NOTE: *In the spring of 1988, Jón Geirsson and Snævarr Guðmundsson made the first ascent of the ca 500m southeast face of Skarðatindur, starting on the far left before working up right toward the summit. The ascent took five hours and was graded TD+ WI5. A second route, climbing directly to the last section of the 1988 line, was added in 2007 by Stéphane Benoist, Jean-Baptist Deraeck, Sébastien Ibanez, and Sébastien Ratel to give Jökullélé (TD+ M5 WI4; AAJ 2008).*

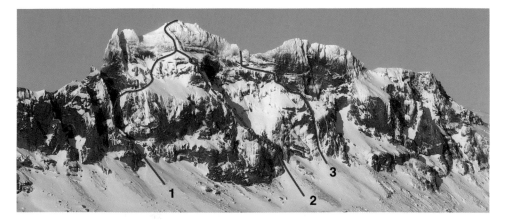

The southeast face of Skarðatindur is about 500 meters high, and the approach can take three to eight hours. (1) Geirsson-Guðmundsson (1988). (2) Jökullélé (2007). End of the Line (2020). *Bjartur Týr Ólafsson*

Matteo Mucci below the rime-ice towers of the east face of Hvannadalshnjúkur, descending from a new route on the west face. The approach to Hvannadalshnjúkur from Hnappavellir climbs the low-angled glacier slopes of the caldera on the left. *Bjartur Týr Ólafsson*

HVANNADALSHNJÚKUR, WEST FACE, HNJÚKAÞEYR

HVANNADALSHNJÚKUR (2,110M), LOCATED on the northwest edge of the Öræfajökull caldera, is Iceland's highest summit. The west face had four existing lines, the first climbed in 1986. The face is seldom visited: The approach is outrageously long, and it is generally in good condition during October when the ice climbing season is still just around the corner.

In October 2016, Þorsteinn Cameron, Matteo Meucci, and I had climbed the west face by a partial new route. In October 2020, Matteo and I wanted to try a more direct line up the face—most routes veer right in the upper section. Anticipating a big day, we decided to leave from Hnappavellir [a hamlet on Route 1 to the south-southeast of the mountain, best known for its nearby sport climbing] and use skis to save time on the way down.

On the 13th, after a long approach in the dark, we reached the saddle between Dyrhamar (the Gate) and the summit cone of Hvannadalshnjúkur, where we left the skis, dropped down the west side, traversed north, and began climbing over bergschrunds and up steep snowfields that form the lower part of the face. After a long spell of simul-climbing 55° snow, we spotted what we had been hoping to see: a beautiful, 110m blue-ice line straight up the middle of the uppermost face. We stopped for a minute to discuss whether the route was too ambitious and steep for our off-season form, but concluded by saying to each other, "Who are we kidding? This is the line we came to climb!"

An 80m section of WI3 took us to the base of the ice fall. I led the first steep pitch of brittle alpine ice; after 55m of sustained climbing at WI5-, I eventually got a rest and belay on a ledge. The next pitch provided similarly sustained climbing (WI4/4+) up to the summit plateau. From here, a 10-minute walk got us to the top. We had stunning views in all directions and enjoyed the moment before descending to our skis.

We named the route Hnjúkaþeyr, after the warm, dry wind that descends from the mountains, similar to the Föhn in the Alps. [*Editor's Note: The online version of this report includes extensive notes on the geography and history of Hvannadalshnjúkur climbing.*] 📄 📷 ▶

— BJARTUR TÝR ÓLAFSSON, *ICELAND*

RÓTARFJALLSHNJÚKUR, WEST FACE, DRAUPNIR

ON OCTOBER 16, Árni Stefán Haldorsen and Íris Ragnarsdóttir Pedersen climbed the west face of Rótarfjallshnjúkur (1,848m). This peak lies on the southern rim of the Öræfajökull, a large, ice-filled caldera that last erupted in 1727, almost due north of Hof. There are five peaks on the rim that exceed 1,800m, including Hvannadalshnjúkur, Iceland's highest summit.

The two climbers started the approach to Rótarfjallshnjúkur by 4WD and then walked to around 1,200m, where they stepped onto the glacier. Moderately angled but crevassed terrain led to the base of the south ridge. They then climbed the west face in three pitches: 75m, 60°; 55m, 60–75° snow/névé; 30m, AI3. The team used ice screws, Spectres, nuts, and snow stakes.

From the top of the face, they followed the ridge northeast for a few hundred meters to the top. Just before the summit is a 15m arête that is quite sharp and gave a precarious passage. The climbers descended east to regain their approach route. ▣

– *INFORMATION FROM* THE ICELANDIC ALPINE CLUB

ICELAND / AUSTURLAND

ÞVERÁRTINDSEGG, NORTHEAST FACE, SINFUL PLEASURES

ÞVERÁRTINDSEGG (1,554M) LIES around 16km northeast of the famed Jökulsárlón glacier lagoon on Iceland´s southeast coast. The normal route is via glaciated slopes to the north (F, probably first climbed in 1932), but its most impressive aspect is the northeast face, about 400m high. Until 2020, this face had seen only one known ascent, a bold line directly up the center, climbed in May 2003 by the accomplished Icelandic alpinists Ívar Finnbogason and Einar Rúnar Sigurðsson. The first 320m of the route were a mixture of steep snow and ice, interspersed with harder sections of WI3 and 4. The last 80m were either vertical or overhanging, and the route was graded TD+ WI5+.

The approach to the east side of the mountain starts by 4WD up the broad Kálfafellsdalur valley, followed by a trek up the Eggjadalur valley and an arduous ascent of 1,000m up steep snow slopes and the Skrekk Glacier. At 2 p.m. on April 26, having made that long approach, Aliesya Bozhitzya and Eugene Glibin, two Ukrainians based in Iceland, started a new route to the left of the 2003 line. They began at a snowy rib to the left of the couloir leading to a large rock triangle that disgorges rockfall almost constantly.

The first three pitches of adequately protected WI3/4 went well, with Bozhitzya enjoying her first multi-pitch ice climb. Then things got more tenuous on thin ice covered with avalanche-prone snow. Three pitches of poorly protected climbing at WI3 R took them to a southeast-facing spur at around 10 p.m. Beyond was a 50° couloir of deep snow, but to reach it the two first climbed the spur for a pitch, with each climber on opposite sides of the ridge, with the rope between them. Two pitches in the couloir and a further pitch (M4 R) with no protection brought them to the summit ridge. After 50m along the narrow crest, they stood on the summit at 1:30 a.m., greeted by a fine display of northern lights.

Descending the northern slopes, they were troubled by what appeared to be headlamps in the valley below, and eventually the commotion of helicopters. Friends had become concerned they hadn't made it home. By the time they returned to their vehicle, they had been out for 23 hours. The route was named Sinful Pleasures (D/D+, 11 pitches, WI4 M4 R). ▣

– *INFORMATION FROM* THE ICELANDIC ALPINE CLUB

NORWAY

LYNGEN PENINSULA, JIEHKKEVÁRRI, SOUTHEAST FACE, SKI DESCENT

IN THE EARLY morning of April 28, Eivind Jacobsen and I made the first ski descent of the 1,100m southeast face of Jiehkkevárri (1,834m), the highest mountain in the Lyngen Alps. The line had been climbed only once, solo, in 1979 by Dave Nicholls. [*Nichols was a highly talented U.K. alpinist and officer in the Royal Marines, who during the 1970s was a group leader of the Mountain and Arctic Warfare Cadre in Norway.*] This was also the last remaining face on the peak without a ski descent.

In Sjur Nesheim's guide to the Lyngen Alps, the southeast face is described as 55° snow and ice

The southeast face of Jiehkkevárri, with the line of the 2020 ski descent marked. *Hamish Frost*

with a pitch of M4 guarding the last 30m to the top of the face, above which gentle slopes lead to the summit. It is a line with plenty of exposure and objective danger, so ideal conditions are crucial. The first part of the route, slanting up a ramp, is exposed to serac fall, and much of the route lies above cliff bands and below large cornices.

On the 27th we left Lyngsdalen with bivouac gear, so we could get a look at the face that evening before an early start. The year 2020 was unusually good for snow in the Lyngen Alps, and the forecast for the previous several days was for moist fresh snow before a drop in temperature, then remaining overcast without much wind. Our hope was the snow would stick to the steep, icy face and then "dry out." This would give us a short window in the middle of the night and early morning of the 28th to ski the face in good powder before the sun increased the risk of avalanches and cornice collapse.

We started at 2 a.m., finding the hoped-for conditions, with about 20–30cm of fresh snow. This made for an exhausting bootpack, but we were able to climb the whole route without using the rope. Apart from a few icy patches, and a sun crust on the last 50m to the top, we found superb skiing conditions. We used the rope to belay while we removed the cornice from above, and then skied the whole line clean.

The name Jiehkkevárri comes from the Sami language, where "Jiehkke" means glacier and "várri" mountain. Steep lines have been skied on other facets of the mountain, with the northeast couloir now a modern classic, seeing a couple of descents each winter, as foreseen by the late Andreas Fransson. The Swede had referred to the southeast face—then unskied—as the Brenva Face of the Arctic.

— FINN HOVEM, *NORWAY*

TYSFJORD REGION, STETIND, SOUTH PILLAR VARIANT, GOLDFINGER

I HAD PLANNED a solo expedition to Greenland in 2020, but due to the pandemic, I had to find an alternative. Northern Norway immediately sprang to mind. I had first seen the famous pyramid of Stetind (1,391m), Norway's "Anvil of the Gods," in 1998 while on honeymoon with my wife, Daniela. Such wild mountains and granite walls are mostly unknown in my home country.

After a few roped solo routes to warm up, and once the rough Norse weather offered a fair window, I headed for my main goal: the south face of Stetind.

I climbed the easy terrain on the initial 800m face without protection, hoping to continue up the Guldfisken Route (Norwegian 6). However, rockfall had covered the ledges on the vertical wall with rubble, so I discarded this idea. Over to my right was a prominent dihedral. It looked good, but it ended below smooth slabs. Would I be able to continue up these? My biggest passion is to explore unknown ground: If I don't know what to expect, there will be a lot of adventure. Achieving this while climbing solo poses the biggest challenge.

Following the dihedral and slabs, I reached the South Pillar (a.k.a. Sydpilaren, Norwegian 6, Hertzberg-Naess, 1936) at about two-thirds height, free climbing and back-roping with traditional protection. I continued up the pillar, and after a further 10 hours reached the summit at midnight. Strong winds made the descent difficult, but I reached my camp by the Tysfjord after a 20-hour round trip, tired but happy. I named my variant to the South Pillar—the middle third of the route—Goldfinger (6b+). [*Editor's Note: Jasper subsequently soloed long routes on Kugelhorn, Rundtind, and Eidetind; details and exceptional photos are at the AAJ website.*]

The South Pillar route on Stetind ascends the sunlit face on the right. *Robert Jasper*

— ROBERT JASPER, *GERMANY*

KAISEPAKTE, ARÊTE LA NIEHKU; LATJOVAGGE, CASCADE DE QUARANTINE

MOSTLY FREE TO climb around the country throughout the pandemic, my wife, Anna Backlund, and I did two new routes in northern Scandinavia. On February 22, we climbed a five-pitch line on the far left side of the northeast face of Kaisepakte (a.k.a. Gaisevarri, 1,205m), which rises above the E10 Highway, southeast of Abisko. The face is notable for a big ice section, around WI4+, which used to stay in climbable condition from early October until mid-June. Climate change has seen to that, but it is still a long ice climbing season in this area.

Our route, Arête la Niehku (Dream Arête, WI5 M6), is an eye-catching line with steep dry-tooling, thin ice, snowy ledges, and an interesting cornice to finish. The line forms more or less every year, though getting the timing right can be difficult: The ice falls off quite easily, and protection can be tricky in the compact rock. A few days later, I went back with Jan Axelsson and made the second ascent.

In the first week of April, Anna and I climbed an excellent new ice route in the lower part of the Latjovagge (Laddjujohka) valley, about halfway up the 20km walk to the Svenska Turist Foreningen Fjallstation, which is the main hut on the southeast side of Kebnekaise (2,096m), Sweden's highest mountain. We named our four-pitch route Cascade de Quarantine (WI6). Due to climate change, far more ice in this area forms now than it did 10 years ago.

— KRISTER JONSSON, *SWEDEN*

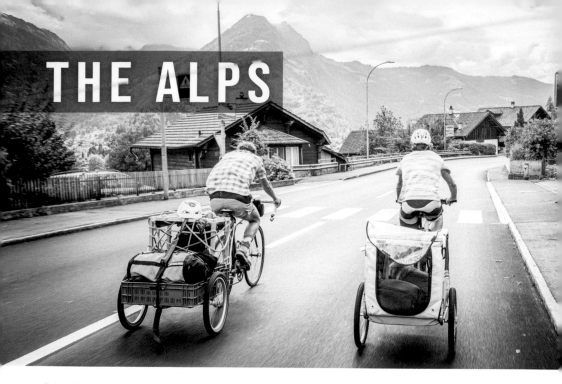

THE ALPS

[Above] Sébastien Berthe and Nicolas Favresse towed the gear for a nearly four-week trip, plus their dogs, for about 650 kilometers. [Opposite] Favresse on Des Kaisers Neue Kleider. *Damien Largeron (both)*

THE ALPINE TRILOGY BY BIKE
A LOW-IMPACT APPROACH TO A LEGENDARY SET OF CLIMBS

BY SÉBASTIEN BERTHE, *BELGIUM*

IT WAS JANUARY 2020, and I was looking for a project for the summer—something really different, a challenge that would test my limits, but also something with less environmental impact than an expedition involving many planes. After some research, an idea began to emerge: the Alpine Trilogy, three legendary 8b+ (5.14a) multipitch routes in the Swiss, Austrian, and German Alps, opened by three legendary climbers, all in 1994. The three routes—Silbergeier in the Rätikon Group of the Swiss Alps (Beat Kammerlander), Des Kaisers Neue Kleider in the Kaiser Mountains of Austria (Stefan Glowacz), and End of Silence in Bavaria's Northern Salzburg Alps (Thomas Huber)—are similar in difficulty and length, but each has its own character and style.

Doing any one of these routes reflects a great performance in the world of high-level multi-pitch climbing, but doing all three is a challenge that only a handful of climbers have managed to achieve—and they had never been done in one summer. Ambitious certainly, but undoubtedly possible! After the pandemic canceled all of my planned trips for the year, and after realizing the three routes were relatively close to each other, I wondered: Would it be possible to do them without fossil fuels? Could I find all the ingredients for a real expedition without taking three planes and two buses to some far-flung destination? Cycling seemed to be the way.

In July, three weeks before the ideal start date for the project, everything seemed ready. Most COVID-19 restrictions had been lifted in Europe. Photographer Damien Largeron had signed on, and I'd found a dog sitter for Kroux, my canine partner. However, I still had a little problem to solve: No partners were lining up. Who would be crazy enough to embark on such a project?

Then one morning my phone rang and I heard the soft voice of my Belgian compatriot Nicolas Favresse. His exploratory trip to the big walls of Norway had just been aborted due to the pandemic, and he was looking for a Plan B. Without further ado, I suggested he get on his bike and join me in three weeks. He immediately and enthusiastically agreed, but then there was silence on the phone. I could almost hear him thinking, hesitating. "I'm in, but I have a condition," he said. I expected the worst: time limits, electric assistance, a sweep vehicle. "We have to take the dogs with us," he explained. Shit, I found someone crazier than me!

On August 2, our train to the base of the Rätikon, our first objective, entered the station in France. I took stock of the team: Bintje, a fiery young dog of an undetermined breed. Kroux, cat lover and border collie–golden retriever mix. Damien and his photo equipment. Nico with his guitar and me in my best pink tights. Somehow our nomadic caravan all got on board. We were underway.

Silbergeier is probably the most famous of the Trilogy and was the perfect route to test our fitness. Nico had climbed the route almost 10 years earlier, and I had given it a try without completing it. We'd quickly know whether this quest could become reality or would stay a dream.

After hours of climbing and sweating on incredible gray limestone, we reached the crux, a technical and bouldery pitch on small crimps. Try after try, Nico and I unlocked the sequences together. One of us found a foothold, the other imagined tricky beta for the hands. A few hours and falls later, we both clipped the anchor after a fierce fight! It was just in time, as melting snow from the top of the wall was flowing dangerously close to the key holds. We each had freed all the pitches, both of us leading the pitches graded 8a and harder.

Ten days later, after a quick bonus send of Headless Children (260m, 8b), also in the Rätikon, we have made our way to the Wilder Kaiser and are resting on an uncomfortable ledge for yet another try at the final crux of Des Kaisers Neue Kleider. "Don't fall asleep, you have to wake Nico in 30 minutes for his try!" I tell myself. "Concentrate, look at the stars, do not fall asleep, do not fall asleeeee…."

I'm awakened by Nico readjusting his position on the ledge. The silent, dark night of the Wilder Kaiser is punctuated by Damien's snoring. "Are you ready to attack?" I whisper to Nico. He responds by turning on our single dim headlamp. His eyes are tired but wide open, and I can see unwavering determination.

After 18 hours of climbing and nearly 20 tries to redpoint the route's four pitches of 8a or harder, Nico sets off for a final attempt on this last pitch, rated 8b+ (5.14a). The first section, a steep and terribly technical dihedral, is executed to perfection. He grabs the jug before the final, easier section with a cry. Only a few more easier moves to go—the victory is not far!

Earlier in the night, however, we both had fallen at these final moves before the anchor. In that moment, I forget my fatigue, my hunger, my thirst. In the light of the headlamp, fighting with slippery footholds, Nico climbs slowly and cautiously. In a few moves, he is trembling and breathing hard. I shout encouragement, giving back the support he has offered me through-out the day. He arrives at the final move, grabs the jug, and clips the anchor, and our cries of joy break the calm silence of the night. Despite our doubts, despite the morning rain, wet pitches, and numerous falls, we have completed Des Kaisers Neue Kleider on our first (long) day on the route, again both freeing all the pitches, and each leading the ones 8a and harder.

We had been climbing, pedaling, and walking for two weeks by then. I wanted a real adventure, and the ingredients were all there: flat tires, high mountain passes under the sun and in the snow, multiple thunderstorms, soaked, dried, resoaked, paradisiacal moments and urban bivouacs, rockfall, big falls, dips in lakes and rivers each more bucolic than the last. Calf pain replaced pain in the fingertips and vice versa. The sweet sound of barking dogs followed in our footsteps as we biked, camped, and climbed through the Alps. Bintje and Kroux seemed to enjoy their new way of life each day. Running alongside our bikes or riding in the carts, sleeping outside next to their owners—what else does a dog need?

We were ahead of schedule and optimistic. Aside from the skin on our fingers, we felt partic-ularly fit. Our buttocks had become accustomed to our saddles and no longer cried out in pain each time we got on the bikes. We relished in slowly discovering these landscapes while carrying only the bare essentials (with the exception of a plastic flamingo and a guitar). It also seemed the pedal strokes boosted our climbing volume, our stamina, and even our resistance. Sprinkled with a few hangboard sessions, this seemed to be a recipe for success.

On August 20, after another 50km of pedaling, getting lost for more than three hours in the bushes, and a series of particularly slippery footholds in run-out terrain, we topped out The End of Silence in the Berchtesgaden massif. Our skin was in tatters, the Trilogy complete.

What a joy to combine a high-performance goal with a close-to-home adventure! What a joy to climb and travel while minimizing our impact, right in the midst of a worldwide pandemic. Perhaps these kinds of adventures are the future.

SUMMARY OF ACTIVITY: Sébastien Berthe and Nico Favresse were the first climbers to complete the Alpine Trilogy in a single summer season. They redpointed each route ground-up and in a day. From August 2–28, 2020, the two biked a total of 650km between the climbs. With time and energy to spare after completing the trilogy, Berthe and Favresse pedaled to the Eiger and made a one-day, team-free repeat of Odyssee (1,400m, 8a+). 🔲

TRANS-SWITZERLAND BIKE AND CLIMB

IN AUGUST 2020, Caro North (Switzerland) and Ines Papert (Germany) undertook a bike and climb journey from east to west across Switzerland, pulling trailers with all their gear and food (about 40kg each) and climbing classic multi-pitch routes of the Swiss Alps.

Departing from Feldkirch, Austria, on August 10, the two spent a month traversing the coun-try, pedaling about 600km and climbing Intifada (220m, 7a+) in the Rätikon, Peruvian Dancing Dust (7a+) on the Teufelstalschlucht above Andermatt, Excalibur (350m, 6b) in the Wendenstöcke, Deep Blue Sea (320m, 7b+) on the north face of the Eiger, and La Fête des Pères (300m, 7a) on the south face of Gastlosen. They finished the trip on the French border with an alpine traverse of les Aiguilles Dorées in the Mont Blanc massif.

– ANDY ANDERSON

THE ALPS AND DOLOMITES: MAJOR ASCENTS

WITH COVID-19 RESTRICTING top European climbers' travels, there were inevitably many fine ascents throughout the Alps and Dolomites. The following is a small but representative selection of the big Alpine adventures carried out during 2020, some of them before the pandemic surfaced in Europe.

Arguably the most notable ascent in the Mont Blanc Massif, and indeed the Western Alps, was not a new route at all but the second ascent of the legendary Phantom Direct on the Grandes Jorasses.

The south-southeast face or Tronchey Wall rises 1,400m from the Pra Sec Glacier to the summit of Pointe Walker (4,208m), making it the tallest in the range. The lower section is characterized by steep, compact granite, while the upper sports a pronounced central pillar. Italians Alessandro Gogna and Guido Machetto were the first people ever to cross the Pra Sec Glacier, when in August 1972 they climbed the wet, steep lower wall of the southeast face, experiencing Eiger-like stonefall, then the more enjoyable central pillar to the summit of Pointe

Foreshortened view of the Tronchey Wall, seen from the upper Pra Sec Glacier. (1) Original Route (1,400m, probably ED2 VI A2, Gogna-Machetto, 1972). (2) Phantom Direct (1,400m, ED2/3 VI/5 or 6, Grassi-Luzi-Rossi, 1985). (3) Plein Sud (VI/5 M6+R, 2010), climbed to blank rock a couple of pitches below the Tronchey Ridge. *Marcello Sanguineti*

Walker. Their route likely has never been attempted since and is probably ED2 in today's currency.

Later, the visionary ice climber Gian Carlo Grassi saw another possibility: ephemeral ice smears leading to the huge gully right of the pillar, which in turn leads to the Tronchey Ridge. Over many years he made six "reconnaissance" attempts until, in June 1985, following the snowiest winter for years, he found the ice smears beautifully formed. With Renzo Luzi and Mauro Rossi, Grassi reached the base of the gully to find…no ice. What to do? The three made a delicate and irreversible 200m rising traverse over snow-covered slabs to reach a hanging couloir or depression left of the central pillar, rising toward the top of the Pra Sec Ridge. Grassi's intuition paid off: It was in excellent condition. With a storm closing, threatening to trap the climbers in a vast avalanche funnel, they unroped and climbed rapidly over technical ground to the summit. Since then, a repetition of the Phantom Direct (a.k.a. Gianni Comino Memorial Route: 1,400m: ED3 VI/5 or 6) has been among the most sought-after ascents in the Alps, Grassi having wisely predicted his route "would not be repeated for a long time."

In January 2020, ice routes in the Mont Blanc Range were in splendid condition. On the 21st, Yann Borgnet and Charles Dubouloz, after driving from their homes in Annecy, France, left the valley at 4 a.m. in a temperature of -12°C, and reached the start of the route at 9.30 a.m. Experiencing high wind and poor visibility on the difficult upper section, they arrived on the summit 10 hours later, only two hours faster than the 1985 ascensionists, having just repeated the longest ice climb in the Mont Blanc Massif. They reached the Boccalatte Hut at 4 a.m. the following day.

The Epéna in Winter

IN THE VANOISE, west of Mont Blanc, the Epéna (3,421m) was one of the last "big peaks" in the Alps to be climbed (1900). The north face—almost 3km wide and up to 750m high—is revered by the French mountaineering community due to the relative isolation, tranquility, and height of this Alpine wall. The limestone on the north face is compact yet often friable, with many small, downward-sloping holds and poor protection, even if using pitons, and the descent on the south side is long and complex. Making the first winter ascent of this face had been a coveted project for decades, and in February 2019 it finally fell to Léo Billon, Julien Ravanello, and Benjamin Védrines, who succeeded on the classic northwest spur of the Pointe Orientale (765m, TD 5c, Rod-Schneider, 1966).

Manu Pellissier made his first foray onto this face almost three decades ago, and for the last 20 years he has watched for viable ice to allow a winter-conditions ascent; on one attempt he was forced to bail just 130m below the top of the Rod-Schneider. Finally, in 12 hours on November 27, with Luc Mongellaz and Jessy Pivier, he completed the first ascent of The Fridge (900m of climbing, 5c M5 WI5) on the north face of the Brèche Perdrieux (3,251m), the col between the Pointe Orientale (3,348m) and Pointe Centrale (3,307m). The three started at the base of the 1966 Rod-Schneider, then worked up the depression to the right, arriving on the summit ridge with the feeling of having achieved something special.

Three days previously, in order to prepare a descent route on the north side, this same team had climbed a west-facing 500m gully at M5 WI5, mostly on new ground, between Pointe Occidentale (3,293m) and the 3,321m Petite Glière to the southwest, equipping it for eight rappels. From the top of The Fridge it took the trio three hours to traverse over the Centrale and Occidentale summits to reach the top of their equipped descent, crawling through the night along the sharp and difficult ridge. They regained their car 20 hours after leaving. The news quickly spread, and the route was repeated by two parties just three days later.

Winter Valtournenche Traverse

Francois Cazzanelli and Francesco Ratti on top of Punta Lioy (3,816m) on the Grandes Murailles Ridge. At far left is Punta del Cors (3,852m), to its right the south face of the Matterhorn, and in the far distance Monte Rosa. *Damiano Levati | Story Teller Labs*

LONG RIDGE TRAVERSES or enchainments in the Alps enable climbers to have a full Himalayan experience in length and difficulty (minus the high altitude). There were several remarkable high-level journeys in 2020, but probably the most outstanding was a winter traverse around the northern rim of the upper Valtournenche, the vast bowl south of the Matterhorn, completed by Cervinia guides Francois Cazzanelli and Francesco Ratti. Moving from east to west and then southward, the pair linked the Furggen chain, the Matterhorn, and the Grandes and Petites Murailles—a total of 20 summits, 51km distance, and 4,800m of ascent. They had attempted this project in the winter of 2019, only to fail near the end due to impassable cornices.

At 7 a.m. on January 20, the two Italians left the hut by Theodul Pass (3,295m), and by 1 p.m. on the 23rd they had descended to the valley from the Col des Dames, southwest of Mont Blanc du Creton (3,406m), the last peak of the Petites Murailles. Their first night was spent in the Carrel Hut, having traversed the Matterhorn, and the second and third at the small Perelli and Paoluccio bivouac huts situated on the Murailles ridge. They climbed along the lengthy east ridge of the Dent d'Hérens but did not go to the summit, instead aiming directly for the Col des Grandes Murailles and the Perelli. Minimum temperatures were -23°C.

The first continuous traverse of the sharp and technical rocky ridges of Grandes and Petites Murailles was made over three days in the summer of 1940. Seven years later, another Italian team linked the Matterhorn with a traverse of the Grandes Murailles, also with two bivouacs. In 1985 Cazzanelli's father, Valter, with Marco Barmasse (father of well-known alpinist Hervé Barmasse) made the first winter crossing of the Grandes and Petites. In August 2018, Francois Cazzanelli and Kilian Jornet traversed the Grandes and Petites Murailles in just under 11 hours.

Cazzanelli returned in September 2020 and with Nadir Maguet traversed the Matterhorn via the Furggen and Italian ridges, then continued to traverse the frontier ridge west over the Dent d'Herens to the Valpelline, the whole ca 35km odyssey completed in less than one day.

Ice Climbs on the Piz Badile

FURTHER EAST, GOOD ice/mixed conditions on the Piz Badile are extremely rare and ephemeral. Local knowledge is crucial. Toward the end of November, Matteo della Bordella and Silvan Schüpbach heard from Marcel Schenk, the preeminent connoisseur of the mountain in winter, that conditions appeared to be perfect. They set out from the Sasc Fura Hut on the 26th with no set plan, plowing through deep snow to reach the start of the north ridge. From here they followed a vague ledge system left across the northeast face for around 400m—thin, poorly protected ice over slabby rock— to below Linea Bianca, the visionary 1978 rock route by Igor Koller and Stanislav Silhan that was the first to breach the steep, poorly protected slabs right of the Cassin Route. The pair followed this "white line," front-pointing delicate thin ice and mixed to M6, to reach the north ridge, where they continued to the summit and

Silvan Schüpbach climbing the thinly iced Linea Bianca section of Crossway of Friendship. *Matteo Della Bordella*

spent the night in the Redaelli bivouac hut. They called their line into Linea Bianca the Crossway of Friendship. This was not the first time Linea Bianca had been climbed during the winter season, but it was the first as an ice/mixed route.

The following day, Schenk himself, along with David Hefti, combined two of his own 2016 routes: Amore di Vetro (800m, M5 R, a beautiful sliver of ice between Memento Mori and the Cassin) and Nordest Supercombo (M7 R) to create Amore Supercombo. The two Swiss found "unbelievable" conditions on Amore Supercombo and even managed to place a few ice screws. Even so, the route had very long runouts. But the word was out, and this new combination only had to wait three days before receiving a second ascent.

Dolomites

THREE OF THE most active climbers in this region, Martin Dejori, Titus Prinoth, and Alex Walpoth from the Val Gardena, managed to solve the "last great problem" of the Pala di San Lucano when they forced a direct route up the great, ca 1,150m south face of the Terza Pala. Guardian of Dreams, climbed from November 1–4, is 1,400m or 34 pitches in length and has a crux pitch of VIII+ A0, which Prinoth climbed with just three pegs and Walpoth, coming second, freed at IX. The whole

Alessandro Baù on pitch seven of Space Vertigo (21 pitches, 8a), Cima Ovest di Lavaredo. *Giovanni Danieli*

route was protected with removable gear, including around 35 pitons—no bolts were carried. The route, which has largely excellent rock and lies between the 1972 Anghileri-Gogna-Lanfranchi-Rava on the left and the 2019 Leduc-Vanhee, was climbed ground up.

Among the other highly active climbers here, particularly when it comes to creating big, bold routes without recourse to bolts, are Alessandro Baù and Nicola Tondini. Demonstrating that independent exploration is still possible on the most famous rock faces in the world, in 2019, with Claudio Migliorini, they completed Space Vertigo on the north face of Cima Ovest, to the right of the classic Via Jean Couzy. Rigorous in their approach, opening each pitch from below without using aid, it took three years to finish their dream project, which requires "strong arms, a very good head, and obligatory 7b climbing, often some way above protection." (Due to the nature of the rock and for portaledge camps on the wall, the belays were bolted, but no protection bolts were used.) The route was done, but the team had not yet freed it in a single push.

In September 2020, the three returned, hauled portaledges and provisions to a point at one-third height, and on the 9th began a free ascent from the ground. Due to slightly damp rock, they were only able to complete three pitches the first day, so they returned to the ground for the night. Next day they jumared their ropes and, with two nights at the portaledge camp, freed the remaining difficulties. On the fourth day they completed the 21-pitch route to the summit. The crux is 8a; five pitches are 7c or 7c+, and another eight are 7a to 7b+. Each pitch was led by at least one member of the team. The route is certainly one of the hardest in the Dolomites.

Also from Cima Ovest comes the remarkable story of Lukasz Dudek (Poland), who made an audacious roped solo of Alexander Huber's 2007 route Pan Aroma (550m, 8c) on the north face. With Jacek Matuszek, Dudek already had made free ascents of Bellavista (8b+) and Project Fear (8c) on the same face, and the Spanish route (8b+) on the Cima Grande. Dudek prepared for Pan Aroma by working two days on the route in 2019 with a friend, and did several dozen roped-solo ascents of sport routes up to 8c in Poland.

After inspecting the route alone in July, on August 7 he completed every pitch free on his first attempt and reached the summit after 17 hours on the face. While the roof pitches are spectacular, Dudek says it is the long 60m rightward traverse, the original pitch six, that provides the technical crux. He had timed his ascent to arrive at the meat of the route around midday, when the temperature on this shadowed wall would approach maximum, keeping his fingers warm and the pump at bay. But, then, timing was the crucial factor for of all these reported adventures, where the protagonists very clearly "seized the day." ◙

— LINDSAY GRIFFIN

JORDAN

JEBEL RUM, QUEEN OF THE DESERT

WADI RUM IS well known for adventure climbing—bolted routes hardly exist. The reason for this, other than local traditions, is the soft sandstone. Many first ascensionists here have reported that expansion bolts could not be tightened because the holes did not have the proper dimension after drilling.

Lead-bolting on Queen of the Desert. *Tobias Wolf Collection*

In February, two teams—Chris-Jan Stiller and I, and a French group led by Jonathan Crison and Arnaud Petit—planned to open long bolt-protected routes in Wadi Rum. Each team had a different approach to solving the problems with the soft rock. The French planned to use removable bolts (Petzl Coeur Pulse) during their ground-up ascent, replacing them later with permanent glue-in bolts. Our idea was to use expansion bolts thicker and longer than the 10mm ones commonly used in hard rock, increasing the contact between steel and rock. In the end, our strategy was to bring drill bits with different levels of wear for our 110mm-long and 12mm-wide bolts: one brand new (12.5mm), one well used (11.5mm), and one really old and worn (10.8mm). As a backup, we brought some epoxy adhesive to glue in the belay anchors and bolts that could not be tightened.

After warming up with Rock Empire (485m, 7c) and 55 Steps to Hell (300m, 7b) on the east face of Jebel Rum (1,754m), we headed into the desert to find a wall of our dreams. We spent many days exploring different walls and testing the rock quality, but none of them came even close to Jebel Rum. The last option was a line on the left side of Jebel Rum, which Arnaud had pointed out. The proposed line would start on Towering Inferno (300m, 7a) before splitting off to the right for another four to six pitches.

After climbing two pitches on Towering Inferno, we quickly realized the rock quality was indeed better than anything we'd seen. We immediately started to make our way up new ground. After two days of work, we had finished our route to the top, establishing ten new pitches. We also wanted to find an alternative to the Towering Inferno start, as the first three pitches of that route are always busy and require a full trad rack. On our redpoint day, we bolted two pitches to the left of Towering Inferno, ground-up, and continued to free Queen of the Desert (450m, 7a+) in a five-hour push.

Overall, we placed 110 bolts on the route and at belays, and now it is possible to climb Jebel Rum with only some quickdraws and two or three small cams. Our success is due to the fact that we brought the worn drill bit (11.5mm). The 12.5mm drill bit was useful on rock with black patina, but in softer rock it left holes much too big. 🗎 📷 🔍

— TOBIAS WOLF, *GERMANY*

LA VOIE DU COEUR: *Jonathan Crison and Arnaud Petit led a team of six young French climbers on the first ascent of a direct 12-pitch line starting to the right of Towering Inferno and Revienta o Burilla. La Voie du Coeur is completely bolt-protected and goes at 7c+ (7b obligatory), with the best rock in the first five pitches. The French reportedly had difficulty with both their expansion bolts and their glue-ins in the softer rock on the upper half. Topos for the new routes on Jebel Rum are at the AAJ website.*

GEORGIA

GEORGIAN DREAM
A NEW ROUTE ON USHBA SOUTH'S STEEP NORTHWEST FACE

BY ARCHIL BADRIASHVILI, *GEORGIA*

CLIMBING A NEW line up the most iconic peak of the Caucasus—Ushba (south peak, 4,710m; north, 4,690m)—is a dream for many alpinists. The mountain is famous for being harsh, complex, and dangerous. I remember moments as a teenager cautiously searching for "my line" on this magic mountain, but every logical route on all six faces of this double-summited peak appeared to have been climbed. Giorgi Tepnadze and I wanted a new, bold line, climbed in a lightweight style, which would test our longtime friendship and team experience.

In 1946, Georgians made the first ascent of the northwest face of Ushba South, but 25 years were to pass before the large upper wall—the Rockband—barring access to the summit, was finally breached. The 1971 Artsishevskiy Route (6A) climbed a corner on the left, while the 1972 Grigorenko-Prigoda Route (6A) took a corner on the right. Both teams spent two weeks, using siege style, to complete their routes, and since then there have been only a handful of ascents (*AAJ 2017*).

We aimed to climb the center of the Rockband, beginning at around 4,200m. This area is gently overhanging and very compact; melting snow from above drops like a waterfall over the wall, fortunately not touching our proposed line. We planned to go fast and light, with the flexibility of switching to big-wall style on the Rockband.

Our preparation was intense. Starting in June we climbed in the Chaukhi Range and the Tetnuldi group, then the 1962 Mishlyaev Route (1,700m, 5B/6A) on Ushba South, and finally a new route on Ailama (*see report below*).

After a 15km hike on September 9, at midnight we started approaching the face via a glacier labyrinth and many moderate pitches of unroped climbing up a rocky spur to gain the Georgian Shelf. Crossing this early in the morning, when it was free from the threat of falling ice, we then roped up and began simul-climbing, then pitching, up the lower northwest pillar. In the afternoon we stopped at a small ledge.

On the morning of the 11th, we started up new ground, climbing a dozen pitches of cold ice up a large icefield. Above, we reached the base of the Rockband via mixed terrain and several tricky sections with powerful pull-ups. The first two pitches on the headwall were crumbling granite, leading to the start of the really steep climbing. While belaying, I melted snow to give us each four liters of water for the coming days. A tough pitch brought us to the only ledge on the wall, and we settled into our second bivouac on this tiny stance.

The next day we climbed two overhanging pitches, and the higher we progressed the harder it became. Following this section on the rope involved much spinning and big swings. Free climbing was no longer possible. Without a portaledge it would be impossible to sleep higher on the headwall, and we weren't sure of the line to take. The situation

The northwest face of Ushba South. (1) Jivljuk, 1962. (2) Artsishevskiy, 1971. (3) Original Georgian line on face, 1946. (4) Badriashvili-Tepnadze, 2020. (5) Grigorenko-Prigoda, 1972 (Badriashvili-Tepnadze variant is shown in AAJ 2017). (6) Mishlyaev-Kosmachev, 1960. In 1958, Mishlyaev and Nikolaenko climbed the line of route 5 as far as the final rock band, then made a rising traverse across the snow terrace to the left to finish up 3. *Giorgi Tepnadze*

rapidly became clear: We either had to bail—just 300m below the summit—or commit to climbing throughout the day and night until we reached a place where we could at least sit. The weather was cold and stable, but soon our water would be finished.

We spent a second night on the tiny ledge, and on the 13th jumared our rope and pushed hard for the top. As the sun was setting, I was below a roof, experiencing a section of loose rock, maybe one pitch shy of the top of the wall. At this point I fell, taking a lump of fractured granite and three pieces of protection with me. Much of our equipment was now wearing out or had already broken. When the night wind started to howl, Giorgi took the lead, and I began to sing to provide us with encouragement.

As he searched for an exit on brittle ice, Giorgi's ancient talisman—a short Cassin ice hammer—broke, and with almost no protection he made a bold lead of the last few meters of difficult icy rock. At 1 a.m. on the 14th, I heard his jubilant shout from the top of the wall.

We built a ledge, rehydrated, napped for a few hours, and woke tired but in exceptional spirits. After a few hours on moderate but extremely loose new ground, we reached the top. One hour of calmness, enjoying a clear sky and the surrounding mountains, restored our strength. We got off the mountain the same day (our fifth) by making an eight-hour descent of the 1937 Gabriel Khergiani Route (5A/5B) on the southeast face, reaching Becho village at midnight. Our 1,700m new route was graded 6A/6B UIAA VI/VII A4. 📷

USHBA'S CLIMBING HISTORY: *Archil Badriashvili has prepared an extensive chronology and descriptions of significant routes on the north and south peaks of Ushba, a mountain with dozens of routes rated 5B (TD+/ED). Readers will find this useful survey and photos at the AAJ website.*

CAUCASUS MOUNTAINS, TETNULDI, WEST FACE

ON OCTOBER 16, a young Georgian mountaineer, Temur Qurdiani, added a route to the west face of Tetnuldi (4,858m) in the Svaneti region, a hard solo ascent that he graded 5A. Qurdiani and three friends camped at 3,600m on the 15th. Early the following morning all of them crossed the relatively complex glacier to the foot of the face. While the others headed for the classic route up the southwest ridge, Qurdiani crossed the bergschrund at around 4,000m and climbed directly through ice and mixed terrain to reach the ridge 700m higher. The first ice section was around seven to eight pitches, with short, steep sections. Above came the crux: a 200m granite wall, with snow-covered slabs, ice-filled cracks, and short, tricky overhanging sections. From the top of this wall, a steep snow slope in poor condition led to the southwest ridge. Qurdiani reached the summit after four hours of free soloing, then descended the southwest ridge. 📄 📷

— ARCHIL BADRIASHVILI, *WITH INFORMATION FROM* TEMUR QURDIANI, *GEORGIA*

The 2,000-meter southwest face of Ailama, showing the new Georgian route and bivouac sites. Earlier routes up the face are not shown. Descent was via the left skyline. *Archil Badriashvili*

AILAMA, SOUTHWEST FACE

AILAMA (4,547M) IS the highest summit in Lower Svaneti and one of the outstanding peaks in the Caucasus, lying on the frontier ridge around 7km southeast of Shkhara. The broad, 2,000m southwest wall was climbed by numerous routes in the 1960s and '70s, but the closing of the Ailana Training Camp in the late 1980s, and the consequences of the Russia-Georgia war, left the region almost uninhabited. Only a handful of ascents have been recorded since, the last of them two decades ago.

Giorgi Tepnadze and I arrived in Svaneti with big ambitions: First was a new route on Ailama's southwest face, and then a long-awaited dream of climbing a new route on Ushba (*see report above*). We invited Levan Lashkarashvili to join us for the first adventure.

We reached the foot of the face on September 2 and followed a rarely climbed direct route to the upper face. Even though this is a logical start, it is too loose to enjoy. That day we bivouacked at around 3,500m.

Early next morning, when the face was free from rockfall, we started up a line between the Central and Third Pillars (both 5B routes); the latter was climbed by the last mountaineers to visit this face, in 2001. We mostly climbed free, enjoying steep, varied, and sounder granite; we had to move fast, as this lower part of the face is threatened by objective danger. It was fun until Levan broke a big hold, which took off the nail of his little finger. He patched it up and then, to our surprise, continued climbing at the same pace. The day ended with a steep headwall and a mixed exit to a bivouac site we dug into ice. We had climbed 13 pitches that day.

On September 4 we climbed more ice than rock, leading directly to the wide, snowy summit. The weather was perfect, and the vast panorama of surrounding mountains gave an impression of isolation. We descended by the northwest ridge. This is complex 4A/4B: at first steep snow and ice to a saddle, then onward, passing a pinnacle on the north flank, to a second saddle, where we rappelled to the southwest. We bivouacked partway down, after spending three hours constructing a good spot in the rock. On our fourth day we made three more rappels and then crossed a glacier, luckily finding a way beside a melted icefall. Anchors were impossible to construct on the glacier-smoothed rock. Eventually we reached the base of the mountain, where we had a cold bath in a spring, looking up at the southwest face.

It is a special kind of adventure to climb neglected mountains, re-exploring their high faces and experiencing their energy. Our route was 5B V/V+, gaining 2,000m, with 850m of new ground. 📄 📷

— ARCHIL BADRIASHVILI, *GEORGIA*

CHAUKHI RANGE, AGMASHENEBELI, NORTH PILLAR, MIF

IN AUGUST 2019, Ukrainians Alexey Litovchenko, Yaroslav Reva, and Vladimir Roshko put up a new route on the north face (Sindaura Wall) of Agmashenebeli (3,854m). The route largely lies between the Badriashvili-Tepnadze Route (2015) and the Lukashvili (1982), the original route up the northwest face. After a day scoping the wall, the three began on August 20, made two bivouacs on the face, reached the summit at midday on the 22nd, and made a third bivouac on the descent of the west ridge. The route, named MiF (after their climbing coach, Mityukhin Fedor), has 760m of elevation gain and 17 roped pitches on rock that was sometimes quite loose. Seven of these involved aid, up to A3, and the overall grade was 5B. 📷

— *INFORMATION FROM* ELENA DMITRENKO, *WOMENGOHIGH.COM, RUSSIA*

RUSSIA

CAUCASUS MOUNTAINS

PIK URAL EAST, SOUTHEAST FACE

THE BEZENGI AREA is the highest region in the Caucasus, with six of the range's eight 5,000m peaks. I'd never been there, but the pandemic gave me the opportunity to visit. In mid-August, Sergey Nilov and I drove for 24 hours in Sergey's old Toyota to reach the Bezengi Alpine Camp.

After a short period of acclimatization and a couple of days on nearby climbs, we began to search for a more significant goal. We were prevented from accessing the main ridgeline by border guards, but unexpectedly we found a potential new line elsewhere. We were lucky: Pik Ural East (4,273m) is neither the biggest nor the most famous of these mountains, and maybe this is why the left side of the southeast face remained untouched.

We were joined by our good friend Eugene Yablokov. We took one day to reach the face from the camp, half a day to reconnoiter, and another half day to fix the first three 50m pitches. Sergey took the lead and generally used aid up to A2.

Next day, August 20, we jumared the ropes and continued above to the summit. The ascent took 10 hours. The first five pitches are the crux, with free climbing up to 6b; above, the terrain is relatively easy and enjoyable, at least if you are lucky enough, as we were, to have the warmth of the sun. The descent took a further six hours. The face is 600m high, with an average angle of

60°. Belays were bolted on the first five pitches, and several protection bolts placed. Hooks and cams were useful. The overall grade was 5B. 📷

— DMITRY GOLOVCHENKO, *RUSSIA*

SIBERIA

SAYAN MOUNTAINS, ULA-GOL, EAST FACE

ULA-GOL (2,911M) RISES above the Ulan-gol Valley in the Eastern Sayan Mountains, about 200km west-southwest of Irkutsk. From near the village of Hoito-gol, it takes seven to ten hours to walk to the Ulan-gol and then north up the valley to a base camp. In winter, this approach is made easier by traveling on the frozen river. A further three-hour walk leads to the 890m east face of Ula-gol.

In 14 hours on March 27, Alexey Boyko and Pavel Tkachenko (Russian) climbed this face at 4B UIAA V-/V. The pair left camp during the night and started up the face at 5 a.m., at times moving simultaneously. They recorded 15 pitches to the summit, although some of these are 200m in length (the total climbing length was over 1,200m). The climb was done throughout in crampons, with difficult mixed pitches and dry-tooling on granite. From the summit, the main ridge was followed northwest toward the next peak, Perm, until it was possible to descend a snow couloir on the northeast face, then slant north to reach the valley. Camp was regained at 9:30 p.m. 📷

— *INFORMATION FROM* ALEXEY BOYKO, *RUSSIA*

SOUTH MUYSKY RIDGE, EIGHTEEN CLIMBS

IN 2019 A small team organized by Evgeny Glazunov visited an area of the South Muysky Ridge, northwest of the town of Baunt in the Russian republic of Buryatia, about 200km east of the northern tip of Lake Baikal (*AAJ 2020*). They made the first ascents of several granite peaks and climbed some striking routes.

One year later, Glazunov returned with 11 other climbers: Grigory Abramov, Alexey Boyko, Evgenia Leontyeva, the brothers Andrey and Dmitry Panov, Alena Panova, Polina Penkina, Anastasia Ramazanova, Daria Sycheva, Anatoly Syshchikov, and Pavel Tkachenko. In less than three weeks, this group tallied a truly impressive list of new routes and first ascents of peaks. [*An excellent map of the area, detailing both expeditions' routes, is at the AAJ website.*]

The team reached Baunt on June 27 and next day transferred to a giant all-terrain vehicle,

The all-terrain approach vehicle en route to South Muysky Ridge, with a nautical assist. *Evgenia Leontyeva*

which carried them to the point where their trek into the mountains would begin. After waiting out a period of heavy rain, they walked north for around 25km with heavy packs over two days, June 30 and July 1, through feasting mosquitoes, to reach a base camp in the valley south of Pik Kart (2,661m).

On July 2, Abramov, Glazunov, and Sycheva opened the bidding by making the first ascent of Pik Modelistov (2,590m) at 1B. The Panov brothers headed to a buttress at the northern end of Pik Kart's west face, where they climbed Sounds of Youth (600m, 12 pitches, 5A 6c). The rest of the team transported equipment to a spot below Kart's west wall, hung it out of reach of hungry animals, and scoped possible routes.

Next day, Abramov, Ramazanova, and Sycheva climbed the north ridge of Pik Admirala Makarova (2,544m, first climbed in 2019) at 3B, while a party of three women, Leontyeva, Panova, and Penkina, and the separate team of Boyko and Tkachenko, put up two new routes on the west face of Kart.

Boyko and Tkachenko climbed the wall more or less directly below the summit in 17 pitches at 5B. The climbing distance was 825m, with difficulties up to 6c+ A2. This was one of the hardest climbs of the expedition; the pair recommended a double set of cams and hooks (the Russian Spectre-like drive-ins for thin, blind cracks). The corner system in the upper face had unstable rock, and there were also dangerously loose roofs that the pair fortunately managed to avoid. The route was named Cascade.

[Top] The west face of Pik Kart. (1) Big Chimney. (2) Sounds of Youth. (3) The Choice is Yours. (4) Cascade. (5) 2019 route. (6) Kuhelklopf. All routes except 5 were climbed in 2020. *Evgenia Leontyeva* [Middle Top] Looking northwest from Krasavic to (A) Medikov, (B) Tatyana, (C) Prazdnichnyj Pass, (D) Mechta, (E) Chudovishche, (F) Maksa Fraya, and (G) Bushueva. *Evgenia Leontyeva* [Middle Bottom] The unclimbed east face of Pik Mechta. *Sergey Glazunov* [Bottom] Evgenia Leontyeva (front left), Polina Penkina (back), and Alena Panova on top of Pik Kart, after the first ascent of The Choice is Yours on the west face. *Evgenia Leontyeva*

Dmitry Panov on pitch five (6a) of Kuhelklopf, a 12-pitch route up the west face of Pik Kart. *Andrey Panov*

The three women climbed a buttress well to the left, finishing on the northwest ridge—thus unable to see a bear that visited camp during the climbs. The route involved friction climbing and some aid where the corners were too wet to free climb. The lower wall took 13 hours, above which eight easier pitches were negotiated during four hours of twilight and darkness. They spent a short but cold night huddled together on a ledge (eventually invaded by mosquitoes) before reaching the ridge via a couple of pitches early the following morning. They continued to the summit via the east flank. The three women arrived at camp at around 10:30 a.m. to be greeted by much-needed borscht and tea. They named their 16-pitch route The Choice Is Yours (5B 6a+ A2).

The team was not yet done with Pik Kart. Glazunov and Syshchikov were attracted by the prominent chimney system on the left side of the west face, left of Sounds of Youth. They completed Big Chimney in 12 pitches (615m of climbing, some moving together) at 5A with four pitches of 6c. On the same day, Penkina, Ramazanova, and Sycheva climbed the northwest ridge (2A).

Most of the group then returned to the first camp to bring up more food for the second part of their trip. While they were away, Penkina and Ramazanova climbed Pik Polyarnikov (2,466m, first climbed in 2019) via the east flank and south ridge at 1B, and the Panov brothers returned to Kart, where they climbed a new line to the right of the 2019 Glazunov-Oleneva-Tkachenko route. The new route was named Kuhelklopf (685m of climbing, 12 pitches, 5A, generally 5c–6a with one pitch of 7b). This route finishes via the last three pitches of the 2019 route.

On the 9th, all 12 climbers crossed north over Razvedchikov Pass to a campsite in the Vetvistaya Valley, and then stayed there throughout the following day in heavy rain.

On the 11th the team planned to cross Alenka Pass to the north and drop into the valley below Pik Mechta (Dream Peak, 2,590m). Before leaving, Leontyeva "decided to climb along the ridge above camp in order to take some photos, but as sometimes happens, I didn't manage to stop in time and ended up on a summit, which I named Pik Altair." The route was 1B. She was late back to camp and received a telling-off for not taking a radio with her. That evening the team crossed the pass and placed a new camp below the southwest face of Pik Mechta.

Perhaps the finest new route achieved during the expedition was Der Fliegende Hollander (The Flying Dutchman), a logical line up the middle of the 800m southwest buttress of Mechta. Glazunov, Panova, and Syshchikov started up the wall at 5 a.m. on July 12 and climbed 22 pitches (generally 40m to 50m) to reach the summit at 4:40 p.m. They were back in camp by 7:30 p.m. Despite heavy rain during the middle of the ascent, the team climbed the entire route free, with seven pitches of 6b and above, and a crux of 6c. The first third is mostly steep slabs, after which the line follows a succession of chimneys and cracks, for a total climbing length of 1,110m and an overall grade of 6A. Der Fliegende Hollander lies to the right of the route climbed by Glazunov, Oleneva, and Tkachenko in 2019.

On that same day, Boyko and Tkachenko made the first ascent of the south ridge of Mechta, gain-

ing a pronounced notch at the foot of the ridge via the southwest flank. They met the previous team on the summit. The 550m route was 4B with some pitches of 6b/6c. At the same time, Abramov, Leontyeva, Penkina, Ramazanova, and Sycheva climbed four new peaks on the east side of the valley. They first reached Prazdnichnyj Pass, then headed north to Chudovishche (2,577m). Returning to the pass, they headed south along the crest, crossing Tatyana (2,446m) and Medikov (2,548m) to reach Krasavica (2,549m). The overall grade of this excursion was 3B III.

The southwest face of Pik Mechta. (1) Original 2019 route. (2) Dragon. (3) Der Fliegende Hollander. (4) South Ridge. *Evgenia Leontyeva*

The 13th was a day of rest for all except the Panov brothers, who had stayed in Mechta base camp the previous day to coordinate radio communications. The brothers put up what is now the easiest route on the southwest face, climbing between the original 2019 route and Der Fliegende Hollander. Starting with 200m of easy climbing up a rightward-sloping weakness, Dragon continues with 750m of climbing, mainly at 4–6a with one pitch of 6b.

On the 14th, Glazunov and Syshchikov made the first ascent of Pik 2,420m, on the opposite side of the valley from Mechta, naming it after the great Yekaterinburg mountaineer Alexey Bolotov (southeast flank and spur, 2B). At the same time, Penkina, Ramazanova, and Sycheva repeated the north ridge of Pik Tatyana (2,446m, 1B) from Prazdnichnyj Pass.

The following day, Boyko, Glazunov, Syshchikov, and Tkachenko tried the impressive east face of Mechta, reaching it by crossing a pass they named Molodets. However, unlike the west side of the mountain, the east face proved monolithic, with little in the way of natural protection. This forced them into placing bolts and fixing some rope. Late in the day, low on bolts and after a broken drill bit, they were washed off the wall by a heavy thunderstorm. On the 16th they removed their ropes and retreated to camp.

Meanwhile, Grigory Abramov had slipped away from camp and soloed the peak immediately north of Pik Alexey Bolotov, naming it Pik Stega (2,452m, 3A) in honour of a deceased friend. The Panov brothers, Alena Panova, and Penkina made an interesting traverse, reaching Chudovishche from Prazdnichnyj Pass and then continuing east along the ridge over peaks 2,600m and 2,627m, which they called Pik Maksa Fraya and Pik Bushueva, respectively. Although a lot of this was III and IV, toward the end of the traverse there were two pitches of 6a. They descended east to the valley and then walked back over Prazdnichnyj Pass. The overall grade was 4A.

It was time to head for home. The Razvedchikov Pass had proved high and unpleasant during the approach to Mechta, so the team decided to try another route out from the mountains, spotted during the ascent of Alexey Bolotov. Crossing Parabola and Papanina passes, with heavy rucksacks, while "drowned in obscurity and mist," was one of the memorable moments of the expedition. In one long day of nearly 24km, they reached their first approach camp, and after a second long day arrived back at Baunt on July 18. They had left nothing behind in the mountains. ◙ ⚲ ▶

– **EVGENIA LEONTYEVA** *(EVGLEON.RU), WITH ADDITIONAL MATERIAL FROM* **ALEXEY BOYKO**, *RUSSIA*

KAZAKHSTAN

Kirill Belotserkovskiy on the last pitch of a new route on the west face of Pik Trud. *Grigoriy Chshukin*

PIK TRUD, WEST FACE

STARTING IN THE 1930s, a large Soviet climbing camp operated in the Middle Talgar Gorge. In summer it hosted hundreds of alpinists from all over the USSR. A 1979 mudflow devastated the camp, with most of the buildings destroyed or buried under massive boulders. Since then, the number of visiting climbers has greatly reduced, and in the early 1990s Talgar became part of the Almaty Nature Reserve and no one was allowed to enter the gorge. Later it reopened, but the lack of good trails, the considerable bureaucracy involved in acquiring a permit, and a little bit of corruption all combined to keep most climbers away.

Though difficult to reach, the highest summit in the area, Pik Talgar (4,973m), and nearby Pik Trud (4,636m) are less than 35km as the crow flies from Almaty, the largest city in the country. Routes on the west face of Trud were mostly put up from the late 1950s to 1980s. The rock is a type of granite, mostly solid. The only attempt to climb a new route on the west face in recent years took place in 2015, when Tursunali Aubakirov and I tried a line to the right of the Tyatinin Route (1959). We ran out of steam and bailed less than half a pitch from easy ground.

I decided to finish the route in May with Grigoriy (Grisha) Chshukin. The approach took two days, crossing two passes and traversing about 30km of forest, glacier, and moraine. At noon on our second day, we camped on the moraine of the Kroshka Glacier. We decided to take a rest day, and that evening I scrambled up to a col from which I could see our prospective descent route. It looked like a gentle snow ridge. Hah!

We started at 2:30 a.m. on May 28. In 30 minutes we reached the base of a snow couloir leading up to our chimney system. Above the snow, we climbed two steep but straightforward ice/mixed pitches to reach a section of rotten ice covering a vertical wall. Five years earlier, this had been a pure ice pitch. Now I had to torque my tools into a shallow crack and gently tap into the thin ice above.

A couple of pitches higher, I found myself stemming, pushing, and puffing in a gently left-ward-leaning chimney. There was climbable ice inside, but the walls held a thin layer of verglas, beautiful as candy. It was hard but fun climbing until I reached a sort of ice chockstone, where it simply became hard—but, hey, it doesn't have to be fun to be fun! I scraped holes with my picks, as hitting the chockstone feature was just too scary, and slowly scratched up to a belay.

Above this, a loose, overhanging chimney led to the 2015 high point. Back then, I'd had a fright-ening time trying to aid past loose blocks, trying two different lines before thankfully dropping part of my aid kit and having to bail. This time I was wiser and had brought rock shoes.

The corner had a blank vertical wall on one side and an infestation of loose blocks on the other. I had to place my feet on the tiny features of the vertical wall and press those loose things with my palms. The climbing was 6b, but a totally different pitch from a 6b at the crag. Fortu-nately, it was the last hard pitch. Seven easier pitches got us to the summit, during which time a stone hit me on the eyebrow. There was blood over my face and my sunglasses were broken. Never mind—keep climbing!

We arrived on top at 7:30 p.m., spent only a few minutes, and then rushed off down the northeast

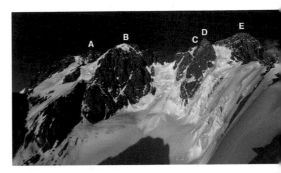

ridge. First we downclimbed to a notch between gendarmes, then made seven rappels to the northwest from Abalakov anchors to reach the ridge I had seen from the col. It was already dark. There was no moon, and the pale stars gave us no light. The snow on this ridge, which connects Pik Trud and Pik Extra, became wet and unsupport-ive, the crust collapsing under one's weight. This went on for two dreary hours until we reached a notch where a couloir leads southwest down to the glacier. During my inspection two days earlier, the midsize scree slope had looked better than it now felt, but it wasn't as rough as trail breaking through deep, wet, crusted snow.

We reached the tent 23 hours after leaving. I drank a little water and crawled into my sleeping bag. Grisha—younger, stronger, and hungrier than me—was already rattling pans and cook-ing something to eat. We felt the 1,200m route to be Russian 5B, M6 WI5 6b. 📷

– **KIRILL BELOTSERKOVSKIY,** *KAZAKHSTAN*

[Top] **Looking approximately northeast at (A) Pik Talgar (4,973m), (B) Pik Talgar South (4,900m), (C) Pik Talgar Southeast, (D) Pik Daugava, and (E) Pik Trud (4,636m).** [Bottom] **The 1,200m west face of Pik Trud. (1) Popov Route (5B, 1984). (2) Tyatinin Route (5B, 1959). (3) Belotserkovskiy-Chshukin Route (5B, 2020). (4) Yun Route (5B, 1982). (5) Gorbunov Route (5B, 1983). This line is approximate, as no report exists for this route and no one appears to have climbed it since the first ascent.** *Kirill Belotserkovskiy (both)*

KYRGYZSTAN

Seen from the Laylak Valley, the nearly 1,500-meter north face of Rocky Ak-su is in front, with Snowy Ak-su (5,355m) behind. The Nose Direct is the leftmost of several lines that climb directly up the north face headwall; it lies about 50 meters to the left of the original Nose (Shabalin, et al, 1994), adding eight new pitches up very steep rock. Many other routes are not shown. *Elena Dmitrenko*

PAMIR ALAI / KARAVSHIN

AK-SU NORTH, NORTH FACE, NOSE DIRECT IN WINTER

FROM SEPTEMBER 20 to October 7, 2002, two legendary alpinists, Pavel Shabalin (Russia) and Ilyas Tukhvatullin (Uzbekistan), climbed the Nose Direct on the north face of Ak-su North (a.k.a. Rocky Ak-su, 5,217m). They made 11 portaledge camps and graded the route 6B 5.9 A5 (1,950m of climbing). Shabalin led every pitch (*AAJ 2004*). This was his 10th ascent of the wall, each by different a route, including the original Nose Route on this face, climbed in 1994.

Nearly 20 years after the first ascent, this time in winter (January 2–8, 2021), the Russians Ratmir Muhametzjanov, Alexander Parfenov, Nikolay Stepanov, Alexey Sukharov, and Vyacheslav Timofeev made the second ascent of Nose Direct. Winter ascents of this 1,460m-high north face are highly respected in the Russian climbing community, and in this case especially so, as the ascent was made in less than half the time of the original climb (6.5 days up; one day for the descent). While this can be put down to progress over the last 20 years, a bigger team and swapping the leader every day also certainly helped.

The team reached the area in December, using 11 horses to transport their equipment through fresh snow to a ruined barn in the Laylak Valley, where they made base camp. The temperature there hovered around -25°C, but this must have felt balmy to the Siberian contingent, who were experiencing -37°C at their homes before leaving for Kyrgyzstan.

The team acclimatized by carrying gear to the foot of the wall at about 3,800m—seven hours and 700m of ascent through snow sometimes up to waist deep—and by climbing Pik Badigan (4,660m).

Once on the route, they used two portaledges, one hanging below the other; they had to make hasty repairs the first night when one of the supporting bars broke. Approaching the Nose, the prominent prow on the headwall, they found hard, run-out sections of thin ice. Parfenov led the route's difficult aid (which he felt was not A5), taking one fall above the crux.

On the last day of the ascent, Ak-su reminded them it was winter, with a fierce gale that covered their face masks with heavy frost. However, by the time they were on the final 200m of relatively easy climbing, the wind had died and the sun appeared, giving them a brief respite before starting their rappel descent of the face. 📷 🔍

— *INFORMATION FROM* **ANNA PIUNOVA,** *MOUNTAIN.RU, RUSSIA*

PAMIR / TRANS ALAI

WESTERN ZAALAYSKIY RANGE, VARIOUS ASCENTS

THE TRANS-ALAY MOUNTAINS delineate part of the border between Kyrgyzstan and Tajikistan, with the Western Zaalayskiy (various spellings) lying about 75km west of Pik Lenin. Our research showed this subrange to be nearly unexplored by mountaineers, offering around 20 potential objectives between 4,500m and 5,500m.

In August 2019, our team of six—Steve Graham, Stuart Hurworth, Jared Kitchen, Emily Thompson, Andy Vine, and I—flew to Kyrgyzstan's second city of Osh and met local support organized by ITMC. We approached the Altyn Daria Valley in the Western Zaalayskiy by 6WD in two days, establishing a comfortable base camp (3,170m) on August 13 at a dusty nomad pasture.

Andy Vine descending the southwest glacier (Deception Route) on Ak Chukur. At distant left is Bel Uluu Mont Blanc (5,402m), while in the center is Pik 5,284m. *Stuart Hurworth*

Google Earth and Soviet military maps had been used to identify possible approaches to advanced base camps and viable peaks in three subvalleys to the west of the main Altyn Daria. However, after a few days, we had not yet located suitable animal transport, so all six of us carried loads to a moraine camp at 3,950m in the Bel Uluu Valley. [*This valley was visited in 2019 by a French-Russian pair of climbers; see AAJ 2020.*] Graham, Hurworth, Vine, and I carried on to an advanced base on a rubble-covered glacier at 4,450m, and from there, on the 19th, completed the first ascent of Ak Chukur (4,970m GPS), via Deception Route (PD). This was an easy glacier ascent with a final pitch of mixed climbing to a small rock platform overlooking a precipitous 1,500m drop to the Altyn Daria. [*This mountain is directly north, across the valley, from the peak climbed in 2019.*]

The other two western valleys identified from advance research—Kaska Suu and Min Terke—proved challenging to access due to several dangerous river crossings. The team therefore looked to the east of the Altyn Daria, where Kitchen and Thompson undertook vital reconnaissance, and by the time the Ak Chukur team returned, two further objectives had been identified.

On the 23rd, Graham, Kitchen, and Thompson made the first ascent of Pik a-boo (5,122m GPS, so named as it remained hidden for most of the climb) in an unnamed side valley 2km northeast of base camp. The climb followed the north glacier (AD-), with several mixed and ice sections, to a snow arête, then a small rock pinnacle summit.

Meanwhile, in order to establish advanced camps for our climbs further to the northeast of base camp, our fixers had succeeded in arranging for donkeys and a horse from a nearby village.

On the 25th, from an advanced base at 4,005m in the Kok Kikki Valley, Hurworth and Vine made the first ascent of Broken Peak (5,122m GPS) via the Golden Tower Traverse (at PD+), the only rock ridge climbed during the expedition.

On the 27th, from a second advanced base in a southern side valley of the Kok Kikki, Graham and Kitchen forced a route through difficult crevassed terrain, much of the time on steep bare glacier. Using dozens of ice screw placements, they eventually summited Ak Kalpak (5,112m GPS) via a route they named North Ridge Chasm Route (D) due to the complex crevasse system on the final stretch to the summit. On the same day, Hurworth, Vine, and I attempted a similarly steep route directly up the north face of the glacier below Pik 5,084m. We retreated at 4,480m, having moved too slowly on bare glacier ice.

There is significant potential in the Western Zaalayskiy, but future expeditions should note that, apart from glacial retreat, two factors need to be considered carefully. The first is river crossings, which can be extremely hazardous in these parts; a large team from the International School of Mountaineering (ISM), with significant experience, expertise, and equipment, were forced to turn back from their approach up the Min Terke valley in 2019. The second will be the interpretation by the resident army commander of the extent to which a border permit allows access to certain areas. We were barred access to the upper reaches of the Altyn Daria (as was the ISM team) and the side valleys toward and beyond Tersager Pass.

The Min Terke group appears to have excellent objectives between 4,900m and 5,300m. From our limited information and first-hand views, we speculate there is potential for a small expedition to access it via a northern approach using animals rather than vehicles.

Our team had a rich experience in a remote area, which was remarkably easy to reach within three days of leaving the U.K. Sadly, this proved to be the last expedition for Andy Vine, who in February 2020 died in a Scottish avalanche. [*The online version of this report has coordinates for each peak.*] 📷

— ANDY STRATFORD, *U.K.*

EASTERN ZAALAYSKIY RANGE, PIK КӨПӨЛӨК (PIK BUTTERFLY), WEST RIDGE

IN AUGUST 2019, we made an exploratory expedition to the Eastern Zaalayskiy, close to the border with China and Tajikistan. Our primary goal was a new route on the highest mountain in the region, Pik Kurumdy (6,613m), which has probably been climbed only twice. However, due to difficult weather conditions and limited time, we changed our target to virgin Pik 4,890m, which we had spotted on the map as an attractive alternative.

We established base camp at around 3,600m in the valley of Kyzyl Su, on the west side of the glacier. On August 21, we crossed the glacier to the east side and continued east, up scree and rocky slopes, to a bivouac at about 4,200m near the ice tongue coming down from the cirque below Piks 4,892m and 4,890m.

Next day we reached the cirque about 100m higher, crossed it, and started to climb the north face of the west ridge. Gaining the ridge required six pitches of ice up to 60°. We then followed the crest to a small basin at about 4,650m, where it was possible to set up a comfortable camp.

Looking southeast into the Eastern Zaalayskiy Range. (A) Pik 4,892m. (B) Pik Көпөлөк (Pik Butterfly, 4,890m). The 2019 ascent followed the west ridge, slanting down to the right from the top. (C) Pik 5,262m. (D) Pik Alexander Gybaev (5,368m, first climbed in 2008). (E) Pik 5,086m. (F) Pik 5,068m (G) Pik Molly (4,748m, first climbed in 1999). (H) Zarya Vostoka (a.k.a. Eastern Sunrise, 6,349m, first climbed in 2000). (I) Pik 5,998m. *Ivan Zhdanov / Dmitry Shapovalov Collection*

On the 23rd, we left the tent with lighter packs and followed the ridge upward, simul-climbing the whole way on exposed but easier terrain. There was one 40m section of 55–60°. We avoided the rocky parts, which were very brittle.

We reached the summit at 10:30 a.m., and our altimeter recorded a height of 4,892m and a position of 39.523750°N, 73.682990°E. We regained the tent, spent another night there, and the next day descended to base camp, with some rappels. Our "rack" had been seven ice screws and a snow stake.

We named the summit Pik Көпөлөк, which means "butterfly" in Kyrgyz. While climbing, we'd been surprised by a large number of butterflies, most likely carried up by air currents from the meadows below. We graded the 600m route D WI3 50–60°. 📷

— MAŁGORZATA ILKIEWICZ *AND* MACIEJ NIEŚCIORUK, *POLAND*

TIEN SHAN / ALA ARCHA RANGE

PIK FREE KOREA, NORTH FACE, BARIN, SOLO FIRST ASCENT

PIK FREE KOREA (Pik Svobodnaya Korea, 4,740m) isn't just another mountain for Dmitry Pavlenko—it's the summit of his dreams. He has climbed the north face 35 times, and soloing a new route had been one of his most cherished ambitions. However, he believed the last logical unclimbed line to solo was completed during the winter of 2015 (Cheremnyh-Syschikov, 32 hours nonstop). Pavlenko was mistaken.

In 2019, Pavlenko had a strong desire to attempt the Kustovsky Route (6A) toward the left side of the face, which hadn't had an ascent since the first in 1969. Studying this route, he was surprised to find a beautiful and logical line cutting through it, finishing out right to the crest of the east ridge.

Starting in November, he made four separate trips to the mountain to work on

Upper left half of the north face of Pik Free Korea. More than 25 routes and variations ascend this face; only the two referenced in this report are marked. (1, red) Barin (Pavlenko, 2020). (2, yellow) Kustovsky Route (1969). *Lindsay Griffin*

Pavlenko has done new routes on Makalu and Jannu, yet this one was his "cherished dream."

the new route, including one in December on which he celebrated his 51st birthday on the wall. The route had extensive and sometimes dangerous aid climbing and some loose rock. Above the roof that caps the rock wall, there was ice up to 80°. Here, he broke the pick of one of his tools and was forced to climb around 100m of 40–50° hard ice with only one tool, with little protection.

On March 11, at the end of pitch 13, he reached the summit ridge. The day was surprisingly sunny and calm. He rappelled the route and returned to an empty Korona Hut, drained, declaring, "I will never be able to force myself through such a test again." He named the route Barin (6A A4) in memory of a "good friend and cool guy," Edik "Barin" Mamykin. 🗎 📷

— *INFORMATION FROM* **DMITRY PAVLENKO**, *RUSSIA/KYRGYZSTAN,* *AND* **ANNA PIUNOVA**, *MOUNTAIN.RU, RUSSIA*

TIEN SHAN

WESTERN TORUGART-TOO, VARIOUS ASCENTS

JENNA AND ROB Hughes-Game, Robin Ohlsson, David Ryan, and I arrived in Bishkek during an August 2019 heat wave. One of our concerns about climbing late in the season was that we might be resigned to snowless peaks. However, at the end of our two-day transit south, as we rounded the last corner and passed the military checkpoint, the much-envisioned Torugart-Too came into view: snow-capped, but only just. Two years of planning and now we could breathe.

None of our team are elite-level climbers. We are in the moderately fit, height loving, heavy-breathing category. Our goals were peaks around 5,000m, so remote and obscure that others might not have considered them worthwhile for an expedition. We'd chosen an area of the Torugart-Too about 10km to the southeast of that visited by a U.K. team in 2008 (*see AAJ 2009*). We had 15 days at base camp to acclimatize and attempt at least one peak.

Our first ascent, on August 30, was on a peak behind camp, climbed by the northwest ridge. The rock quality proved to be extremely poor (as we discovered on subsequent climbs as well), which meant gendarmes were not easily passed. We found solid snow/ice at 4,400m and climbed 50° slopes to the summit, which we named Pik Ketiley (4,710m, AD). With one peak in the bag, and psych high, the next day Dave, Jenna and Rob attempted the most westerly of our objectives. They turned around at 4,300m due to altitude sickness and an encounter with unpassable, shattered buttresses.

On September 3, all but Jenna ascended a high point along a border ridge southwest of Pik Ketiley. An extremely long and arduous walk-in was rewarded with easy climbing on the finest of scree (yes, easy scree!) on the most westerly of three north-facing spurs. This led to a steep, rocky summit that we named Nomad (4,622m, F/PD-).

With the weather holding, and Jenna having now been at base camp for five days straight, talking to grazing cattle, it was decided to make another attempt on the western peak that had eluded her, Rob, and Dave earlier. On the 7th, these three hiked up a different valley in order to give a closer approach to the snowline. They gained the northeast ridge and pitched hard ice until it eased, then continued together to the top. This was named Pik Jaksi Adamdar (4,766m, PD-).

Looking south on the approach to Pik Burkut, the prominent pyramid left of center on the Kyrgyzstan-China border. The first ascent zigzagged up the north-northeast ridge, facing the camera. *Derek Billings*

For our final attempt, we headed for a more easterly rocky peak that wasn't initially on our radar. Due to the rock quality previously encountered, we were hesitant to press our luck. However, on the 9th, Robin and I decided to have a look at the north-northeast ridge. In the most bitter conditions met on the trip, we managed to stand on our fourth previously virgin summit, which we named Pik Burkut (4,737m, AD+). [*Coordinates for all peaks climbed are at the AAJ website.*]

A huge snowfall the following day prompted an early departure from base camp, and we were back in Bishkek on the 11th. As mediocre climbers, standing atop four previously unclimbed peaks was far beyond our expectations, helped immensely by near-perfect weather. 📄📷🔍

– DEREK BILLINGS, *U.K.*

KUILU RANGE, WOLF PEAK, NORTH-NORTHWEST RIDGE

TUCKED AWAY TO the south of the Terskey Alatau Range and west of the Inylchek Valley is the compact range known as Kuilu (Kuylyu). The first recorded expedition to the Kuilu Range took place in 1937, when a team led by I. Cherepov made the first ascent of the highest summit, Pik Konstituzii (5,281m). Soviet expeditions sporadically visited the area, and more recently a succession of mostly British teams (largely from the International School of Mountaineering, led by Pat Littlejohn) explored the western end of Kuilu. The last visit, in 2016, concentrated on the Kindyk Glacier in the northeast of the range (*see editor's note below*). In 2018, Rob Reynolds and I decided to visit the Oroy Glacier, the next valley west of Kindyk, which as far as we could tell had no prior visits.

We established base camp at 3,349m on August 24. Bad weather allowed little progress until the 29th, when we established a high camp in a small amphitheater on the west side of the valley below a 4,631m summit (4,648m on Soviet maps). We dubbed this Wolf Peak. On the 31st we climbed the north-northwest ridge, with 400m of 45° ice covered with a thin layer of snow (PD). 📄📷

– JON BURGESS, *U.K.*

CLIMBS IN THE KINDYK VALLEY: *In August 2016, Miles Gould and Andrew Vine (U.K.), though not the first visitors, were probably the first to climb from the Kindyk Valley. From an advanced base camp at 3,830m, they made first ascents of Tülkü Chokusu (4,605m) via the East Kindyk Glacier and east ridge (PD), and Karga Chokusu (4,714m) via the east ridge (PD). They also climbed two minor peaks west of advanced base: Töö Chokusu (4,554m) via the West Kindyk Glacier and north ridge (PD), and Suurdun Chokusu (4,444m) via the south ridge. A full report is at the AAJ website.*

TAJIKISTAN

Approaching the ice-streaked, 1,000-meter lower north face of Pik Communism. The 2020 route followed the curving gray ice line starting above the right-hand climber. *Winter Snow Leopard Project*

WINTER SNOW LEOPARDS
NEW ROUTE ON PIK COMMUNISM AND A MILESTONE IN WINTER CLIMBING

BY LINDSAY GRIFFIN, *WITH INFORMATION FROM ANNA PIUNOVA, MOUNTAIN.RU, RUSSIA*

FIVE YEARS AGO, Sergey Seliverstov from Kyrgyzstan came up with the idea of the Winter Snow Leopard: completing the five great high-altitude mountains of the former USSR in winter. Thirty years ago, before there was a name for the feat, legendary Kazakh Valery Khrishchaty was on target to complete the set, having made the first winter ascents of Pik Communism (a.k.a. Kommunizma or Ismail Samani, 7,495m) in February 1986, Pik Lenin (7,134m) in January 1988, Pik Pobeda (7,439m) in February 1990, and Khan Tengri (6,995m) in February 1992. Tragically, Khrishchaty was killed during the approach to Khan Tengri in 1993, before he could complete a winter ascent of Pik Korzhenevskaya (7,105m), the last of the five.

In January 2018, Seliverstov and three friends climbed a new route in winter on Korzhenevs-kaya (*AAJ 2019*), leaving him only Pik Communism in Tajikistan to complete his Winter Snow Leopard goal.

Seliverstov and 12 other climbers from Russia and Kyrgyzstan flew to Moskvina Base Camp (3,680m) on January 9, 2020. They split into four teams headed by Vitaly Akimov, Mikail Danich-kin, Seliverstov, and Pavel Vorobyov. Approaching up the Valtera Glacier, the team dug a large snow cave below the north face of Pik Communism at 4,960m, then subsequently stocked it. For their ascent, the climbers chose a new, steep, but relatively safe line on the 1,000m north face, lead-ing to the upper plateau at around 6,000m. This lay a little to the right of the original route up the wall, the August 1971 Bezzubkin Route (5B), which finishes up the north ridge of Communism. The new line is between the Bezzubkin and Chochia (1988, 5B) routes on the lower north face.

With no suitable place to establish a camp on the wall, the team climbed and fixed 32 pitches. The first section was the steepest, with the crux, a passage of vertical ice, at around 5,350m. The

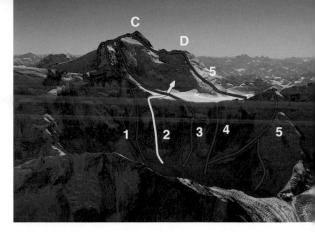

The north face of (C) Pik Communism (7,495 meters) as seen in winter from Pik Korzhenevskaya. (D) Pik Dushanbe (6,960 meters). (1) Bezzubkin Route (1971). (2) Barca (2020). Above the plateau, the 2020 team climbed the face left of Route 5 (Borodkin) to reach Pik Dushanbe. (3) Chochia (1988). (4) Czechoslovak Route (Belica-Mareka, date unknown). (5) Borodkin Route (two starts, 1968). *Winter Snow Leopard Project*

next third of the face was less steep, perhaps 60–70° in parts, but with the characteristic bulletproof blue ice of winter. Arranging protection here proved difficult. The top section was less complicated (50–60°), but proved to be hard work at this altitude and low temperature; the minimum temperature recorded down in base camp—about 2,000 meters lower—was -33°C. It took the team 18 days to establish Camp 2 just below the plateau at 6,000m. This camp and the wall below never received any sun, but they were at least sheltered from the strong winds, sometimes up to 100 km/h, that blew across the plateau.

From Camp 2, the team had to cross the plateau, climb up to Pik Dushanbe (6,960m), which is traversed on the normal (Borodkin) route, and then follow the ridge east of Communism to the summit. Danichkin's team went first and established Camp 3 in a snow cave at 6,200m on the far side of the plateau. On January 29 they climbed the northern slopes of Dushanbe and placed their Camp 4 a little below the top of this peak. They attempted the summit next day but were driven back by a storm.

Meanwhile, Seliverstov's group crossed the plateau and placed a camp above the snow cave at 6,450m. On the 30th they climbed to 6,900m, below Danichkin's camp, and put their tent in the shelter of a huge serac. The next day, Viktor Filinov and Alexander Moroz from Seliverstov's team started from this camp before dawn, and after a difficult time reached the summit just before 2 p.m., completing the new route, Barca, with an overall grade of 6A. (This also was the second winter ascent of Pik Communism.) Later the same day they were followed by Maxim Cherkasov, Mikail Danichkin, Andrey Erokhin, and Artur Usmanov, all leaving from the higher camp. The calm, sunny weather was somewhat offset by a temperature of -47°C. They returned to their respective Camp 4s, and then all climbers descended to base camp.

After two days' rest and with the only forecasted weather window beginning on February 7, Alexander Moroz, Alexey Usatykh, and Seliverstov climbed back to their Camp 4, moving faster due to better acclimatization. The wind next day was predicted to be 50–70 km/h, yet in the morning it didn't seem bad. All three made the summit between 11:35 a.m. and 1:10 p.m. Seliverstov thus became the first Winter Snow Leopard, and Usatykh, who arrived last on top, the second. Moroz became the first person to climb the mountain twice in a single winter season.

Back at Camp 4, they were told the forecast still predicted 80 km/h winds on the 9th, and were strongly advised to descend to the plateau the same day. They reached the snow cave at 11 p.m. It was the right decision, as the following day was wild at high altitude. The trio continued down, stripping the ropes on the lower north face, and were back in base camp that evening.

In the meantime, Danichkin and Usmanov had been part of a team making an alpine-style push on Korzhenevskaya, which lies about 13km due north of Pik Communism. They followed the route Ol'cha, opened by Seliverstov in the winter of 2018. A few minutes after Usatych reached the summit of Pik Communism, Danichkin and Usmanov stood on top of Korzhenevskaya, with Danichkin thus becoming the third Winter Snow Leopard. ▣ ▶

PAKISTAN

The north ridge of Falak Sar is the left skyline, seen from the approach to the west. The traditional approach reached the ridge from the far side. *Ahmed Mujtaba*

SWAT-KOHISTAN MOUNTAINS

FALAK SAR, NORTH RIDGE VIA NEW START FROM NORTHWEST

A Pakistani team climbed a significant new variation to the north ridge of Falak Sar (5,918m), the highest peak of Swat. The team was from Lahore—Hamza Anees, Ahmed Mujtaba (expedition leader), and Adnan Saleem—and is an example of a growing trend of Pakistani alpinists from the "lower regions" taking on more technical climbs.

The team chose to reach the crest of the north ridge, which was first climbed as early as 1965 and possibly earlier, by pioneering an approach from the northwest rather than the established route along the northeast spur. The advantages are a much higher base camp and more direct route to the summit, avoiding some of the difficulties of the lower north ridge. However, it is steeper and more crevassed. The three walked east from Beigabad, following the usual approach to the northeast spur, then moved south and entered a parallel valley rising more steeply west toward the north ridge.

After three nights at base camp (4,223m), they moved to an advanced base at 4,750m. This involved negotiating an icefall and crevassed glacier. From here, their climb to the summit took four days, with camps at 5,072m, 5,430m (just below the crest of the ridge), and in a snow cave at 5,808m. This was Mujtaba's third attempt on the mountain. In 2014, following the standard approach, he reached 5,330m, and in 2019, via the new approach from the northwest, he reached 5,072m. 📄📷🔍

– LINDSAY GRIFFIN, *WITH INFORMATION FROM* AHMED MUJTABA, *PAKISTAN*

Falak Sar's Climbing History: *The chronology of ascents on Falak Sar ("Road to Heaven") has some uncertainties. In the summer of 1957, two New Zealanders reported the first ascent of the mountain, approaching the northeast spur and north ridge from Beigabad to the west. Then, in July 1965, after driving from Germany, a four-man expedition led by Stefan Rausch climbed Falak Sar, thinking it was still unclimbed. They followed the same general route up the northeast spur and north ridge, and, upon their return, were surprised to discover the first ascensionsts' account, which did not mention the significant obstacle of rock towers on the lower ridge and described the summit as a plateau* big enough to play a game of rugby, whereas the Germans had to crowd onto a little summit dome.

In July 1990, Hermann Warth from Germany and Ang Choppal Sherpa from Nepal made the first traverse of the mountain via a new route on the south face. The two climbed about 25 pitches (40–50°) to reach the west ridge, then followed this to the summit. The elevation gain was around 1,100m. Warth noted that the northeast and northwest faces of the mountain posed significant challenges. To date they remain unclimbed. [Additional details on Falak Sar climbs are at the AAJ website.]

KARAKORAM / GHUJERAB MOUNTAINS

KARUN KOH SUBGROUP, DIH SAR, ATTEMPT AND TRAGEDY

JAKUB BOGDAŃSKI AND Michał Ilczuk returned to the northern Karakoram in September for a second attempt on unclimbed Dih Sar (reported as either 6,200m or 6,363m). In September 2019, they reached around 5,950m on the southeast face (*AAJ 2020*).

The two Poles began their 2020 attempt on September 30. At around 5,800m, while traversing to a possible bivy site, Bogdański slipped on steep ice and fell 40m. He badly bruised a shoulder and ribs. Ilczuk rappelled to him, cut out a platform, and sent a distress message with their Garmin inReach. A rescue was initiated, involving seven mountaineers from Shimshal and assisted by a military helicopter. Ilczuk began to feel ill, and despite the efforts of Bogdański, he died during the night of October 1. The following day, Bogdański descended to rescuers under his own steam, rappelling from V-threads. More details, including information on a new approach to the mountain, are at the AAJ website. 🗎 📷

— JERZY WALA, *WITH INFORMATION FROM* JAKUB BOGDAŃSKI, *POLAND*

CHASHKIN GROUP, VARIOUS ASCENTS

DURING THE SUMMER, I was looking for a destination for my guided group. Kyrgyzstan and Kazakhstan were closed because of COVID-19, but suddenly I got word that Pakistan was opening its borders, so I contacted Mirza Ali Baig from Shimshal. One day after Pakistan opened to tourists on August 9, I flew to Islamabad, with the rest of our German team following a couple of days later. With Mirza Ali, we started our trek from Shimshal on the 15th, reached Purien-e-Sar after two days, and on the third walked a further 4km to establish base camp at 4,950m, immediately south of the Chashkin Group.

The weather had been excellent on the approach, and except for a few morning rain showers, continued to be fine for the next seven days. Wasting no time, on the 20th, Mirza Ali, Arshad Karim, Patrick Münkel, Gabriel Stroe, and I left base camp at 5 a.m. and headed for Peak 5,770m. Rocky terrain led to a ridge, which we followed to around 5,400m, then slanted right across snow and boulders to reach a 40–50° snowfield. We followed this to a saddle in the ridge at 5,700m. We turned right and climbed the last section of the northwest ridge (60°) to the summit. We were all back in base camp by early afternoon, naming the new summit AM Peak (standing for Astrid Maria) and grading our route 450m, AD- 60°.

Two days later, Arshad, Gabriel, Patrick, and I set out at 4:30 a.m. for Chashkin I (6,035m on Polish map, 36°31'24.71"N, 75°29'46.90"E), not knowing that an ascent and ski descent had been reported in 2019. From around 5,300m, a snowfield led into the left couloir on the south-southeast face. After a narrowing (55° hard ice), we continued on 45–50° névé slopes, and at the

top of the couloir traversed right across blocky ground (II and III) to the col between the west and east tops. The main (east) summit is a rock tower and was climbed from the north by a pitch of about 50m (steep snow and about 10m of M4/M5). We reached this top near midday, measuring it at 6,105m. Patrick also climbed the west top (ca 6,080m), a relatively easy ascent from the col over a snow arête.

We descended with around nine 60m rappels and two short sections of downclimbing along the central couloir on the southsoutheast face, then rejoined our approach route and were all back in base camp by 6 p.m. The 700m route was graded TD- M4/5 60°.

On the 24th, Patrick, Markus Hohle, and I decided to try a rock tooth of 5,820m on the ridge between Chashkin I and AM Peak. We left base at 6 a.m. and reached the bottom of the snow couloir that led up to the col to the right (southeast) of the tooth. This was 400m high and mostly 50–55°. At midday, just a few meters before reaching the col, Markus slipped and slid about 60m. Fortunately, his injuries were not too serious, but once at base camp he was evacuated by helicopter. We dubbed our route as far as the col Johnny Danger Couloir (AD). 🔲

[Top] The upper south-southeast face of Chashkin I and the lines of ascent (1) and descent (2) in 2020. The highest point is on top of the right-hand rock buttress. The reported 2019 route followed the rocky ridge in between to reach the snow slope between the summits. *Felix Berg* [Bottom] The true (east) summit of Chashkin I as seen from the lower west top. The 2020 ascent followed the steep snow and a short section of mixed on the left skyline. *Patrick Münkel*

– **FELIX BERG,** GERMANY

EDITOR'S NOTE: *In 2019, Tico Gangulee (USA) reported making the first ascent of Chashkin I by the central spur on the south-southeast face, followed by a traverse of the summit and a ski descent of slopes farther east, part of this in quite poor weather (see AAJ 2020). On returning from Pakistan, Felix Berg read reports of this ascent and was troubled by the descriptions, particularly as the final pitch was hard and there was no visible rappel anchor on or near the summit. In response, Gangulee noted that he made several rappels (as much as 60m total) on the east flank of the northeast ridge of the summit tower in whiteout conditions, leaving a piton and an ice screw lower down. Berg and others also analyzed Gangulee's photos and compared them with Berg's own images. Based on the position of nearby and distant peaks seen in these images, Berg feels certain at least three of the photos reportedly taken during the 2019 ascent were taken further to the east, in the vicinity of the rock tooth attempted in 2020. As a result, Berg believes his party made the first ascent of Chashkin I. Gangulee did not respond to an invitation to comment on this report.*

KARAKORAM / HISPAR MUZTAGH

AMBAREEN SAR, SOUTHWEST RIDGE

AFTER RETURNING HOME from my August expedition to the Chashkin Group (*see report above*), I organized another trip to Shimshal from November 7 to December 4. David Langanke, my companion from Germany, and I reached Shimshal village on November 10 and spent three days giving ice climbing training to local guides and climbers, mostly on the snout of the Malangutti Glacier. This program was supported by the Pakistan Youth Outreach Foundation, my travel company SummitClimb, and Black Yak Global.

David and I then joined six Shimshali trainees for an attempt on Yeer gha Tag (a.k.a. Shimshal Sunrise Peak, ca 5,750m), which is east of the village, on the opposite side of the river. On the 18th we placed a high camp at 4,830m, but called off the ascent due to deteriorating weather. Later, I climbed alone to a triple-summited tooth of around 5,280m on the ridge left of Yeer gha Tag's summit.

Toward the end of the month, we received a forecast for clear weather and decided to explore the Momhil Glacier. We left Shimshal village on the 25th and trekked up the Momhil valley until, on the 27th, we turned left into a side valley (Ambareen Cwm), where we camped at around 4,600m.

At 2 a.m. on the 28th we set off for an easy-looking snow dome on the north side of the valley, slanting up the south face to reach its southwest ridge. Due to the poor snow conditions, we stayed on rock ridges (50° UIAA III) and reached the top (ca 5,900m) at midday. Here, we discovered there was a higher summit a bit further. We continued unroped along the ridge until, some distance in front of David, I reached a corniced high point. We regained camp a few hours after dark, and in a round trip of 15 hours. [*Editor's Note: Berg reached the summit labeled on maps as Ambareen Sar (6,171m, 36°25'54.40"N, 75°7'20.05"E). The only previously known ascent was on July 17, 1987, by Austrians Robert Gruber, Kurt Lapuch, and Christine Schmid (who most likely gave the peak its name). These three moved higher up the cwm and climbed the south face/ south spur to the top section of the southwest ridge.* 🗎 📷]

– FELIX BERG, *GERMANY*

MUCHU CHHISH, ATTEMPTS VIA SOUTH RIDGE OF BATURA VI

DESPITE VERY FEW foreign expeditions reaching the Karakoram in 2020 due to COVID-19 restrictions, two teams headed for Muchu Chhish (7,453m), generally considered to be the second-highest unclimbed peak in the world—and the highest for which it is possible to obtain a permit. (The highest unclimbed summit is Gangkar Punsum, 7,570m, in the Bhutan Himalaya.) Muchu Chhish lies almost 2km east along the main watershed (the Batura Wall) from Batura VI, in the direction of Pasu Sar (7,478m).

All attempts to climb the mountain have followed a prominent ridge that extends to the south from the Batura Wall. This was the route followed in 1983 by a Polish-German team led by Wladyslw Wisz that made the first ascents of Batura V (7,531m) and Batura VI (7,462m), the two most easterly summits of the Batura Group (not Batura IV, as reported in *AAJ 1984*). The objective of Muchu Chhish suitors has been to repeat the 1983 route to the top of the Batura Wall and then make the committing ridge traverse to the east, all of it above 7,200m.

The first expedition in 2020 to arrive at base camp on the Muchuhar Glacier was a three-member team from the Czech Republic: Pavel Ben (a former mayor of Prague and member of the Czech parliament), Jiri Janak, and Pavel Korinek. The trio was not able to enter the area until late

The south side of the Batura Massif. (A) Batura IV (7,594m). (B) Batura III (7,729m). (C) Batura II (7,762m). (D) Batura I (7,785m). (E) Batura V (7,531m). (F) Batura VI (7,462). (G) Muchu Chhish (7,453). (H) Pasu Sar (7,478m). The route line shows the unrepeated 1983 Polish-German route to Batura V and VI via the south ridge, attempted by 2020 teams as a way to reach unclimbed Muchu Chhish (G). *Jon Bowles Photography*

August. In the past this would have been considered the end of the climbing season in this area, but climate change has pushed the season later: In 2019, members of this team had inspected the approach and enjoyed almost three weeks of perfect weather during September.

The lower south ridge of Batura VI is very sharp, necessitating a long traverse across its west flank. The Czechs did this from their Camp 2 at 5,300m, reached via 60+° mixed terrain. They traversed about 100m below the crest across 50–70° ice and snow, before climbing up to the ridge-line (80°) at 6,400m. This was a 12-hour endurance test on front points. After two nights here in snowfall, the team retreated. Lack of acclimatization had led to slow progress (the team felt it was hard to acclimatize to any meaningful height in the Muchuhar valley), the high campsite was poor, and the weather was unsettled. They left base camp on September 7.

Two days later, Philipp Brugger (Austria) and Jordi Tosas (Spain) arrived. These two spent much of September acclimatizing and inspecting the route. On the 28th, Tosas left base camp at 4,000m, picked up Brugger, who had been staying at 5,000m, and progressed to 5,800m, at which point Brugger decided not to go any higher. Both descended to base camp, and the next day Tosas headed back up alone, carrying skis. He reached more than 6,900m on the ridge but decided the avalanche risk would be extremely high on the slopes above. He stepped into his skis and descended all the way to the glacier, in ideal skiing conditions and great weather.

In 1999, Luis Lopez's six-man Spanish team established three camps on the south ridge and reached a height of 6,650m, then abandoned the mountain in poor weather. In 2014, Phil De-Beger, Tim Oakes, and Peter Thompson attempted the same line in alpine style. They found hard ice in the lower section, making progress too slow to complete the route in a lightweight style, and retreated from 6,000m (*AAJ 2015*).

— LINDSAY GRIFFIN, *with information from* JORDI TOSAS, *Spain*

KARAKORAM / PANMAH MUZTAGH

PEAK 5,470M, YAARI COULOIR (NOT TO SUMMIT)

THE AIM OF our small Belgian expedition was the first winter ascent of Lukpe Lawo Brakk, the highest of the Snow Lake peaks. [*Lukpe Lawo Brakk (6,593m) was climbed, possibly for the first time, in 1989 by a British expedition via the west ridge. New Zealanders climbed the southeast ridge two years later.*] Steven Maginelle, Jean-Francois Spelmans, and I planned to approach the mountain on skis with sleds, and employed porters from Askole to take us to a base camp at Shatung

(4,138m), before the Biafo Glacier. However, a period of very heavy snowfall meant that we were unable to progress faster than one km/h. We decided to opt for a nearer objective.

On December 10 we skied to the foot of Peak 5,470m (Polish Wala map), which forms the cornerstone between the Uzun Brakk and Biafo glaciers. A long couloir on the south-southwest face led up to the southeast ridge; we called it the Yaari (Friendship) Couloir. We climbed around 1,000m (graded AD), taking the right branch above 4,890m. At 5,170m, around 10m below the crest of the ridge, the snow became hip-deep and unstable. We turned around and descended.

After this we explored possible routes on Shatung Brakk, the small peak northeast of base camp, and on the south-southeast flank of Dongbar Peak (6,282m, no recorded ascent). There are a number of possible routes up Dongbar, but the southern flanks are composed of rotten rock. 📖📷

– SOFIE LENAERTS, *BELGIUM*

KARAKORAM / TAGAS GROUP

NANGMA VALLEY, SHINGU CHARPA, HISTORICAL ASCENT BY WEST FACE

IN 2000, THE Corean Alpine Club sponsored six climbers to make the first ascent of Shingu Charpa (a.k.a. Great Tower, ca 5,900m; various heights have been reported, from 5,600m to over 6,000m). The team established base camp on July 7 in the Nangma Valley at 3,870m, and then proceeded to fix nearly 700m of rope to Camp 1 (4,100m). Bad weather followed, but after several days, twin rainbows appeared in the west, a signal for them to commence climbing.

On July 16, Bong Jeong-ho, Hwang Young-soon, and Shin Dong-cheol left base camp and reached the top of the fixed lines by 2 p.m. The climb above initially followed a large couloir on the west face and became more difficult above 4,300m. There was a section of 80°, and protection was difficult. After climbing three pitches above the end of the fixed ropes, the three retreated to a small ledge, where they bivouacked.

The following morning, with gear drenched by the previous evening's drizzle, they worked quickly to escape the couloir. Overcoming a large chockstone with water cascading down both sides, and with several big leader falls, the team exited the couloir to the crest of a spur on the west face. They found a tent platform 50m to the right at 4,700m.

On the 18th, Bong and Shin climbed 200m up the spur, while Hwang dried out their gear in long-awaited sunshine. Next day, all three jugged to their high point. At 5,000m, Hwang was hit by rockfall, though fortunately without serious injury. Multiple leads of 5.9 to 5.10 led to a bivouac site at 5,110m, where they slept on separate ledges. On the 20th, only five more pitches were completed, as time was lost when a stove was dropped. Fortunately, they had left a second stove at the previous bivouac, which was retrieved. That night they were again forced to bivouac on separate ledges at 5,250m.

Shingu Charpa (ca 5,900m) from the north. The Korean first ascent (2000) climbed the shaded west face from the top of the obvious snow couloir. The prominent north ridge (facing the camera) was attempted several times in the mid-2000s. The east face (left) was climbed in 2007. *Kelly Cordes*

Next day, in mostly clear sky, they climbed rock up to 5.11b, bivouacking at 5,350m. On the 22nd, they reached a point 300m from the summit. That night was long, windy, snowy, cold, and sleepless, the food almost all gone. At 9:20 a.m. on the 23rd, after climbing 200m of snow and 100m of rock, the three stood just below the summit. Bong carefully approached the large cornice and hammered in a snow stake. The three then retreated safely down the route, abandoning around half their fixed rope. The Korean Route had climbing up to 5.11b A2.

In 1999, these same three climbers had attempted Amin Brakk in the Nangma Valley, almost completing the line first tried in 1996 by a Basque team (*AAJ 2000*). In 1997, they were part of the Korean team making the first ascent of the central pillar on the west face of Gasherbrum IV, with Bong Jeong-ho reaching the summit (*AAJ 1998*). 🖼

— **PETER JENSEN-CHOI**, *COREAN ALPINE CLUB*

TAGAS VALLEY, PATHAN PEAK AND PATHANI PEAK

IN 2016, FRENCHMAN Mathieu Maynadier visited the Lachit Valley, and during the trek out he saw several relatively accessible big walls in the Tagas Valley. (This is the next valley west of the Lachit, running north-northeast from the village of Tagas/Thagas.) Maynadier returned in July 2018 with an international team comprising Nicolas Favresse, Jean-Louis Wertz (both from Belgium), and Carlitos Molina (Argentina).

Probably the first foreign mountaineers to explore this valley, the team approached via a good path and aqueduct, establishing base camp on an alpine meadow. Their first attempt on one of the rock walls ended well below the top due to poor quality granite. They then turned their attention to the west side of a beautiful rock tower in the cwm of the Second Tagas Glacier, above the East Upper Tagas Glacier (as designated on Jerzy Wala's Polish map). The summit, approaching 6,000m, was named Pathan Peak; it lies on the ridge northwest of "Ogre" (6,058m).

The first attempt was straight up the front face of the pillar, but after two days they bailed: There were few natural lines, and the rock was mostly choss. A less steep line was then chosen on the left flank, and the team spent three days fixing the first 300m, installed a portaledge camp, and then spent another two days fixing a few more pitches and making a push for the top. While better than expected, the rock was still mediocre for much of the climb. All four reached the summit at 5 p.m. on August 4, having climbed 900m at 6b A1 (estimated to go free at 7a).

The descent began well, and by 10 p.m. they had reached the top of the fixed ropes and began removing them as they descended. At the top of the last rope above the portaledge, they decided to place one of the few bolts on the route. This was around 10m lower than the original anchor, placed above a loose ledge. Favresse and Mayandier had just completed fixing the new anchor when the ledge above, on which Molina was standing, collapsed. Maynadier was hit and suffered a concussion, an open fracture of the right elbow, and two compressed vertebrae. When Maynadier came around, he was incoherent but able to be lowered to the portaledge, from which a rescue call was made. The next morning he was in better shape and was able to descend to the base of the wall. At midday, an Army helicopter evacuated him to Skardu.

The rest of the team spent the following week recovering gear from the wall; one of the portaledges was completely crushed by rockfall. On the 15th, in a nice weather window just before their departure from the valley, Favresse and Molina climbed the west side of Pathani Peak, to the north of Pathan. An initial 300m snow ramp led to a steep ridge, then an ascent of this ridge at 6a M6. The route Pathani was completed in a 17-hour round trip from camp. 🖼 ▶

— *INFORMATION FROM* **NICOLAS FAVRESSE**, *BELGIUM*

KONDUS GLACIER: ALISON PEAK, EAST RIDGE; PEAK 6,000M, ATTEMPT

IN SPRING 2019, inspired by a photo taken two years earlier by our friend Marcello Sanguineti (*AAJ 2018*), Maurizio Giordani asked me to join him, Massimo Faletti, and David Hall on an expedition to the Kondus Valley. Our goal was to climb some of the beautiful untouched rock towers near the head of the K6 Glacier, between Link Sar and the east face of K6. As far as we knew, not only had no one tried to climb these formations, no one had explored the area, and the biggest question mark was how we would reach the base of these mysterious towers.

Seen from the southeast, unclimbed Alison Peak (ca 5,100m+); the glacier is at around 3,600m. (1) Start of Welcome to the Jungle (Ballard-Focchi-Nardi, 2017), ending at ca 4,400m. (2) Giordani-Hall attempt (2019). (3) Ma-ma Natura on the east ridge (Della Bordella–Faletti, 2019). This pair rappelled the southeast face from their high point. *Marcello Sanguineti*

In late June we established base camp (ca 3,600m) at the end of the military road in the Kondus Valley, at the same place as the American team that later made the first ascent of Link Sar (*AAJ 2020*). We had planned only 17 days at or above base camp, and we spent the whole of the first week trying to work out how to approach the towers. After getting lost on the glaciers and trying to negotiate scary crevasses and steep couloirs, we realized our objectives were out of reach in the limited time we had available.

For Plan B, we turned to Alison Peak (ca 5,150m), named in 2017 by Tom Ballard and Daniele Nardi. This summit, rising directly above the west side of the Kondus Glacier, is still unclimbed. On July 2 and 3, Massimo Faletti and I climbed the east ridge but stopped below the summit. Avoiding the unattractive lower southeast face, we started from a big grassy terrace that was very easy to reach from the right in 1.5 to 2 hours from the glacier. The climbing on the pillar was varied and more difficult than initially expected, with steep cracks, very technical slabs, and ice or snow ramps. The rock was solid and enjoyable, but not excellent. We reached the end of the steep section, at around 5,000m, after 22 pitches, and then continued along the gently angled ridge (II-III) for a couple of hours. At this point, lack of food and fatigue prompted us to descend. We made 20 adventurous single-point rappels through the night down the southeast face to regain the grassy terrace.

While we didn't reach the summit, we thought our efforts deserved a name: Ma-ma Natura (about 835m of climbing, 7b A2, climbed clean). While we were climbing, Maurizio and David had moved left from the grassy terrace and attempted a line up the center of the southeast face, climbing 11 relatively short pitches until forced down by bad rock.

A few days later, David, Massimo, and I tried to climb the peak (ca 6,000m) immediately above and southeast of base camp. On our first day, the route-finding was tricky due to the many different couloirs and subsidiary summits on the northwest flank of the peak. Eventually, we reached a nice flat area at about 5,400m and bivouacked. That night, Massimo and I set off for the summit. After several hours in deep, inconsistent snow, we had reached around 5,600m when Massimo started to feel sick. I continued for another hour on easy terrain, but at about 5,800m (and after 2,200m of ascent), when it began to get steeper and technical, I also turned around. 🖼 🔍

– MATTEO DELLA BORDELLA, *ITALY*

Tsewang Namgyal leading the first pitch of Whiskey Shadow (WI4+/5). The ice during this ascent in early 2021 was considerably leaner than it was during the first ascent in 2020. *Vishal Rautela*

EAST KARAKORAM

NUBRA VALLEY ICE CLIMBS

In December 2019, I asked Indian climber Karn Kowshik if I could join him and his friends later in the winter for some ice climbing exploration in India. I had met Karn at the February 2018 Michigan Ice Fest and learned of his tremendous enthusiasm for the developing ice climbing scene in his home mountains. In January 2019, a small group of American climbers accompanied Karn to the Spiti region to participate in the ice festival that he and some friends had organized (*see AAJ 2020*). I was intrigued by the possibility of another ice climbing venture to northern India.

Karn responded positively, and after consulting with Ladakhi mountain guides Tsewang Namgyal and Rigzin Tsewang, they welcomed me to join their exploration of the Nubra Valley. Waters flowing south out of the Siachen Glacier in northernmost India travel through the Nubra on their way to joining the Shyok River near Diskit village.

I flew to India in early March. On March 5, after warming up at a 25m ice crag near Leh, the nearest city to the Nubra Valley, we drove over the 5,359-meter Khardung La, which is kept open year-round by the Indian military to maintain a link with outposts along the borders with Pakistan and China. After stopping at Rigzin's sister's house for a delicious meal, we continued up the valley to the government guest house in Panamik Hot Sulphur Springs. The next morning, we climbed on a nearby waterfall in the Podong Valley that Rigzin and Tsewang had explored earlier in the winter. The 15m step of near-vertical ice, called Podong Cake, was only a 30-minute hike from the guesthouse, south of the village.

The Podong introduced me to the "hidden gems" of ice climbs in this extremely dry environment. While there was absolutely no green vegetation anywhere in March, many of the side valleys were fed by creeks that drained the vast terrain above. The only climbs I saw were in such canyons.

The next day we headed to Murgi village, on the west side of the Nubra River, and to the impressive falls nearby. Rigzin and Tsewang had tried Murgi's ice earlier in the winter, getting partway up the 70m first pitch. This steep waterfall was a continuous and stellar WI4+, among the best

pitches of this grade I've climbed. Above this 70m pitch, the ice-filled gully rose through the deep cleft at about WI3. Tsewang led us to a belay stance in a small recess on the right side of the gully, about 30m up. The next 35m pitch continued up the gully on beautiful grade 3 ice, curving around right and out of view before leveling out in an almost flat, frozen creek. Two rope-stretching 70m rappels brought us to the ground, where some villagers had been observing our progress. It felt good to accomplish the defining route of the village, if not the valley. The men named the route Whiskey Shadow (140m, WI4+/5).

We rested the following day by taking part in a Buddhist ceremony in nearby Taksha village. There was no social distancing on this day, as we crowded into a small room and sat cross-legged on the floor with 50 others, eating a delicious lunch and listened to the monks' chanting.

[Top] Rigzin Tsewang leading Luxury, a new route from 2021 at Nubra Adventure Club Crag. [Bottom] Participants in the first Nubra Ice Climbing Festival, held in January 2021. *Vishal Rautela (both)*

On March 9, we traveled to another climb that Tsewang and Rigzin had explored earlier in the winter; they had been unable to pass a 15m, difficult-to-protect rock step. We drove about 30 minutes south of the guesthouse on the west side of the valley to a small hamlet called Youlkham, where an obvious drainage extends to the west. The approach took about 45 minutes into the canyon.

After an initial 10m WI3 ice ramp, the frozen creek led into a steep-sided canyon for about 300m until it was blocked by the rock step. Unfortunately, the rock was now running with water and coated in algae! This unappetizing step blocked access to an attractive 25m column of vertical ice. While it appeared that one *might* be able to leave the gully and scramble around the step, I thought it would be more aesthetic to climb directly. I spent the next hour climbing this difficult little step and bringing Rigzin up to the creekbed above. Meanwhile, Tsewang and Karn had discovered they *could* scramble around this step to the right and rappel back into the creek from the side.

Fortunately, the 25m ice column was steep and well-formed, reminding me of one of the vertical steps of The Professor Falls back home in Alberta. We took turns leading the WI5- pitch, and then, with everyone satiated, we rappelled the rock step and descended the right-hand creek bank back to our car. They named the route Ladakhi Scouts.

During the following days, we explored the Nubra area to the south and north, finding several potential ice climbs as well as miles of beautiful granite buttresses. We had picked some of the low-hanging fruit in the area. There will be much new climbing in coming seasons. [*Editor's Note: The first Nubra Ice Climbing Festival, with 28 participants, was held in January 2021. In addition, Rigzin Tsewang, as president of the Nubra Mountaineering Association, organized the Nubra Valley Women's Ice Climbing Festival in the first week of March 2021, with 46 participants. Despite ice conditions that were not as good as those in 2020, many new routes have been climbed. As of March 2021, there were at least 16 ice routes in the valley.*] 📄📷

— CARLOS BUHLER, *CANADA*

TASHISPA RI, NORTH RIDGE

OUR HIMALAYAN CLUB team for the Satti Valley consisted of Abhijit Dandekar, Rajesh Gadgil, Atin Sathe, and I, supported by Pasang Bhote, Pasang Sherpa Pemba Norbu, Phuphu Dorje, Sangbu Sherpa, and a team of low-altitude porters from Nepal. We had visited the valley in 2005, during an Indo-American expedition (see *AAJ 2006*), and had explored the glaciers and peaks at the northeastern end. We now planned to explore the Lung Tung Nala in the southwestern section.

We arrived at Satti village (3,300m) in the Nubra Valley on July 26, 2019. Ascending the Satti Valley brought us to a point at 4,250m from which we had to descend diagonally to the river at 3,900m and our planned intermediary camp. Negotiating the loose scree and exposed slabs was nerve-racking work, even with light loads. The route was prone to rockfall if it rained, so even in the slightest showers we had to stay put. As a result, we were only able to move to the intermediary camp on the 29th. After a difficult river crossing, we reached base camp at 4,823m on August 1. We were now at the junction of the Spang Chenmo and Lung Tung valleys.

[Top] Rajesh Gadgil near the head of the Lung Tung Glacier with unclimbed peaks 6,160m (left) and 6,190m to the southwest. [Bottom] Unclimbed Peak 6,170m on the southern rim of the Lung Tung Glacier. *Divyesh Muni (both)*

On August 7, after establishing an advanced base at 5,300m on the terminal moraine of the Lung Tung Glacier, we climbed onto the glacier to be met by an awesome view. On the left rim were peaks 6,489m, 6,277m, and—furthest away—Peak 6,104m. The right-hand rim, running southwest then west from Peak 6,104m, held peaks 6,160m, 6,190m, and 6,170m. I felt like a child on my birthday. So many gifts to be opened!

On the 11th, all but Abhijit, who needed to return to Mumbai, shifted to a high camp at 5,900m, and the next day we climbed Peak 6,104m at the head of the Lung Tung Glacier. We ascended easily for 150m onto the northwest ridge, which we followed to the summit, arriving at 11 a.m. We had been lucky to climb Peak 6,104m on one of the few good weather days, so we decided to name it Tashispa Ri, meaning "good fortune peak." 📷 🔍

– DIVYESH MUNI, *HIMALAYAN CLUB, INDIA*

LADAKH

GUIDE RI, NORTHEAST FACE

THE LADAKH MOUNTAIN Guides Association (LMGA) organized an expedition in September 2018 to the Skitmang region of southeast Ladakh, about 140km from Leh. Our objective was unclimbed Peak 6,364m. Participants were Dorje Angchuk, Kunga Dorje, Tsewang Gyalson, Stanzin Norbu, Skalzang Rigzin, Rigzin Tsewang, Tsewang Tundup, and Jigmed Wangchuk.

From the beautiful village of Skitmang, we walked two hours with no porters, carrying packs between 28kg and 32kg, to reach our first camp below the Skitmang Gompa (a nunnery). The next day, September 30, we reached base camp at 5,250m in a further five and half hours. We had a great view of three 6,000m peaks above, and in the opposite direction glorious Chakula, sometimes called the "Matterhorn of Ladakh."

At 3:30 a.m., we had a light breakfast and set out for the summit via the northeast face. More than 60cm of new powder made it quite difficult, but after nine hours, with everyone taking turns to break trail, we were on top. The descent took four hours, the sun-softened snow now making it quite hard work. We were back in base camp that night. We named the peak Guide Ri. 🔍

– LADAKH MOUNTAIN GUIDES ASSOCIATION, *INDIA*

EDITOR'S NOTE: *Guide Ri lies at 33°19'52.97"N, 78°10'47.38"E, north of the Pologongka road pass. Nearby peaks include Pologongka (6,632m), Chakula (6,529m), and Thugje (6,148m). A brief climbing history of these mountains and description of the activities of the Ladakh Mountain Guides Association are at the AAJ website.*

HIMACHAL PRADESH

KULLU: ALI RATNI TIBBA, SOUTHWEST PILLAR; MANIKARAN SPIRES, PEAK 5,394M, EAST PILLAR, AND PEAK 5,200M, NORTH FACE

AT THE END of August 2019, Franziska Dünßer (team doctor), Veronika Hofmann, Jana Möhrer, Dörte Pietron (team trainer), Laura Tiefenthaler, and I traveled to the Malana Valley, southeast of Manali, as the last stage of the German Alpine Club's three-year program for young female alpinists (DAV Expeditionskader). We originally wanted to visit the Zanskar Valley, but due to the Kashmir conflict we had to reorganize our expedition two weeks before departure.

Our new goal was Ali Ratni Tibba (5,490m) and the Manikaran Spires. It is not clear how many of the spires remain unclimbed, but one of the highest, Peak 5,394m, was climbed in 2008, via the south face, by Janet Bergman, Ben Ditto, Pat Goodman, and Freddie Wilkinson from the USA. We decided to go to the north side of the spires, because this would allow access to Ali Ratni Tibba. However, we had very little information, since the last expedition from the north may have been in the late 1970s.

We flew to Delhi and from there took a car for 16 hours to Naggar. We then walked four days over Chandra Khani Pass to the end of the Malana Valley, just before the entrance to the side valley leading south toward the northwest side of Ali Ratni Tibba and the north side of the Manikaran Spires. It took a fifth day to cross the river and set up base camp on a perfect meadow at around 3,360m. It would be better and faster to drive to Malana village, from which it is possible to reach base camp in one long day (or two days if using horses to carry equipment; however, the last bridge is not passable for horses).

Peak 5,394m and the 2019 route More Rice on the east pillar. The peak was first climbed in 2008 by the south face. *Dörte Pietron*

[Left] Laura Tiefenthaler and Jana Moehrer on Ali Ratna Tibba. The fine rock pillar to the south above Tiefenthaler is the Obelisk. The aiguilles visible lie south of the Pass of the Obelisks, and some were climbed by British teams in the 1960s and '70s. *Raphaela Haug* [Right] The southwest pillar of Ali Ratni Tibba and (1) upper part of the original 1969 route up the west ridge (more or less on the lower left skyline) and (2) Flying Backpack (2019). The 1971 route, climbed in snowier conditions than shown here, started near the bottom right of the image and slanted left up the south face. *Dörte Pietron*

We established an advanced base at 4,700m on a glacier plateau between Ali Ratni Tibba and the Manikaran Spires. All of our climbs started from this camp, which became increasingly hard to reach as melting snow exposed crevasses.

During our five-week stay, we had a lot of unstable weather, with daily precipitation, including some thunderstorms, and only one week of "climbable" weather. Temperatures were quite warm at the beginning, when the freezing level was far above 5,000m. However, by the end we were measuring -4°C in base camp. There was a lot of rockfall and approaches were quite difficult and dangerous. We would recommend visiting the area earlier in the year in the hope of finding colder temperatures and better conditions in general—but keep in mind the monsoon season. There is good rock climbing potential in the area, especially on the north face and northwest pillar of Ali Ratni Tibba, as well as the north face of the so-called "Obelisk." We found it impossible (it would require a sort of via ferrata) to reach the South Malana Glacier from the end of the Malana Valley: It is a very steep gorge with a raging river, but might be possible earlier in the year, when the entire gorge is covered by snow.

We climbed three peaks during our stay. Hofmann and Pietron climbed one of the Manikaran Spires—Peak 5,200m—from the north via a glacier hike and some easy scrambling. The GPS gave an altitude of 5,120m. Ali Ratni Tibba was climbed in a day (September 9) via a partial new route up the southwest pillar to join the original route on the peak in its easier upper section. Moehrer, Tiefenthaler, and I completed the ascent, which we called Flying Backpack (600m, 6a). The GPS recorded an altitude of 5,410m. On September 12, Hofmann, Moehrer, Tiefenthaler, and I climbed a new route up the east pillar of Peak 5,394m, which we named More Rice (420m, 6b+). Our GPS recorded a height of 5,320m. [*Coordinates for these peaks are at the AAJ website.*] 📷

– RAPHAELA HAUG, *GERMANY*

ALI RATNI TIBBA'S CLIMBING HISTORY: *The early climbing on Ali Ratni Tibba was somewhat dominated by climbers from the U.K. After earlier reconnaissance by British expeditions, Fred Harper and Margorie-Anne Harper, Dave Nicoll, and Chris Radcliffe made the first ascent of the peak over two days in May 1969, climbing a north-facing snow ramp below the west face to reach the west ridge,* *which they followed (snow, ice, and UIAA IV) to the summit, with one bivouac (around 1,500m, D+/TD-). Expeditions in 1971 and 1973 climbed the south face and upper southwest ridge, as well as the west face and southeast ridge. More details are with this report at the AAJ website.*

KULLU: SPEED ASCENTS

INDIAN ULTRARUNNER Kieren D'Souza moved to Manali in 2016 to concentrate on trail running. When COVID-19 put an end to global competition in 2020—and influenced by performance ascents made by international mountaineers—D'Souza decided to attempt speed ascents of local peaks. He ran up and down popular Friendship Peak (5,287m) and then, on October 1, made a 19 hour 38 minute round-trip from Manali (2,050m) to the summit of Deo Tibba (6,001m). The full story is at the AAJ website. 🗎

– LINDSAY GRIFFIN

SPITI: SUVITA LUNGPA BASIN, PEAK 6,015M, SOUTH RIDGE

IN AUGUST 2018, I joined a small expedition to northwest Spiti led by Dr. Kallol Das from the Kolkata section of the Himalayan Club. The objective was to introduce beginners to the craft of self-reliant Himalayan climbing. We chose the Suvita Lungpa basin after reading Arun Samant's detailed reports from his 1994 expedition. This basin is mainly formed by four unnamed glaciers (known as I, II, III, and IV), which merge to form the Suvita Nala, flowing north to meet the Spiti River near Losar. In 1994, Samant's team climbed a number of peaks at the heads of these glaciers, including Larimo (5,995m) and Num Themga (6,024m) at the head of Glacier I (*see AAJ 1995*).

On August 19, we established base camp at 4,500m and later a high camp at 5,100m on Glacier I. On the 23rd, Partha Das and I climbed Larimo by its south ridge, the route taken by Samant's team in 1994. We then noticed that the unnamed peak to the north (map height 6,015m) was not too distant and connected by a straightforward ridge. While Partha remained, I went for it and soon was on top, where my altimeter read 6,005m. As far as I can ascertain, this was the first ascent. The difficulty was thought to be AD. [*Note: On the Leomann map to the region, Larimo is incorrectly marked as Larimo II, and Peak 6,015m as Larimo I.*] 🗎 📷

– ANINDYA MUKHERJEE, *INDIA*

SPITI: KANAMO, FIRST WINTER ASCENT

KANAMO (THE WHITE Lady, 5,974m) lies to the northeast of Kibber, among the highest inhabited villages in the world reached by road. The Spiti region gets substantial snowfall, making it one of India's prime destinations for winter sports. [*Editor's Note: The road through Spiti is increasingly kept open through winter to provide military access to strategically important regions. Similarly, Lahaul has gained winter access due to the opening of a new tunnel under Rohtang Pass.*] In summer, Kanamo is a straightforward and popular trek, but the mountain had never been attempted in winter.

In February, I organized 26 members of the Snow Saboteurs, a specialized military mountaineering team, for an attempt on Kanamo. We arrived near the Kibber village monastery on February 23 and waited out a period of bad weather. On March 1, a team of 20 started from Kibber at 3 a.m. After a long and tiring ascent through many feet of soft snow and then scree overladen with thin snow, we reached the summit at 1 p.m. We were back in Kibber by 8 p.m. 🗎 📷 🔍

– JAY PRAKASH KUMAR, *INDIA*

KINNAUR, BASPA VALLEY: DEVBHOOMI AND ALPBANDARIOL, FIRST ASCENTS; CHARAS, WEST FACE, NARESH GOOD

Markus Kärle, Roman Mayerl, Christoph Schranz, Magnus Stangl, and I visited the Baspa Valley between October 9 and 25, 2019. The year previously, Hansjörg Auer, Max Berger, Much Mayr, and Guido Unterwurzacher had visited this relatively unknown valley and made the first ascent of Peak 6,050m (*AAJ 2019*). Hansjörg wanted to climb there again in 2019 but died in the spring of that year. He and Much had told me about the beauty of the valley and its potential—unclimbed 6,000m peaks and granite faces—so we decided to go.

We flew to Delhi and from there traveled two days by taxi to the small village of Rakcham in the Baspa Valley. On October 10 we hiked up the Gor Garang Valley to the so-called Rakcham Plateau, where we set up camp for the next few days. We had no porters, wanting to do everything by ourselves. At the plateau, we met Eneko and Iker Pou, who were part of a North Face team expedition.

Over the next two days, Christoph, Markus, and I climbed a new route up the south face of an unnamed granite peak of approximately 5,000m on the west side of the valley. We named the summit Alpbandariol [*coordinates of all peaks are at the AAJ website*] and the route Rehab Line, climbing it clean but not all free (580m of climbing, 7b A2). We estimate the route can be climbed completely free at around 8a. We descended east in the couloir behind the peak to rejoin the valley. The same day, the Pou brothers put up a new route on the next peak further up valley, climbing the east pillar, which they named Miquellink (600m of climbing, 6b, *AAJ 2020*).

[Top] Pitch two (7a) of Rehab Line on Alpbandariol (ca 5,000m). [Bottom] Looking north-northeast across the Rakcham Plateau. Approximate lines of (1) Latin Brother, (2) Rehab Line, and (3) Miquellink, all climbed in 2019. *Gebhard Bendler (both)*

In the meantime, Magnus and Roman had put up a new line on Hace and Charas (ca 4,850m), a peak on the east side of the valley climbed a month previously by the Austrian Alpine Club's Young Alpinists Group (*AAJ 2020*). The Austrians climbed a 450m line on the north face and west ridge at VI A1; Magnus and Roman climbed the more compact slabs to the right at 6b A1 (possibly 7b all free), joining the original line toward the top; they descended without continuing to the summit, naming the 400m route Naresh Good.

Bad weather arrived and we descended to Rakcham village. We were invited to a big Indian wedding party and were impressed by the hospitality, which included heavy applejack (strong brandy)—this area is famous for its apple cultivation.

From Hansjörg and Much, we knew that a pass led west from the Rakcham Plateau to the Saro Gad (valley) and the foot of a peak Hansjörg and others had climbed in 2018, which you can see from the village. When the weather improved, we decided to look at other summits in this valley.

After a night on the plateau, we crossed the pass and went up-valley to around 4,200m, where we set another camp. The journey was far from easy due to extensive boulder fields. At 2 a.m.

on the 17th, we departed for the peak immediately northeast of the one climbed by Hansjörg in 2018. [*These peaks lie on the ridge that runs southwest from Jorkanden (6,474m).*] We snaked up the left side of the southeast face, finding ice and mixed terrain up to 70°, to reach the southwest ridge, which we followed (one 50m section of 70° ice) to the summit. By early afternoon we were on top. We named the peak Devbhoomi ("Land of the Gods," 6,057m).

We returned to the village and decided to focus on a few short rock routes accessible from the main valley. Christoph repeated Luger Hammer (8a+, first climbed around eight years ago by Alexander Luger), while I climbed a nice crack to the right that I named Bendler Hammerl (7a+). 📷

– GEBHARD BENDLER, *AUSTRIA*

KINNAUR: JUPKIA, SOUTH-SOUTHWEST FACE

IN 2002, SEVERAL members of the Climbers' Circle, a Kolkata mountaineering club, trekked from Uttarakhand to Himachal Pradesh. While crossing Gibson Pass, they noticed a peak to the east of Borasu Pass. This was later identified as Jupkia (6,279m, 31°14'5.84"N, 78°32'2.39"E), and it remained on the club's wish list until 2017, when I was part of a team that climbed the mountain.

We first headed by road to Sangla, a small village in the Baspa Valley, acquiring Inner Line permits from the district headquarters. (Jukpia is close to the Tibetan border, about 12km southwest of the better-known Rangrik Rang; see *AAJ 1995.*) Continuing east through Chitkul and then south toward Borasu Pass, we established base camp on the Jupkia Glacier moraine at 4,680m.

Over the next few days, we placed Camps 1 and 2 on the southwest side of Jukpia, the latter at 5,610m, at the head of a side glacier that rose toward the mountain. Above, a depression rose to the east, reaching a col below the south side of Jukpia. On September 2, after two false starts halted by severe snow squalls, four of us left high camp at 11 a.m. and climbed the south-southwest face, passing many crevasses and reaching the summit at 4:50 p.m. We regained our top camp at 7:30 p.m., and the following day descended to base camp to celebrate a carefully nurtured wish of almost 15 years. Our team was Buddhadeb Das, Arun Kanti Das, Rana Das, Rajib Sanyal, Prakash Shaw, and summiters Nagraja Pai, Pasang Sherpa, Pemba Tsiring, and me (expedition leader). 📖📷🔍

– ABHISHEK DAS, *INDIA*

GANGOTRI

WEST HARSIL HORN, FIRST ASCENT VIA WEST-SOUTHWEST RIDGE

HARSIL VILLAGE (CA 2,400m) lies on the main road from Uttarkashi to Gangotri, about 30km before the latter. The name Harsil may derive from the horns of a deer—in this case referring to twin rock peaks around 5km to the south across the Bhagirathi River. The Harsil Horns more or less form the end of the long northwest ridge of Srikanta (6,133m) in the far western Gangotri.

The westernmost and seemingly the higher of the two summits (4,823m, 30°59'26.18"N, 78°45'15.70"E) was attempted in November 2019 by a team from the Nehru Institute of Mountaineering (NIM), Uttarkashi, with an aim of promoting trekking and tourism in this region. Heavy snowfall prevented an ascent, but a useful reconnaissance was achieved.

In June 2020, with their outdoor courses canceled due to COVID-19, the NIM and its principal, Col. Amit Bisht, organized another attempt. The team reached base camp at 3,620m on the 22nd, and on the 25th carried out a reconnaissance of the route to a high camp at 4,387m. The

The Harsil Horns from the north. The first ascent of the west peak (right) was in 2020 from the col to the west of the mountain (not visible). *Nehru Institute of Mountaineering*

latter part of this involved steep, snow-covered slopes interspersed with rocky outcrops.

The team moved to high camp on the 27th, and the following day five members—Col. Bisht, Lt. Col. Yogesh Dhumal, Hav Thinlass Gyalpo, Shri Shivraj Singh Panwar, and Shri Saurav Singh— left for the summit at 4 a.m. Steep snow led to a col west of the summit, and then the climbers ascended the south flank of the rocky west-southwest ridge. Fixing ropes where deemed necessary, the five reached the top at 9:30 a.m. The team descended safely to base camp the same day. 📷

— *INFORMATION PROVIDED BY* **AMIT BISHT**, *NEHRU INSTITUTE OF MOUNTAINEERING, INDIA*

ATAL PEAKS, FIRST ASCENTS

IN OCTOBER 2018, the Nehru Institute of Mountaineering and the Uttarakhand Tourism Development Board jointly organized an expedition to attempt peaks in the area of the Raktaban (a.k.a. Raktavarn) Glacier. The venture was highly successful, with the eight-member team, led by Amit Bisht, summiting four previously unclimbed peaks.

The team was established at the 3,700m Bhojbasa base camp by October 8 with the main aim of climbing Peak 6,566m. This high summit sits on the long ridge that separates the side glaciers that run south from Sri Kailas West and Sri Kailas to the Raktaban Glacier.

After establishing Camp 2 at 5,100m on the glacier west of the ridge [*sometimes called the Shyamvarn Glacier*], the climbers first summited two peaks, 6,086m and 6,126m, along the ridge. On the 15th, from Camp 2, they ascended the glacier north to camp at 5,900m, below the col that separates Peak 6,566m and Peak 6,557m. From here, on the 16th, all eight members reached the col, turned north, and were on the summit of Peak 6,557m by around 11 a.m. Returning to the col, five members of the team then made the difficult ascent of Peak 6,566m, negotiating steep ice walls and arriving on top at 3:30 p.m. They returned to their top camp 18 hours after leaving.

This was the first known attempt on any of these peaks, which were named Atal I (6,566m, a.k.a. Shyamvarn Parvat), Atal II (6,557m, just north of Atal I), Atal III (6,126m), and Atal IV (6,086m), after the late prime minister Atal Bihari Vajpayee. [*Coordinates and additional information at the AAJ website.*] 📄 📷 🔍

— *INFORMATION PROVIDED BY* **THE NEHRU INSTITUTE OF MOUNTAINEERING,** *INDIA*

NEPAL

MUKUT HIMAL

MUKOT HIMAL, HISTORICAL FIRST ASCENT FROM THE WEST

OFFICIALLY OPENED IN 2014, Mukot Himal (a.k.a. Mukut Himal, 6,087m) lies north of Dhaulagiri on the ridge running south from Hongde (6,556m) to Sita Chuchara (6,611m). The "Mukut Himal" region, north of Dhaulagiri II, was reconnoitered in 1954 by Jimmy Roberts (U.K.), who appears to have climbed two small peaks to the north and west of Hongde from the village of Mukut. Reports in the AAJ in 2015 and 2016 describe the first official ascent of Mukot Himal but hint that the mountain was likely climbed in the 1960s. In fact it was, and now we can provide details.

Camp 1 on Mukot Himal in 1967. Behind lies the northwest face of Peak 5,975m, which may still be unclimbed. *F. Charles Dufour*

In the autumn of 1967, Johannes Noordijk led a seven-member team from the Netherlands, which left Pokhara on October 4 and arrived in Mukut village on November 9 after a long trek via the Barbung Khola to the west. The same day they established Camp 1 in the valley west-southwest of Mukot Himal and north of Peak 5,975m. After placing Camp 2 on the 10th at about 5,425m, below the peak's west ridge, the next day Fons Driessen, Michael von Mourik Broekman, Phu Dorje Sherpa, and Tenzing Gyatso Sherpa climbed up the west ridge, then slanted up the north-northwest face to reach the last section of the north ridge, which they followed to the summit. This was a very different route to that followed by the 2015 teams, which approached via the next valley to the north and reached the north ridge at a lower elevation.

On the same day, November 11, other members of the team attempted Peak 5,975m, stopping on the summit ridge around 60m below the top. This peak lies southwest of Mukot Himal, has an impressive northwest face, and may still be unclimbed. 🖹 🖻

— LINDSAY GRIFFIN, *WITH INFORMATION FROM* RODOLPHE POPIER, *HIMALAYAN DATABASE, FRANCE,* *AND* FLORENTIN CHARLES DUFOUR, *THE NETHERLANDS*

LANGTANG HIMAL

KYUNGKA RI II, SOUTHWEST FACE AND SOUTHEAST RIDGE

ON DECEMBER 8, Dawa Sangay Sherpa, Mingma Sherpa, Tenjing Sherpa, four local porters, Kukur (a lovely, crazy dog that followed us from Langtang village), and I set off from Kyanjin Gompa (3,870m) for the Shalbachum Glacier. After a long day on wild moraine, we made base camp at 4,570m, and on the 9th, another full day of dangerous, unstable moraine, we set Camp 1 at 5,325m, just before the glacier ice. Two porters remained here, while the next day the rest of

Camp 1 by the Shalbachum Glacier with (A) Kyungka Ri II, (B) Kyungka Ri I, and (C) unnamed peak (ca 6,300m). The ascent of Kyungka Ri II followed obvious glacier slopes to the ridgeline, then left up the southeast ridge to the top. *Sophie Lavaud*

us continued up to Camp 2 on the glacier at 5,630m.

Leaving the dog in the company of the remaining two porters, Dawa, Mingma, Tenjing, and I set off at 2 a.m. on the 11th and climbed up the southwest-facing slope above to reach the ridge between Kyungka Ri I and II. In the autumn of 2017, the summit of Kyungka Ri I (6,599m) was reached by climbing this slope, then turning right along the northwest ridge to the top (*AAJ 2018*). We climbed more to the left on the southwest slope, with a few steep sections and huge crevasses making this rather technical and difficult. At the ridgeline, we headed left up the southeast ridge to reach the summit of Kyungka Ri II (official height 6,506m) at 10:40 a.m.; my GPS measured an altitude of 6,522m. During our descent, we left three V-threads, four snow stakes, and one ice screw. Continuing down the glacier, we reached Camp 1 at 4:30 p.m.

That night we had 15–20cm of snow. Next day, with the dangerous moraine still to descend and our four porters not equipped for snow, we decided to call a helicopter, and in three separate lifts were transported to Kyanjin Gompa. 📷

— SOPHIE LAVAUD, *SWITZERLAND*

MARIE RI, HISTORICAL ASCENT, EAST FACE TO SOUTH-SOUTHWEST RIDGE

IN LATE 1996, Jean-Christophe Lafaille planned a bold, solo, clandestine ascent of the southwest face of Xixabangma during the first few days of the official Nepal-China winter mountaineering season (December 1–February 15). He would start from Langtang, follow the Langtang Glacier north to the border at Hagen's Col, and cross it to the foot of the southwest face. Lafaille was accompanied by Jean-Michel Asselin, then editor of the French magazine *Vertical*, and four Sherpas (Amchu, Dorje, Gyalzen, and Zangbu).

The group trekked up the Langtang Glacier to the foot of Hagen's Col, but deep snow made progress much slower than anticipated. When they reached the slopes leading to the col and found them to be hard ice, they retreated.

During the return journey, they camped near the junction of the Langtang and Kyungka glaciers, where Lafaille was attracted by a prominent peak (6,140m on the HMG-Finn map; 28°18'0.91"N, 85°40'58.68"E) on the long east-northeast ridge of Kyungka Ri I (6,599m). On December 1, he left camp early and reached the summit in a little over seven hours. He climbed a steep, fluted eastern face of 250m to reach the crest of the south-southwest ridge at around 5,800m, and then followed this to the summit, negotiating a 70° ice step high on the crest. Lafaille christened the peak Marie Ri after his daughter, who would be two years old the following day. 📷

— RODOLPHE POPIER, *LA CHRONIQUE ALPINE-FFCAM, WITH INFORMATION FROM JEAN-MICHEL ASSELIN, FRANCE*

LUZA PEAK, SOUTHEAST FACE AND SOUTH-SOUTHEAST RIDGE

PROJECT LUZA WINTER was a joint expedition of some young, independent Sherpas from the village of Phortse, with the aim of uplifting our standards as professional climbers, even though we are not IFMGA-certified: Urken Lendu (a.k.a. Lendhup) Sherpa, a 27-year-old freelance mountain guide with multiple ascents of Everest, Lhotse, and Manaslu; Lhakpa Gyaljen Sherpa (26), a guide who has climbed Everest, Cho Oyu, Cholatse, and many smaller peaks; and me, a freelance mountain guide who began my climbing career with an Everest expedition in spring 2012. Every winter I instruct ice climbing courses at the Khumbu Climbing Center, and I've also climbed in the Alps, with ascents of many peaks. Phortse, in the Khumbu, lies at an altitude of 3,840m and has the highest concentration of Everest summiters in the world (83 at the time of writing).

Luza (5,710m) lies on the long ridge that runs from Kyajo Ri to Khumbi Yul Lha (a.k.a. Khumbila). It used to be snow-capped, but with the impact of climate change it has become an exposed rocky peak. We established base camp in December at 4,900m, above Luza village (Luja, 4,338m) in the Gokyo Valley. After inspecting the peak, our initial goal was to climb a prominent depression/couloir on the northeast face, a wall that never sees the sun in winter. We started early, traversing the snout of the Luza Glacier to the base of the wall. The initial climbing was fun, but as we progressed we began to find looser and more unstable slabs, and eventually retreated by rappelling from rock bollards.

Our second option was the southeast face and south-southeast ridge. On December 17, a moderate one-hour climb over scree and moraine warmed us, as did the early sunlight. We arrived at a fine rock face approximately 150m high. The ridge to the summit was tricky and loose, but we took time to film and arrived at the top at 11:30 a.m. The descent proved more exciting, as we followed the south ridge in part, and we had to be careful not to trigger rockfall. But we managed to get back to base camp before dark. We had hoped to establish a moderate climb for trekkers or rock climbers/scramblers, but we concluded this is not ideal route for beginners. Experienced climbers will have a good day out; we recommend taking plenty of cams and nuts.

Our objectives had been to promote eco-friendly expeditions and winter tourism, and to provide a positive message to the world that Sherpas don't just climb to earn a living. We climb for ourselves. We climb for fun. It is a passion that promotes self-growth. We hope to motivate a newer generation of Sherpa youths to explore new routes and new peaks. [*Editor's Note: Sadly, Urken Lendu Sherpa fell to his death the following month while climbing near Phortse.*] 📄 📷

— PEMBA SHARWA SHERPA, *NEPAL*

The east side of Luza (5,710m) showing (1) 2020 route up the southeast face/ridge to the summit and (2) attempted route up the middle of the northeast face. *Pemba Sharwa Sherpa*

Yuikeung Ho and Xiaohua Yang approach the shoulder on the upper north ridge of Daddomain West during the second day of their climb. *Siyuan Huang*

MINYA KONKA RANGE, DADDOMAIN WEST, FIRST ASCENT VIA NORTHWEST FACE

IN NOVEMBER, Siyuan (Azuo) Huang, Xiaohua (Charlotte) Yang, and I visited the Minya Konka Range, after Siyuan and I did a warm-up climb in the Tatsienlu Massif (see report below). From the Moxi Valley, we noticed a clean line with direct access rising straight to the summit of Daddomain West (6,296m), the unclimbed subsidiary summit of Daddomain (6,380m). This line captivated us.

On the 10th, from a base camp at 4,200m, we walked five hours with food and gear up the valley leading to Daddomain, and pitched camp at 4,865m on the glacier. Pleasant weather over the preceding week meant there was little snow on the glacier: Crevasses could be clearly identified, and fortunately none were huge. We stayed the night, observing that there were no signs of avalanche or rockfall on our proposed line up the northwest face.

Next morning we reached the bergschrund at the bottom of the face in one hour. Surmounting this large obstacle took some time, as the snow was too loose to hold body weight securely. We climbed around the left side at M3. This took us to the couloir in the lower section of the face, where the snow was still unconsolidated but got firmer and more frozen as we continued up. There were also sections of shiny ice.

The weather was excellent, with clear skies. We progressed wherever possible by climbing simultaneously with intermediate protection. Sometimes we belayed, but on the lower half of the route the ice was thin and hollow, with a deep layer of sugar snow beneath. Ice screws were useless, and the rock wasn't much good either, being too loose or brittle. We often had long runouts.

By 6 p.m. we had been looking for a bivouac site for some time, but still found no ledge or stance. Finally we built an anchor at a rock outcrop and dug out a narrow snow ledge for a sitting bivouac at 5,684m.

We started again at 9 a.m., the weather still good. We pitched sections of ice and at 7 p.m. reached a shoulder on the north ridge at 6,200m. The summit was just above, but we decided to stop there, where a large plateau allowed us a relaxing bivouac.

The northwest face of Daddomain and Daddomain West seen from the approach valley. The 2020 team bivied once on the face and once just below the summit. The west ridge, on the right, was partially followed by New Zealanders in 2004 to make the first ascent of Daddomain, bypassing the top of Daddomain West. *Yuikeung Ho*

We left again at 9 a.m. the following morning (November 13) and made a quick ascent of the remaining two pitches. The snow was soft, and we spent little time on the summit before returning to the shoulder. From there we downclimbed 100m of the northwest face to reach ice, where we placed our first Abalakov rappel anchor. We more or less followed our ascent route downward, seeking ice for rappel anchors. Lower down, given that neither the rock nor ice was of good quality, finding anchors took a long time. We reached the bottom after 28 rappels, leaving behind 30m of cordelette and a few pieces of gear.

The route was sustained, but apart from the bergschrund it had no real crux. We named it Good-bye Happiness (1,400m, D+ WI3 M3 75°) as a memorial to our close friends Ng Ka-Kit and Li Haoxin, who died in an avalanche on Liligo Peak in Pakistan in 2019 (*AAJ 2020*). 📷

— YUIKEUNG (KENNETH) HO, *CHINA*

THE FIRST ASCENT OF DADDOMAIN: *The first climb of Daddomain took place in 2004, when New Zealanders Jo Kippax and Sean Waters climbed the west ridge. Rather than traverse over Daddomain West to reach the main summit, they dropped into a snow basin on the south side and followed this to the top, thus leaving the western summit unclimbed until 2020.*

TATSIENLU MASSIF, PEAK 5,600M, NORTHWEST FACE

IN OCTOBER, Siyuan (Azuo) Huang and I traveled to the Tatsienlu Massif, which is southeast of Kangding and culminates in Lamo-she (6,070m). Our base camp was a one-hour drive from Kangding, located at 4,080m on a flat sandbank with a nearby lake.

After some reconnaissance, we decided to go for an unclimbed summit on the long southwest ridge of unnamed Peak 5,624m (PLA map), south of Lamo-she. This summit lies on the right side of the upper valley that rises east-northeast from base camp. We established Camp 1 at 4,800m, following a track on the right side of the valley for six hours before pitching our tent on the start of the scree-covered glacier.

On October 26 we hiked up to the northwest face of our peak, racked up, and began climbing. The route was basically mixed climbing on granite, interspersed with a few terraces. Starting with a few M3 and M4 pitches, we made several traverses and climbed a couloir with good protection. At the time of our attempt, there was little ice on the face, just a thin layer of snow that wouldn't hold our steps securely.

In the upper section we shifted to another couloir, which became slabby and demanding. The rock turned brittle and scrappy, and sometimes the protection was poor. The crux was high on the route: a few pitches of M4 to M5+ to reach a large, triangular snow platform. The pitch below this platform was vertical to overhanging in parts, followed by a chimney. We bivied on the snow platform at 5,464m.

Next morning, we took only what was necessary and slanted up to the northeast ridge. In two hours we were on the summit (approximately 29°55'49"N, 102°3'7"E). We had left our phones and altimeter watches at the bivouac and were unable to measure the peak's height, but we estimate it to be around 5,600m. We returned to the bivy platform and then rappelled the route, using rock gear (no pitons) for anchors. The route gained about 700m, and we graded it D+ M5+. 📷 🔍

— YUIKEUNG (KENNETH) HO, *CHINA*

SICHUAN / QIONGLAI SHAN – SIGUNIANG NATIONAL PARK

POTALA SHAN, NORTH FACE, JIAYOU, SECOND ASCENT

AFTER FOUR PREVIOUS attempts in seven years, He Chuan, Sun Bin, and Wang Zhen completed the second ascent of Jiayou, the route that Yasushi Yamanoi from Japan climbed in 2005 up the north face of Potala Shan (5,428m). Yamanoi soloed the route from June 28 to July 19 in generally poor, snowy conditions, fixing the lower section and then completing the route over seven days in capsule style. He took a further two days to descend and graded the 18-pitch route 5.8 A3+ (*see AAJ 2006*).

In mid-August, the three Chinese climbers made a base camp at 4,650m, 100m below the start of the wall. Starting on August 20, in a single push with a portaledge, they climbed the route in 15 pitches over five days. Most of it follows a large dihedral, and over 70 percent of the route was climbed on aid. They added eight new bolts, on bivouacs, rappel anchors, or to reinforce belays. Like Yamanoi, the Chinese finished their ascent upon reaching the southeast ridge at around 5,350m, still a long way from the summit; they descended to base camp in a day.

Up to a point four pitches below the top, which appeared to be the last of Yamanoi's bivouacs, they found his bolt belays and abandoned gear. At the top of the next two pitches, they found bolt belays and abandoned gear; above that they found nothing.

He Chuan reports that the last two pitches are mainly in a two- to five meter-wide chimney with large jammed blocks. The terrain is 20° less than vertical, not steep like the great dihedral below. Above the last bolt, He Chuan climbed a short offwidth and then a narrow chimney to reach the wide chimney with chockstones; he passed behind or alongside the big chockstones. All this was relatively dry and considerably easier than the main dihedral below, going free rather than on aid. There were no bolts, slings, or any form of rappel anchors visible.

Yamanoi said there had been a lot of snow and ice on the route, forcing him to wear full plastic boots for his entire climb. He felt the last section was probably the hardest, while for the Chinese these pitches were by far the easiest. Yamanoi remembers rock covered by ice, which he climbed without pitons. He climbed around a red pyramid to finish, and in the last part there appeared to be several dangerous hanging flakes. He spent only 15 minutes on the mist-covered ridge before descending, and thinks he used slings for rappel anchors. Yamanoi also remembers leaving a lot of material on the route as he battled to escape an incoming storm.

Despite the absence of evidence from the 2005 ascent on the final section, He Chuan accepts Yamanoi's account, adding that a plastering of snow and ice on the last two pitches would completely change the difficulty of that section. He also notes that a violent earthquake affecting this area in 2008 could have removed jammed blocks and rappel anchors.

Chuan confirmed the base of the wall was at 4,750m, making the route 600m rather than the originally reported 850m.

Potala Shan's summit likely has been reached by only one route, established by Andrej and Tanja Grmovsek from Slovenia in the autumn of 2003. The two climbed the west face (800m, VIII-) to the north (main) top of the broad mountain.

– LINDSAY GRIFFIN, *WITH INFORMATION FROM* HE CHUAN, *CHINA*, XIA ZHONGMING, *GERMANY, AND* YASUSHI YAMANOI, *JAPAN*

The line of Jiayou (Yamanoi, 2005) on the north face of Potala Shan. Both ascents of this route to date stopped at the ridge. The summit is at upper right; the only complete ascent was from the right, via the west face (800m, VIII-), first climbed in 2003 by Andrej and Tanja Grmovsek. *Yasushi Yamanoi* [Inset] He Chuan (circled) on the southeast ridge of Potala Shan. The dark chimney below and right is the top of Jiayou on the north face. *Wang Zhen*

YUNNAN / HENGDUAN MOUNTAINS

YULONG XUESHAN OVERVIEW AND SNOW LOTUS PEAK, NORTH RIDGE

THE YULONG XUESHAN or Jade Dragon Range lies north of Lijiang and is a popular tourist area. The range holds around 18 peaks over 5,000m; some of the mountains are believed to be unclimbed.

The highest summit is Shanzidou (5,596m), which was first attempted as early as 1938 and was climbed in 1987 by Eric Perlman and Phil Peralta-Ramos (*AAJ 1988*). Shanzidou has now been off-limits for many years, out of respect for local religious beliefs; Chinese authorities deny it has ever been climbed. No other peaks in the area are believed to be forbidden to climbers; a climbing or trekking permit may be required.

At the AAJ website, a report by Yannick Benichou describes a recent ascent of the north ridge of Snow Lotus Peak (a.k.a. Xuelian, ca 5,231m) and provides excellent photos of these attractive mountains. 📖 📷

– *INFORMATION FROM* YANNICK BENICHOU, *FRANCE*

In fading light, Merry Schimanski ponders the way through new terrain during the first ascent of The Mile High Club (700m, 22 pitches, 5.12d) on the Airport Wall, above Milford Sound. *Daniel Joll*

SOUTHERN ALPS

MILFORD SOUND, AIRPORT WALL, THE MILE HIGH CLUB

IN RECENT YEARS I have been living between France and the USA, not really spending much time in my native New Zealand. My wife, Julie, is French, and our loose plan was to settle in France when our young son, Sam, started school.

At the end of 2019, we had just finished a three-month road trip in California and headed back to NZ for Christmas—for what we intended to be a 10-week visit. But that was before COVID-19. In February, France began its first lockdown, and India, where I was meant to go in April to attempt Changabang, canceled all tourist visas. Since we were already in New Zealand, which at the time had no COVID-related restrictions, we took the easy option of staying there.

A few months passed. New Zealand went through its own lockdown, which ended on May 13. We emerged with few restrictions, but we certainly weren't leaving the country anytime soon. For two years, I had thought of Changabang daily, and for four months I'd been training cardio almost exclusively. Now I began looking for an outlet for all of the energy I had been saving for Changabang.

There were no standout alpine objectives calling my name in New Zealand, but my friend Merry Schimanski, who was taking a year off work, was keen to help me develop a long rock route. Like me, he has a love of ground-up adventure climbing, and he is also well versed in establishing big granite lines. While we have many nice granite cliffs in NZ, most of them require a long approach, and few have sustained climbing. For me, when it comes to rock climbing, the climbing-to-walking ratio has to be positive.

Located on the northeastern flank of Mt. Sheerdown, which rises out of Deep Water Basin in Milford Sound, the Airport Wall (named for its proximity to the busy airport) is large by New Zealand standards, like a bigger version of Stawamus Chief or Half Dome. Low-elevation and perfect for sunny winter climbing, with an approach of less than one hour, this wall checked all the boxes.

Though no routes had been established, we were not the first to venture onto the Airport Wall. Around ten years ago, Bruce Dowrick and a collection of friends attempted to go ground-up on the central corner line. After fixing lines for 400m through bushy ledges, they bailed 40m up the first pitch of the corner due to some dangerous loose blocks. (This experience was in stark contrast to our line, where we climbed on very solid rock.) Later they returned and rappelled the wall in search of a line. Luckily for us, that's where the exploration stopped. For ten years, the cliff had lain waiting.

Maybe if we had known just how much work the Airport Wall was going to require, we might have picked a different objective. However, who can complain about a big-wall climbing project with a short approach and pitch after pitch of untamed rock?

We started up the wall on June 6. We were aiming for the longest possible continuous rock climb, so we began lower and avoided the bushy terrain that previous attempts had used to access the wall. It took 14 days simply to top out, using aid where needed, and another 16 to 20 days to clean and complete a team free ascent, which we accomplished on August 25. On November 10, supported by Steve Fortune, I made a one-day free ascent, leading all the pitches in 16.5 hours. We called our new route The Mile High Club (700m, 22 pitches, 5.12d).

All told, we spent over 40 days on the wall. The winter days were short, but the temps were quite nice. The views over Milford Sound, with its many peaks plastered in ice, were spectacular. We sank about $4,000 to $5,000 NZD of expenses into the effort, for bolts, brushes, fixed lines, and petrol for the multiple 3.5-hour trips down to Milford from Queenstown. Merry and I had many helpers over the course of putting up the route—a big thanks to Alastair, Jaz, Rachael, Jessy, Jono, James, Anton, Sooji, and Ruari, who all put in hours or days of work, helping to clean and climb pitches. Ultimately, it was all worth it to have a long, challenging line on which to push ourselves.

Let's leave the Airport Wall for ground-up route development. I doubt there is a sunnier, bigger cliff in the country that has more possibility for future generations, and this will give them something to aspire to. Sections of this wall are immaculate. Other parts will take days of cleaning and hard work. No doubt, whoever puts up the next route on this wall is going to have to work for it. 📷 🔍

— **DANIEL JOLL**, *NEW ZEALAND*

Daniel Joll setting up for crux face moves on pitch four (5.12b) of The Mile High Club. *Gavin Lang*

Ruari Macfarlane descending Torres Peak during the first wintertime Torres-Tasman traverse. *Gavin Lang*

SOUTHERN ALPS: SUMMER AND WINTER HIGHLIGHTS

THE NEW ZEALAND summer of 2019–'20 was typified by stable spells of warm, dry weather interspersed between significant storm fronts, the worst of which hammered the South Island ranges in early February, when Milford Sound was drenched by over half a meter of rain in a single day. Despite the fickle weather, plenty of climbers braved the odds, and while there wasn't an abundance of new routes, some noteworthy first ascents were completed. Two notable moderate routes were a new line on the north face of Newton Peak (2,543m) by Michael Eatson, George Loomes, Olivia Truax, and Sam Waetford, and a 400m alpine rock route from the upper Malte Brun Glacier to the crest of the west ridge on Malte Brun (3,198m), by Gavin Lang and Ruari Macfarlane.

The COVID-19 pandemic then placed the country into a state of lockdown from late March through mid-May. Ongoing travel restrictions all but eliminated any chance to climb internationally, which resulted in a glut of motivated climbers stuck in New Zealand—with the net result being one of the most productive winter and spring climbing seasons in recent years.

Daniel Joll and Karl "Merry" Schimanski kicked things off in late May, when they climbed the aptly named Straight Outta Lock Down (175m, 25/5.11d) at Copper Point, a cliff accessed by boat on the south shore of Milford Sound. Bruce Dowrick, Llewellyn Murdoch, and Jon Seddon made the first ascent of Big Fish (150m, 28/5.12d) at the same area, and then Murdoch paired up with Steven Fortune to establish a third route, the seven-pitch Taratahi (24/5.11c). Joll, Schimanski, and Rachel Knott put many days of work into the first ascent of The Mile High Club, a 700m route on the Airport Wall (*see report on previous page*). All four of these routes utilize a mixture of natural and bolted protection while climbing on high-quality granite in a maritime setting, which, despite the proximity to the ocean, maintains a distinct alpine feel.

Ben Dare established two new routes during the annual Darran Mountains winter climbing meet in July. Lit Up (III, 5) takes a line up the right-hand side of the main wall in McPherson Cirque, between the Thrill Frenzy Ramp and 1964 HQ Holden (both by Uren and Vass, 1992). This was followed up with the first ascent of the south face of Pyramid Peak (2,295m) via a sustained ice and mixed route (*see report below*).

July also saw two new routes climbed on the south face of Tititea/Mt. Aspiring (3,033m).

George Loomes and Rauri Macfarlane climbed the 500m Shooting Tahr, IV, 5+ (M5, WI4). Starting up the Whiston-Hyslop (1976) through the lower rock band, they then followed new ground to the Coxcomb Ridge, between Shooting Star (Dare-Joll, 2014) and Thales (Heung-Kirchner, 2016). Meanwhile, Sooji Clarkson and Gavin Lang started just to the left of the Chocolate Fish Route (Beavan-Uren, 1997) to climb a new 300m ice and mixed route to the Coxcomb Ridge: Kia Rapu i Tōku Māramatanga (Seeking the Light), IV, 5 (WI3, M4). To round out the month, Macfarlane, Jaz Morris, and Maddy Whittaker found great ice conditions on the south face of Mt. Joffre (2,091m) when they climbed Antics, III, 5 (WI4), 500m.

In Aoraki/Mt. Cook National Park, Lang and Macfarlane claimed the first Torres-Tasman traverse (Cleveland-Hamilton-Lange, 1951) in winter. After a two-day approach to Katies Col along the Fox Range, the pair traversed over Torres Peak, Mt. Tasman (3,497m), and Lendenfeld Peak, then descended via the "ever dwindling" Fox Glacier to reach the car after a 19-hour day.

Soon after, Bia Boucinhas, Owen Lee, Petrouchka Steiner-Grierson, and Chris Tipper teamed up to climb a new mixed line on the west face of Mt. Humdinger (2,796m): Nota14lol, II, 5 (M4), 300m. On the eastern side of the Main Divide, Macfarlane was at it again in August, when he climbed a pair of new routes on the southeast face of Vampire Peak (2,645m). Firstly, he and Mark Evans climbed Twilight, IV, 4 (WI3), a seven-pitch ice route between Bram Stoker (MacFarlane-McLeod, 1993) and Swiss Virgins (Blackburne-Nash, 1983). The very next day,

[Top] Rauri Macfarlane on Antics, south face of Mt. Joffre. *Jaz Morris* [Bottom] The south face of Tititea/Mt. Aspiring, showing (1) Shooting Tahr (500m, IV,5+) and (2) Kia Rapu i Tōku Māramatanga (300m, IV5). Many other routes not shown. *Gavin Lang*

he set out alone on Single and Searching V, 6 (WI5, M6), a 500m direct line to near the summit, starting from partway up the broad gully of Far From the Madding Crowd. [*Macfarlane's first-person account of this bold ascent is at the AAJ website.*]

Following these climbs, Macfarlane set his sights on the Inland Kaikoura range to climb a single-day triple linkup on the southern aspects of Mitre Peak (2,621m), Point 2,578m, and Mt. Alarm (2,877m). In the process, he climbed three new routes: Milford Wanderer, II 3 (M3) on Mitre Peak; the Central Gully, II, 4 (M4) on Point 2,578m; and finally The Good Shepherd, III, 5 (M5), 250m, on Mt. Alarm.

The last word of the spring season went to Clarkson and Loomes, who climbed a variation to The Band-aid Route (Dickson-McLeod, 1992) on the south face of Mt. D'Archiac (2,875m). Lust, V, 5+ (WI5), adds a new direct start and finish to the route. ▤ ▣

— BEN DARE, *NEW ZEALAND*

The south face of Pyramid Peak, showing Frost Flower (1,200m, VI,6). Flat Top Peak is at left. *Ben Dare*

PYRAMID PEAK, SOUTH FACE, FROST FLOWER

TEN YEARS AGO, I ventured out on my first winter climbing trip to the Darran Mountains. Following an abortive attempt at a then unclimbed route on the west peak of Mt. Crosscut, Al Uren and I stopped off in the upper Eglinton Valley and were rewarded with a view into the head of Mistake Creek, where two prominent features stand guard: the east face of Flat Top Peak and the south face of Pyramid Peak (2,295m), a sweep of steepening snow, ice, and granite that rises 1,300 vertical meters from the valley floor, taking center stage at head of the valley. It was a view that planted the seed for an adventure a decade in the making.

Finally, in July 2020, I decided it was time to become properly acquainted. On July 16, I started walking from the highway around sunrise and arrived at the small lake below the south face of Pyramid not long after midday. I pitched my tent here and continued up. Access to the face was guarded by a jumbled mass of avalanche debris: car-size snow blocks, welded together and haphazardly stacked like a giant game of drunken Jenga gone wrong. After 200m, the debris cone petered out as the slope steepened and entered the first rock band. In a narrow chute, the snow transitioned to firm névé and then water ice as dark rock walls closed in on either side.

Above the confines of the gully, several hundred meters of steep snow and squeaky névé led into the second rock band. I tackled this via a great shield of thin alpine ice leading into a series of interlinked runnels. Hero ice provided first-swing sticks and rapid progress despite the near-vertical terrain.

Viewed from the valley floor, the upper headwall was the only portion of the route that did not appear to hold continuous ice. Thankfully, luck and conditions were on my side, and a thin, ice-choked gully provided a means to advance. Slowly moving through the steep cruxes, I watched the last of the day's light fade away. I finally reached the notch between the twin summits under the cover of darkness, alone with my thoughts and the slightest hint of a breeze.

As I started downclimbing the unfamiliar south ridge of Pyramid, I seriously questioned the logic of not descending into Falls Creek to the northeast, a descent I had already done after a climb back in 2016. But decisions influenced by eagerness can often lack in logic, and for better or worse I had left my tent and sleeping bag back at the head of Mistake Creek, thus committing myself to the long traverse over Flat Top. Bumbling my way through the long hours of darkness, it was well into the wee hours before I finally reached the security of the valley floor.

I called the route Frost Flower, VI, 6 (M5 WI4), inspired by the intricate patterns of the frost formations I saw in the valley. 📖

— BEN DARE, *NEW ZEALAND*

BOOK REVIEWS

EDITED BY DAVID STEVENSON

TO LIVE: FIGHTING FOR LIFE ON THE KILLER MOUNTAIN

ÉLISABETH REVOL. Vertebrate Press (U.K.), 2020. Paperback, 160 pages, £24.

IN THE WINTER of 2013, French alpinist Élisabeth Revol made her first attempt on Nanga Parbat, marking the beginning of a fateful and formative relationship with the "killer mountain." She returned with Polish climber Tomasz Mackiewicz, first in the winter of 2015 and then again in 2017–'18 (Mackiewicz's seventh attempt). On January 25, they completed the second winter ascent—and first by a woman—of the 8,125-meter peak, via a new route up the northwest face, which they had started during their first attempt together in 2015. But as all climbers know, the ascent is just half the story, and what follows is a heartbreaking descent and the nightmarish realities and choices the team must face. The descent, a harrowing ordeal of life and death, comprises the bulk of the story in *To Live*.

Highlights of Revol's book include her exploration of and tribute to her friendship with Mackiewicz, despite their opposite natures, and his physical and spiritual obsession with Nanga Parbat's slopes and stories. Her candor about the wide range of emotions she experiences help convey the complexity of climbing partnerships. Intriguing to all, regardless of climbing ability—and in many ways the most fascinating aspect of the book—are the sections where Revol delves into her motivations for climbing, especially such notoriously difficult objectives; the opposing forces of life and death that high-stakes, high-altitude climbing demands a climber to constantly juggle; and what has kept her climbing in the face of criticism, conflict, and tragic loss. Sometimes this is done through reflective prose and in other instances excerpts from personal journal entries. These insights help the reader better understand Revol and a drive that may be hard for some to grasp.

Also helpful are the copies of texts that occurred between Revol, her husband, and ground crews as a rescue was organized. Despite their sparse nature, these quick exchanges reveal volumes about the tense, terrible nature of the situations that adventure in the high mountains can create.

Similar to the opposing forces of life and death that climbers like Revol and Mackiewicz must balance, so too there is a fine line between self-sufficiency and the contributions of others that may be integral not only to success but also to survival. Details like Revol's reliance on fixed lines set by a Korean team a year prior, and the Herculean efforts of the rescue organizers and climbers, including Adam Bielecki and Denis Urubko, add a layer of vulnerability that again deepens the story, as does Revol's honesty around the trauma experienced in the aftermath of the climb.

Revol's dedication, skill, drive, and passion for Himalayan climbing, in spite of all the tragedy she has experienced, shines throughout the book, as does her compassion for Mackiewicz and those who helped in his retrieval and her own rescue. The book concludes with a sampling of some of the existential dilemmas Revol faced in the aftermath of the climb, and the answers she eventually found would warrant another book. Just as we need more stories by competent woman climbers, so too do we need more ways to tackle not only hard routes but also these universal questions.

— MOLLY LOOMIS

EDGE OF THE MAP: THE MOUNTAIN LIFE OF CHRISTINE BOSKOFF

JOHANNA GARTON. Mountaineers Books, 2020. Paperback, 240 pages, $19.95.

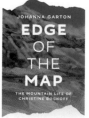

JOHANNA GARTON'S *EDGE of the Map* follows the life and high-altitude climbs of Christine Boskoff, a widely admired and accomplished mountaineer from Appleton, Wisconsin, whose body was found after an avalanche in a remote range of China in 2006. Though Garton spent time trekking in the Himalaya as a young woman, she is not a climber, making her devotion to the story and life of Boskoff, a stranger, all the more moving.

Boskoff was ebullient, open, and unpretentious, her passion for the mountains clear and without ego. "Christine takes pain very well," said Austrian climber Peter Habeler when interviewed about Boskoff for *Outside* in 2001. To be one of the women in the upper echelons of mountaineering at the time required fortitude, and Boskoff had it in spades.

Boskoff's life was impacted by the much-chronicled tragic events of the 1996 storm on Everest that took the lives of eight climbers. One of the climbers who perished, Scott Fischer, was the owner of Seattle-based guiding company Mountain Madness. Boskoff had crossed paths with him in 1995 on Broad Peak, her first 8,000-meter summit. After Fischer's death, Christine and her husband, Keith Boskoff, bought Mountain Madness, shifting Boskoff's relationship with mountaineering from personal to professional.

Garton is methodical, patient, and thorough, and her exhaustive research lays out important mountaineering history, the science and experience of being at high altitude, as well as the tangled cultural and political fabric of Tibet and China. Her prose and dialogue are imaginative and textured. We see Boskoff's smiling face and hear her frustration as she learns the ways of the mountains. We are right next to her as she climbs Broad Peak. We celebrate with her when she summits Everest, but join in her disappointment when she isn't able to do it without supplemental oxygen. Garton takes us to the valley where she was last alive with her partner Charlie Fowler. We feel their last moments as Garton imagines them, tingling while reading what it is like to be enveloped by avalanche, based on first-hand survivor accounts.

I was grateful for Garton's willingness to discuss the often-sidestepped topic of Indigenous beliefs and customs, and how they often are dissonant from the pursuits of the mountaineer. I do wonder if, had she been less emotionally attached to Boskoff's family and her legacy, whether she would have been able to go deeper, further questioning Boskoff and Fowler's decision to pursue a peak, Genyen, that local Tibetan monks had clearly indicated they wanted left alone to the spirits.

In an author's note, we learn that Garton grew up in the same small Wisconsin town as Boskoff, and learned of her disappearance through Garton's own mother, a close friend of Boskoff's mother, Joyce. For four years, Garton's mother, also a writer, poured herself into learning everything she could about Boskoff's life. Within a year of being diagnosed with Parkinson's, Garton's mother handed all of her hard work to her daughter, who inherited it with great purpose.

Christine Boskoff comes across as full of light and joy, despite being drawn to the danger and accepting the potentially dire consequences of high-altitude mountaineering. Boskoff's mother, Joyce, received a giant teddy bear and a dozen roses from her daughter on her birthday, three days after she was killed in an avalanche on the other side of the world. Johanna Garton may not be a high-altitude junkie or a wall rat, but she is a daughter who understands devotion.

– SASHA TURRENTINE

EMILIO COMICI: ANGEL OF THE DOLOMITES

David Smart. Rocky Mountain Books, 2020. Hardcover, 248 pages, $32.

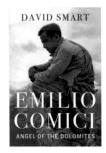

David Smart's new biography of Emilio Comici (1901–1940) draws on a variety of sources to paint a nuanced picture of Comici, a man of genius and flaws who had an oversized but underappreciated—particularly to English-speaking readers—impact on climbing. I knew nothing about Comici when I started reading. I just had the vague sense that his name was as important as other famous Italian climbers of the 20th century, like Bonatti or Maestri. By the end of the book, I'd come to appreciate Comici's impact on so many aspects of the sport. He was the inspiration behind the first artificial wall built to teach climbing, the precursor to modern gyms. He also filmed the first rock climbing documentary, a concept from which I've benefited greatly.

Comici made over 200 first ascents, including the north face of Cima Grande in the Dolomites, one of the "six classic north faces of the Alps," in 1933. Four years later, he soloed the 1,500-foot route in three and half hours. But his biggest contribution to climbing is probably the idea of the *direttissima:* choosing an aesthetic line straight up a face instead of searching for weaknesses. As Smart describes, "By denying modern climbers the option of wandering the mountain for easy rock, the direttissima reconfigured the ethic of adventure for 20th-century climbers and elevated route-finding from a skill to an ideal."

The writing flows along quite nicely, and the book almost felt like it ended prematurely, but I suppose that's the result of Comici's untimely death, at age 39, when a frayed rope broke on easy ground. I couldn't help but wonder if the climbing community would better recognize his name if he had lived longer.

Much of the book made me think of the closing song from the musical *Hamilton*; I kept imagining Comici, who was so concerned about greatness and about how other climbers viewed him, singing the lines: "Let me tell you what I wish I'd known/When I was young and dreamed of glory/You have no control/Who lives, who dies, who tells your story?" I think Comici would be pleased with David Smart for telling his story so well. [*Editor's Note: This book was winner of the Banff Mountain Book Award for Climbing Literature in 2020.*]

— ALEX HONNOLD

ROCK 'N' ROLL ON THE WALL

Silvo Karo. Translated by Gorazd Pipenbaher. Self-published, 2020. Paperback, 304 pages, €25.

I bumped into Silvo Karo and Mauro "Bubu" Bole on the streets of Huaraz, Peru, in 2000. Asked what they'd been up to, Silvo humbly replied, "Just a little climb in the Cordillera." He and Bole had just done the first ascent of "little" Cruz del Sur, an 800-meter 5.12 on La Esfinge, a massive granite bubble in the Blanca. The comment was typical, I'd learn, of one of the world's greatest alpine wall climbers. He was always humble, always downplaying.

In his new memoir, humility is the theme, Silvo is the master. It tells the story of a kid growing up in a tiny Slovenian village before the end of the Cold War, meeting like-minded souls, and of his approach to the very, very hard climbing that grabbed his attention: extreme walls.

In fact, the extreme nature of both the training and climbing in this book is quite mind-boggling. In the summer of 1982, visiting the United States, Silvo did an amped-up version of the standard Colorado-Wyoming-South Dakota tour with 172 routes climbed in "a little over a month." These weren't single-pitch sport routes. Many were multi-pitch routes on the Diamond, Hallett Peak—you get the point. In this book, the 1993 fifth ascent of Wyoming Sheep Ranch on El Capitan is little more than a footnote!

New route after new route in his beloved Julian Alps (many of them approached by cycling or running) are punctuated by climbing trips that seek out the most extreme terrain on Earth. Straight out of the gates in 1983 (at age 23), he climbed a new route on Fitz Roy, followed by more wild Patagonian routes, including two on Cerro Torre. His description of his and Janez Jeglič's ascent of the 1,200-meter line up Cerro Torre's south face is truly the stuff of nightmares. It's terrifying but highly addictive reading for anyone who's ever jugged frozen fixed lines on an alpine wall. It made me feel physically ill. Their ascent of the west face of Bhagirathi III in India, in 1990, is just as soul-throttling, but for Silvo it seems just another run-of-mill "madmen and masochists" outing.

Rock 'n' Roll isn't just a memoir, it's also a peek into that period of the 1980s and 1990s when Eastern Europeans were becoming some of the greatest high-altitude alpinists on Earth. While the Poles were banging out first winter ascents and new routes on the 8,000-meter peaks, other Easterners—particularly the Slovenians—were tearing up both big peaks *and* massive alpine walls, like the ones on Bhagirathi III and Torre Egger. In the tales of these climbs, the Slovenians are jugging torn and frozen ropes, dodging barrages of stones, and hanging in icy corners by their harnesses. You expect death at any second, but somehow Silvo and his wildly talented partners daintily dance between the bullets.

Yet what I loved most about this book is the unforced humility. Silvo took up climbing with his friends, got good, explored his local mountains, then just kept on going. And he looks back at it all as one great adventure, which is the best way to look back at any climbing life, including one of the most impressive the world has ever seen.

— CAMERON M. BURNS

WINTER 8000: CLIMBING THE WORLD'S HIGHEST MOUNTAINS IN THE COLDEST SEASON

BERNADETTE MCDONALD. Mountaineers Books, 2020. Paperback, 272 pages, $21.95.

WHEN A TEAM of 10 Nepalese mountaineers reached the summit of K2 in the waning hours of January 16, 2021, the achievement marked not only a singular feat of endurance and teamwork, but also the closing of a frontier: All the world's principle peaks above 8,000 meters have now been climbed in winter. While it took only 14 years, from 1950 to 1964, for all the 8,000-meter monsters to be climbed for the first time, their winter conquest required 41 more years.

In her latest book, Canadian author Bernadette McDonald delivers a succinct and timely history of this period. Succinct because the author made the deft choice to structure her story with each chapter focusing on a different mountain. Checking in at tidy 272 pages, her narrative drops the reader directly into the fray on the flanks of each peak, delivering 14 epic climbs for the price of one. And timely because the book was released in 2020, some months before the K2 ascent made headlines around the world.

At the heart of the story are the Ice Warriors, a legendary band of Polish mountaineers who embraced "the art of suffering" and successfully summited seven of the 8,000ers, including Everest, in a span of only eight years during the 1980s. Having written extensively about the rich Polish mountaineering tradition (McDonald's *Freedom Climbers: The Golden Age of Polish Climbing* was published in 2011), she is clearly on comfortable terrain, introducing the reader to the key players with ease and adroitly explaining nuances between different cliques that came together behind the Iron Curtain in cities like Zakopane and Katowice.

For many armchair mountaineers, the names are familiar yet their true characters remain only dim outlines. McDonald does a genuine service sketching in their substance here—and the integrity of her work is most visible in the cracks in the legends she exposes. For instance: Did Andrzej Zawada knowingly allow the Polish media to falsely report the first winter ascent of Broad Peak, when those in base camp knew Maciej Berbeka had only reached its rocky foresummit? Was Jerzy Kukuczka so caught up in his race with Messner that he coldly exploited the efforts of his teammates on Dhaulagiri, Cho Oyu, and Kangchenjunga?

As the narrative shifts into the new century, the players broaden into an international crowd, and the sense of collective action embodied by the Poles gives way to a Western sense of individualism. In these latter chapters, McDonald does a good job dissecting complicated intra-team dynamics, particularly those that unfolded on Nanga Parbat and Gasherbrum I, with tragic repercussions. I particularly enjoyed getting to know Élisabeth Revol, Marianne Chapuisat, and Tamara Styś, a trio of gritty *alpinistas* whose contributions may well have been overlooked by less attentive writers.

McDonald is already hard at work revising her book to include the recent ascent of K2, an achievement that will make a fitting finale to this indispensable work. While the Golden Age of Himalayan climbing ended more than a half century ago, I suspect the Frozen Age of high-altitude climbing is here to stay.

— FREDDIE WILKINSON

IN BRIEF

IN *The Moth and the Mountain: A True Story of Love, War, and Everest* (Avid Reader Press, $28), Ed Caesar tells the story of Maurice Wilson, who in 1933 crash-landed his Gipsy Moth biplane on the slopes of Everest, intending to solo the mountain, despite having no climbing experience. Mick Conefrey's *The Last Great Mountain: The First Ascent of Kangchenjunga* (Mick Conefrey, $25) completes his high-altitude trilogy (*Everest 1953* and *The Ghosts of K2*).The world's third-highest peak is under-represented in our literature—this is a welcome addition. *Himalaya: A Human History* (Norton, $40) is a comprehensive look at the roof of the world by Ed Douglas, one of our most gifted mountain writers. The book received a special jury mention at the 2020 Banff awards. *Cliffhanger: New Climbing Culture and Adventures* (Gestalten, $60) is a lavish coffee-table book that takes the pulse of our present moment, edited by Julie Ellison. In *The World Beneath Their Feet: Mountaineering, Madness, and the Deadly Race to Summit the Himalayas* (Little, Brown, $30), Scott Ellsworth recounts the high drama of nations competing to summit the Himalayan giants, culminating in Hillary and Norgay's Everest climb. Jennifer Hull tells the story of the 2015 earthquake in Nepal with special focus on guide Dave Hahn in *Shook: An Earthquake, a Legendary Mountain Guide, and Everest's Deadliest Day* (University of New Mexico Press, $19.95).

— DAVID STEVENSON

IN MEMORIAM

Readers will find additional tributes to climbers who passed away in 2020 at the AAJ website. These include Gail Bates, Howard Peterson, Ang Rita Sherpa, and Frank Tarver.

John Cleare

JOE BROWN, 1930 – 2020

JOE BROWN SEEMED to me a kind of Renaissance master, his medium blank sheets of rock and ice, the lines he drew on them elegant and clever, his tombstone grin full of maverick good humor and the wisdom of his craft. His death at the age of 89 is not only the end of a defining era in climbing but also the loss of an immense creative force. "I'm always happiest when I'm doing something new," he once told the journalist Peter Gillman. And even in his last illness, the preternatural curiosity that fueled his extraordinary life remained undiminished. Even as his body failed, he could and did talk for hours in that searching, teasing way of his: always the explorer, but never overwrought, never self-important.

These days the routes Joe climbed in the 1950s and 1960s are comfortably within reach for even moderately able climbers. That's hardly the point. Routes like Valkyrie, Right Unconquerable, Right Eliminate, Cemetery Gates, Cenotaph Corner, The Grooves, The Rasp, Shrike, Vector, Hardd, and many others are a foundation stone in what British climbing is and means. So much is built on it.

In the early 1970s, as Ken Wilson was assembling the first edition of his compendium *Hard Rock*, he wrote of Joe: "He has brought to climbing a rare combination of attributes: keenness, patience, strength, technical ability, eye for a line, competitiveness and, above all, a subtle and mysterious charisma. Few would deny that his place in British rock climbing remains pre-eminent."

All this, and I haven't yet mentioned his mountaineering achievements, including the first ascents of Kangchenjunga, with George Band, in 1955, the only 8,000m peak first climbed by Britons; Muztagh Tower, climbed in 1956 with Ian McNaught-Davis; and Trango Tower, climbed in 1976 with, among others, Joe's great friend Mo Anthoine, with whom he started the equipment company Snowdon Mouldings.

Joe's appearance in the early 1950s, alongside that of his younger partner Don Whillans, heralded a seismic structural upheaval in the social breadth of English climbing. Working-class climbers galvanized standards, and Joe was at the vanguard of that group, his upbringing having been unusually disadvantaged. He was born in the slums of Ardwick, then a heavily industrialized district of Manchester, the youngest of seven. His father was a jobbing builder who, during the Depression, worked as a merchant seaman. In 1931, when Joe was eight months old, his father suffered a shipboard accident and his injuries became fatally gangrenous. His widowed mother took in washing, and when Joe was old enough to be left in the care of his siblings, she went out to work as a cleaner. One night during the Blitz, in World War II, hiding under the dining-room table, they heard the rattle of an incendiary device coming down the chimney. Moments later the windows of their house blew out. Heading for the local air-raid shelter, Joe saw that his school had also been blown up, "an agreeable piece of news," as he put it in his memoir, *The Hard Years*.

Organized sports, organized anything, seemed dismaying to Joe. He was sacked from the Scouts for refusing to go on a church parade. He tolerated school, but his real education was in the outdoors. As a teenager, Joe explored the fringes of Manchester, camping out, playing and climbing in old quarries, and eventually, inevitably, aged around 16, he came to the gritstone ramparts of Kinder Downfall. He had read Colin Kirkus' *Let's Go Climbing*, and, borrowing his mother's discarded washing line, set out for the crag.

The gritstone climbing of the Peak District came naturally to him. I remember asking him about Right Eliminate, which plenty of strong climbers still struggle on. "I found stuff like that quite straightforward," he replied. "Just over the roof I stopped and jammed my knee in so I could roll a fag [cigarette]."

In April 1951, Joe happened to be at the Roaches on the same day as Don Whillans. Over the next few years their names would become inextricably linked, like Lennon and McCartney, climbing legendary routes in both Britain and the Alps.

Late in 1954, Joe got a telegram from Charles Evans, leader of an expedition planned for the following year to Kangchenjunga, the world's third-highest mountain. That Whillans was not invited prompted decades of speculation and a certain level of resentment. The truth is their personalities were too different for their partnership to have endured, even without Kangchenjunga. Joe reached the summit on what had been a low-key and exemplary adventure. That he might not have the £20 "pocket money" he was expected to bring didn't occur to the organizers, but he managed. In fact, he always did. Until the mid-1960s, when he opened the first of his outdoor shops and began manufacturing his eponymous helmets, money was always tight. By then he was married to Val, who survives, and they had their daughters Helen and Zoe. That didn't stop him from having fun: He had far too much imagination for circumstances to get in the way.

He was an unconventional hero. He was also an inspiration. The difficulties in his early life, which he seemed to have casually sidestepped, earned him the deepest respect. His curiosity and need for friendship kept him engaged, even if being considered a legend was at times a burden. His contribution was immense. "Bloody hell," he told me at the end of one interview, thinking of the world he had encountered and then made his own, "we were bloody lucky, y'know." But if Joe Brown was lucky, then so were we. British climbing would not have been the same without him.

— ED DOUGLAS

EDITOR'S NOTE: *This tribute was adapted from a longer version that appears at the British Mountaineering Council (BMC) website.*

EVELIO ECHEVARRÍA, 1926 – 2020

ON OCTOBER 29, Evelio Echevarría left this world peacefully in his bed, with his family in Colorado alongside. An authority on the Andes and a reference for many generations of climbers in Latin America, he was an intelligent and restless writer, climber, explorer, and much more.

Cameron M. Burns

Evelio was born in Chile and began climbing there in 1947, exploring many untrodden summits. In 1953 he emigrated to the United States, and soon was climbing in his new home. At first he lived in Idaho, working in a hotel, where he met Edwina and married, eventually having four children. He moved to San Diego, worked as a gardener, and began attending the University of California. There and in Colorado, he eventually earned master's and doctorate degrees in Hispanic studies. He taught Spanish and Latin-American literature at Colorado State University in Fort Collins for three decades, retiring in 1994 as professor emeritus.

As a researcher on the history and climbs of the Andes, Evelio had influence worldwide, with articles printed in many languages. In addition to exploring and climbing virgin summits, he studied the precedent climbers dating back to pre-Columbian times, preserving ancient names and legends. Evelio contributed countless reports on climbs in the Andes to the AAJ, and his two-part "Survey of Andean Ascents," published in the journal in 1962 and 1963, was a titanic compilation.

His last published book, *The Andes: The Complete History of Mountaineering in High South America* (2018), is a bible for the Andean climber. This precise work was prepared with handwritten notes and his beloved typewriter, with which he also wrote his letters—he added Spanish accents with a pen. At the time of his death, Evelio was preparing a book about the archaeology of pre-Columbian ascents, a subject he loved. (This book is expected to appear in 2021.)

Others books included *Chile Andinista, su historia* (a history of Chilean mountaneering), *Leyendas de la alta Venezuela*, and *Leyendas de los Andes de Chile* (two books of Andean legends). His goal was to complete a trilogy, with a book of Argentine legends. We had been friends since 1988, and, knowing about this project, I began collaborating with him and later received a big pack of information from the States. Evelio, with his great kindness, encouraged me to finish the work. I wrote *Leyendas de los Andes Argentinos* and dedicated it to him.

Evelio always said he didn't climb very high mountains but instead sought the unexplored ranges all over the Andes, especially in Perú, Bolivia, Chile, and Argentina. He climbed roughly 200 mountains, mostly solo, sometimes with local climbers or friends. He was active into his 80s. As an example, at age 77, he started alone from Chilean territory in the Paso de Agua Negra, reached an untrodden 5,200-meter summit on the international border, and continued to another virgin summit of 5,160 meters in Argentina. He christened this Cerro Olascoaga after an Argentine soldier who was an early climber. Some months later, not knowing this, I also ascended Olascoaga and discovered Evelio's cairn and documents. He was very happy about this.

Evelio is survived by his family in the United States and his climbing family worldwide. Certainly his soul must be watching his beloved Andes from above, searching for new routes and unexplored territory.

— MARCELO SCANU

JOCELYN "JOCK" CHENEY GLIDDEN, 1935 – 2020

JOCK GLIDDEN PASSED away on July 29, at his home in Ogden, Utah, after the balance of pains outweighed the sum of pleasures, and he determined there was no longer any purpose in continuing the struggle against Parkinson's disease.

Jock was born and raised in Connecticut until his early teens, when his family purchased a cattle ranch near the Verde River in Arizona. Here, the family began a romance with the American West and the outdoors which they never abandoned. Jock spent several years on the ranch before attending high school and college in Vermont, graduating from Middlebury in 1958.

While pursuing a master's degree in philosophy at the University of Edinburgh in Scotland, he took up climbing and skiing in the Highlands and the Alps. Jock became a highly accomplished mountaineer, with many new routes in Canada, South America, India, and the United States. In 1968, he made the second ascent of the north face of Mt. Robson in Canada, via a more direct route. Three years later, he and four others did the first ascent of the north face of Huandoy Norte in Peru. In 1972, Jock and George Lowe III climbed the north face of Mt. Alberta in the Canadian Rockies, a route that is still considered one of the great prizes of the range. That same year, he set the speed record for summiting the Grand Teton from the Jenny Lake climber's camp, running up and down in 4 hours 11 minutes, a mark that stood for ten years. In 1974, he was invited to join the USA-USSR Pamir Expedition to climb Pik Lenin (now Ibn Sina) in what is now Tajikistan, a diplomatic effort during the Cold War. Although considered a success, it was also met with tragedy, when eight Russian women died during a summit attempt.

In 1969, Jock obtained his Ph.D. in philosophy from the University of Colorado Boulder. During his time in Boulder, he married Roberta Bannister. (They were later divorced in 2000.) They had a son, Jesse, in 1969, and Jock was offered a professorship at Weber State University in Ogden. He taught philosophy at Weber State for 29 years, retiring in 1998. He almost never drove to work, preferring a bicycle or cross-country skis. He also ran three marathons—his best time was 2:59. He liked this observation from Epictetus: "It is difficulties that show what men are." Though he loved a good challenge, he nevertheless would bring others along who weren't nearly as capable. Whether teaching philosophy or how to place protection in mixed rock and ice, he was generally good-humored and patient.

Jock was a dedicated environmentalist and helped found the Ogden Group of the Sierra Club. He brewed beer, grew wine grapes, and loved apple trees. As his health declined, Jock spent more time at his family cottage in Tabusintac, New Brunswick. There, he took up sea kayaking and was instrumental in donating significant migratory bird habitat to the Nature Conservancy of Canada.

Jock served as a hospice volunteer for over 15 years after retiring, and one of his patients was a sheep rancher, with whom Jock felt kinship because of his teenage years on a cattle ranch. Jock met the rancher's daughter, Josette, and they fell in love. Josette became a cherished member of the family, who unconditionally devoted herself to Jock's welfare during the final years of his life.

– JESSE GLIDDEN

EDITOR'S NOTE: *An additional brief remembrance of Jock Glidden by Peter Lev, a longtime friend and climbing partner, is available at the AAJ website.*

John Cleare

HAMISH MACINNES, 1930 – 2020

ENERGETIC, CREATIVE, ADVENTUROUS, and highly unorthodox, Scotsman Hamish MacInnes was among the most influential British climbers of the 1960s and '70s, and he continued to be an important rescue leader and innovator for many years. Hamish started climbing as a teenager, and from the outset he had big ambitions. When he was 18 years old, he hitchhiked across war-torn Europe, intent on climbing the Matterhorn. Unable to afford hut fees, he made a solo ascent of the Hörnli Ridge, up and down from Zermatt in a day. Hamish then spent 18 months in the Austrian Tirol on National Service, which gave him many opportunities to develop his technical skills in the Eastern Alps.

On his return to Scotland in 1950, Hamish fell in with members of the Creagh Dhu climbing club and started doing new routes in Glen Coe. In February 1953, he succeeded on three longstanding winter problems on Buachaille Etive Mor with 18-year-old Chris Bonington. One of them, Raven's Gully, was the most difficult winter route of the era in Scotland. Ice techniques at the time were rudimentary—MacInnes deployed his characteristic creativity and determination on the route, at times climbing wet rock in socks, wearing crampons on ice, and lassoing a chockstone for a pendulum.

A couple of months later in 1953, he visited Nepal with John Cunningham, intent on making the first ascent of Everest using food dumps left behind by the Swiss the year before. John Hunt's expedition famously got there first, so the Scottish pair made an attempt on Pumori. Beaten back by avalanches, they finally succeeded in making the first ascent of Pingero, a prominent subpeak of Taweche.

Hamish climbed in New Zealand over the next few seasons and did several new routes, including the very fine Bowie Ridge on Mt. Cook/Aoraki. Back in Scotland, he turned to one of the greatest prizes of all: the first winter ascent of Zero Gully on Ben Nevis. Competition was intense and MacInnes tried six times before he was successful in February 1957 with Tom Patey and Graeme Nicol. Another big prize was the first winter traverse of the Cuillin Ridge on Skye with Patey, Davie Crabb, and Brian Robertson. Their success, over three days in February 1965, was a testament to MacInnes' determination to drop everything and go for the route when conditions were just right.

By the mid-1960s, ice climbing was moving on from the step-cutting era. A big technological advance came in 1970 when Yvon Chouinard visited Scotland from the United States. Chouinard had been experimenting with a curved-pick tool that he showed to MacInnes in his workshop in Glen Coe. MacInnes, who had a strong engineering background (he built a car from scratch at the age of 17) had also been working on a new axe design, but with limited success. After talking to Chouinard, he increased the angle of his pick and came up with the Terrordactyl, the first of the dropped-pick tools. MacInnes soon showed their effectiveness by making the first winter ascent of Astronomy, a serious ice climb on Ben Nevis. Terrordactyls went into production later in 1971, and within a couple of seasons grades rocketed.

Hamish returned to Everest in 1975 as deputy leader of Chris Bonington's successful southwest face expedition. Working from an idea initiated by Don Whillans in Patagonia, he designed "MacInnes Box" tents. Rectangular in shape, they had adjustable front legs which allowed them to be pitched on any angle of slope. Typically, Hamish was the only person who knew how to erect them, but they were critical in allowing the team to move up and down the relentlessly steep southwest face.

Back in Scotland, Hamish founded the Glen Coe Mountain Rescue Team. As leader of the busiest search and rescue team in the country for 30 years, he saved countless lives. His engineering prowess led to the invention of the MacInnes Stretcher, a lightweight, foldable design used by many rescue teams today. Hamish's technical safety expertise was greatly sought after by filmmakers, and he was involved in many films, from the *Eiger Sanction* to *Monty Python and the Holy Grail*. He also was a prolific writer, with perhaps his best-known works being *Call-out*, describing his mountain rescue experiences, and an innovative series of Scottish climbing guidebooks.

Hamish died in his home in Glen Coe on November 22. He was 90 years old and had led an extraordinary life. The word "influential" is often used, but for Hamish, nothing could be more appropriate.

– SIMON RICHARDSON

EDITOR'S NOTE: *Simon Richardson wrote a longer tribute to MacInnes that was published at the UKClimbing website.*

MARK POWELL, 1928 – 2020

MARION "MARK" LYLE Powell, was born in Selma, California. His family moved frequently, and when Mark was 15 years old, his parents divorced and he went with his mother to his grandparents' farm in Laton, California. After graduating from high school there in 1946, he enlisted in the U.S. Air Force and served primarily in Alaska; he was honorably discharged just prior to the onset of the Korean War.

Long interested in the mountains, Mark had hiked and scrambled extensively as a boy, often riding tens of miles on his two-speed bicycle to approach his objectives. His technical climbing began in 1954 when he joined the newly formed Fresno Chapter of the Sierra Club's Rock Climbing Section. He quickly learned the basics and began climbing seriously in the company of more experienced climbers such as Don Wilson and Jerry Gallwas, who remembers:

Mark and I first met during Easter week of 1954 in Yosem-

Jerry Gallwas

ite He was obviously eager to do his first climb in the Valley, and the Lower Cathedral Spire seemed an inspiring start. Mark was overweight and slow but enthusiastic. The summit and the rappel down made Mark's day; it was enough to inspire him to get in shape by losing weight and climbing regularly. It was soon clear that Mark was committed to climbing at the highest level, and it was remarkable to see both his dedication and skills surpass that of all his peers—he was climbing in a class with Royal Robbins.

Don Wilson and I had climbed with Mark in Tahquitz in 1955, and we invited him to join us for a trip the next Easter to attempt Spider Rock in the Four Corners area. We drove through the night from San Diego in Mark's chartreuse Ford convertible, arriving at the rim of Canyon de Chelly just at dusk. It was a very cold week in the canyon with high winds. There were many memorable moments, but after a freezing bivouac and an exhilarating summit, we returned to the car late one evening to a victory dinner of a can of peaches and half a jar of pickles.

We planned our next desert adventure for Labor Day. Mark had found a travel advertisement with a photo of Cleopatra's Needle in northwest New Mexico. On Labor Day weekend, the three of us, along with Don's wife, Nancy, made the long drive in Don's VW Bug, a sardine-can experience if there ever was one. The sandstone of Cleopatra's Needle is incredibly soft, and after Don and I had our turns placing pitons with a hammer and removing them with fingers, Mark put in a bolt just below the summit and led to the top. During the drive home we discussed our next desert objective, and it was clear that the Totem Pole in Monument Valley, Arizona, would be the ultimate prize.

In June 1957, the three of us met in Monument Valley, joined by Bill "Dolt" Feuerer. By the time I arrived, they had managed to climb within one pitch of the summit between rainstorms. Mark had done the bulk of the leading and announced that they had saved the summit pitch for me. The winds were gusting to 40 mph, and as Don and the Dolt prusiked they were blown nearly halfway around the spire. The summit photo of the four of us signaled the end of a marvelous collaboration.

The bonds of friendship and loyalties had begun to stretch, and two weeks after the Totem Pole summit photo, when Mark, Dolt, and Warren Harding arrived in Yosemite Valley, Royal Robbins, Mike Sherrick, and I had already begun the first ascent of the Northwest Face (Regular Route) of Half Dome.

As a consolation prize, of sorts, Mark, Warren, and Bill chose to take on the enormous south buttress of El Capitan—the line that became the Nose. With Mark doing most of the leading, the team climbed 1,000 feet in eight days. Due to the traffic congestion in the Valley caused by such a sensational climb, they agreed to suspend their efforts during peak tourist season. Then, on September 20, while approaching one of his favorite long climbs, the Arrowhead Arête, with a novice partner, a foothold broke and sent Mark 40 feet to the ground, resulting in a compound dislocation of his left ankle. Difficulty in initiating a rescue and soil in the wounds contributed to a severe infection, and he was fortunate not to have his leg amputated.

So great was Mark's desire to climb the Nose route on El Capitan that he joined Warren and Bill again in the spring of 1958 to help push the climb higher, despite his still-recovering ankle. By September, Bill had dropped out and Mark spent ten days as part of a party of six pushing the route to 2,000 feet before quitting the effort, feeling that, in his diminished capacity, he was a burden and, further, "was unwilling to cater to Harding's dominance" in that lesser role.

That year Mark married Beverly Woolsey, a climber he had met in Yosemite. They developed a lifestyle of working in the winter and saving money so they could rock climb all summer. Most American climbers at this time were weekend participants, but Mark stood apart in his dedication to staying in peak shape and establishing as many high-standard routes as he could manage before returning to work.

Despite occasional bouts of osteomyelitis and other complications from his ankle injury, Mark continued to establish difficult first ascents through the early 1970s in California, Arizona, Utah, and in the Needles of South Dakota.

Mark pursued his education as well as climbing, eventually earning a B.A. and a master's in geography. He taught geography at Pierce College in Woodland Hills from 1967 to 1995, with a specialty in weather, and served as chairman of the Earth Science Department for many years. In 1974, he remarried to Kriss Lindquist, and they purchased a second home in Idyllwild for climbing purposes. He married a third time in 1999 to Mary McLaughlin, who predeceased him in 2018.

In 2009, Mark's lower leg finally had to be amputated, more than 50 years after the accident. Had Mark not been injured in his prime, the trajectory of American climbing history undoubtedly would have been steeper and its tapestry of achievements far richer. Ropemate and visionary climber Chuck Pratt once wrote that Mark "showed us that climbing can be a way of life and basis for a philosophy." In a 2008 interview, Mark acknowledged savoring that great compliment and concluded, "If there is any contribution I made to climbing, that's it. I showed there was a way of life in pursuing it."

Jerry Gallwas concludes: Mark and I had not been in touch since 1958 but reconnected in 2009 as I was putting together a document recording my reflections of our adventures climbing the three desert spires. His memory was remarkable, and his red pencil corrections to my drafts extremely helpful.

Any party with Mark included would ultimately achieve the summit, had it been Half Dome or El Cap. The rock climbing community has lost one of its most accomplished and little-published pioneers.

— STEVE GROSSMAN, *WITH REMINISCENCES FROM JERRY GALLWAS*

John Cleare

DOUGLAS KEITH SCOTT, 1941 – 2020

IN A CAREER spanning decades, Doug Scott was recognized worldwide as one of the greatest mountaineers of the postwar era. The statistics speak for themselves: over 40 expeditions to Central Asia, countless first ascents all round the world, the first British ascent of Mt. Everest (and by a new route). But what made Doug special was not the height or difficulty or number of ascents—for him, what mattered was *how* you made those ascents.

Like all the best people he was a jumble of paradoxes: tough-guy rugby player fascinated by Buddhist mysticism; anarchic hippy with a deep sense of tradition; intensely ambitious one day, laid back the next. He was as egotistic as any climber, but also demonstrably generous and compassionate, admired universally for his philanthropy. In his Himalayan heyday he resembled a beefed-up version of John Lennon; in latter years, presiding over his gorgeous English garden in moleskins and tweed jacket, he looked more like the country squire.

He grew up in Nottingham, the eldest of three brothers, and started climbing at 13, inspired by seeing climbers when he was out walking with the Scouts. By the early seventies he was publishing regular articles in *Mountain* magazine, and what an inspiration they were, illustrated with his superlative photos. I remember particularly his piece "On the Profundity Trail," describing the first European ascent of the Salathé Wall with Peter Habeler. There was also an excellent series on the great Dolomite pioneers—research for his first book, *Big Wall Climbing*—and a wonderful story of climbing sumptuous granite on Baffin Island.

For an impressionable young student, dreaming of great things, this was all inspiring stuff, and I lapped it up. But it was only much later, when I saw Doug's big autobiographical picture book, *Himalayan Climber*, that I realized quite how *much* he had done in those early days. As well as Yosemite and Baffin Island, there were big, bold adventures to the Tibesti Mountains of Chad, to Turkey, and to Koh-e-Bandaka, in the Afghan Hindu Kush.

All the while, Doug had been working as a schoolteacher in Nottingham. I have no idea whether he planned all along to go professional as a climber, but it was Everest that made that possible. Doug went to Everest twice in 1972, attempting the southwest face unsuccessfully. Then, while in India during the first ascent of Changabang, a message came through announcing a surprise free slot in the Everest waiting list for the autumn of 1975. With little time to prepare another Everest blockbuster, there was talk at first of a lightweight attempt on the regular South Col route, but Doug was instrumental in persuading Chris Bonington that they should go all-out for the southwest face. *That* was the great unclimbed challenge.

It seemed inevitable that Doug should have been chosen for the first summit push with Dougal Haston. In a team of big personalities, he was the biggest personality of all. Perhaps, like Hillary, he wanted the summit more than the others; in Bonington's eyes, he clearly had that extra something—that sheer bloody-minded strength, determination, and ability to push the boat out. Supremely confident, Scott and Haston made an informed decision to continue to the summit even though it was almost dark and their oxygen was nearly finished. On returning to the South Summit and seeing how dangerous it would be to continue down in pitch darkness, they agreed very sensibly to bivouac right there, higher than any other human being had ever previously spent a night, and wait for the morning. It amazes me to this day that Doug was not even wearing a down jacket, yet still managed to avoid frostbite. "The quality of survival," as he put it, was exemplary.

Following the huge Everest expedition, both its architect, Chris Bonington, and Doug realized that the way forward lay in scaling things back down. To my mind, his finest climb was Kangchenjunga in 1979, with Peter Boardman, Joe Tasker and, initially, Georges Bettembourg. It was only the third ascent of the mountain and the first from the north. Ropes were fixed judiciously on the lower, technical face. Up above, they cut loose and went alpine style, without oxygen. Messner & Co. had already shown it was possible to climb to the highest altitudes without oxygen, but they had done it on well-known ground, with other climbers around should things go wrong. This was a big step into the unknown.

It would take too long to list all Doug's other Himalayan achievements, but it's worth mentioning some themes. What was impressive was the way he was always rethinking expeditions. It was his idea to transfer the concept of the extended Alpine summer season to the Himalaya, with loosely connected teams roaming far and wide on multiple objectives, with the family sometimes coming along, too. He introduced young talent to the Himalaya, bringing Greg Child's big-wall expertise to the beautiful Lobsang Spire and east ridge of Shivling, and Stephen Sustad's stamina to the gigantic southeast ridge of Makalu. They didn't quite pull off their intended traverse of Makalu with Jean Afanassieff but, my goodness, what a bold journey it was. In fact, despite several attempts, Doug never quite summited Makalu, nor Nanga Parbat, nor K2. But that is not the point. He didn't give a damn about summits for their own sake—unless they were attained in an interesting, challenging way, they held little appeal. Or he might just decide that the omens—or the I Ching, or his particular mood that day, or whatever—were not right, as happened in 1980, when he left the slightly exasperated Boardman, Renshaw, and Tasker to continue on K2 without him.

When the mood *was* right, there was no stopping him. Among all the climbs I would most love to have done (and had the ability to do!), the first ascent of the Ogre in 1977, with Bonington, Mo Anthoine, and Clive Rowland, must be the most enviable, with difficult rock climbing on immaculate granite, 7,000 meters above sea level, at the heart of the world's greatest mountain range. (Less enviable was the epic descent with two broken legs.) Another visionary climb was the 1982 first ascent of the southwest face of Shishapangma, with Alex McIntyre and Roger Baxter-Jones, discovering the most elegant direct route to any 8,000-meter summit.

I only climbed with him once, when we were both speaking at an Alpine Club symposium in North Wales. There was a beautiful sunny morning—far too good to be shut indoors—so we sneaked over Llanberis Pass for a quick jaunt up Cenotaph Corner. It was 1989 and he was middle aged, but definitely still in his prime. He led with powerful ease and then suggested we continue up another route, Grond, a brutal creation of his old mentor Don Whillans. In the absence of large cams to protect the initial offwidth, he grabbed a large lump of rhyolite, explaining cheerfully, "This is how we used to do it, youth," shoved it in the crack, hitched a sling round it, and clipped in the rope. As soon as he moved up, the chockstone flew out of the crack, narrowly missing my head, but Doug carried on regardless, blithely calm, assured and fluent, supremely at ease with the rock.

Doug's conversation, like his lecturing—or indeed his expeditioning—could be enigmatic, discursive, elliptical, often veering off the beaten track into untrodden side valleys, but always with an undercurrent of humor. And never pulling rank: He was a humble, approachable man, happy to talk with anyone. He had great empathy with the people of Nepal, and this came to fruition in his remarkable charity, Community Action Nepal. At an age when most people in Doug's position would be happy to rest on their laurels, Doug traveled the length and breadth of the United Kingdom on grueling lecture tours, pouring all the proceeds into his charity.

As if this were not enough, Doug also managed in recent years to complete a fine history of the Ogre and to finally publish his long-awaited autobiography, for which he was first paid an advance in 1975. His history of Kangchenjunga will be published this year.

Despite the frenetic pace he set himself and his devoted third wife, Trish, Doug seemed in recent years to have achieved the kind of contentment that many people only dream of. He had a genuine sense of purpose and an assured legacy. He will be missed hugely in the U.K., in Nepal, and all round the world, but most of all by Trish and by the five children of his first two marriages. I feel honored to have known him and glad that if I should ever have grandchildren I will be able to tell them, "I climbed Cenotaph Corner with Doug Scott."

— STEPHEN VENABLES

EDITOR'S NOTE: *This tribute was adapted from a piece published at UKClimbing.com.*

NECROLOGY

In addition, we remember the following AAC members who passed away in 2020:

DILLON BLANKSMA	JANETTE HEUNG	BARRETT MORGAN	DOUG SNIVELY
RHEA DODD	BEN KESSEL	MIE NAKANE	JOHN TIEMAN
JOHN EVANS	VAN LITTLE	JIM RAMSEY	
JOHN FEAGIN	WILLIAM MAY	GEORGE N. SMITH	
FRANK FICKELSEN	DEE MOLENAAR	NOLAN SMYTHE	

INDEX

Compiled by Eve Tallman & Ralph Ferrara

Mountains are indexed by their official names. Ranges, geographic locations and maps are also indexed. Unnamed peaks (e.g. Peak 2,340m) are listed under P. Abbreviations are used for some geographic locations as well as the following: Cordillera: C; Mountains: Mts; National Park: Natl. Park; Obituary: obit. Indexed photographs are listed in bolt type.

INTERNATIONAL GRADE COMPARISON CHART

SERIOUSNESS RATINGS

These often modify technical grades when protection is difficult

PG-13: Difficult or insecure protection or loose rock, with some injury potential

R: Poor protection with high potential for injury

X: A fall would likely result in serious injury or death

YDS=Yosemite Decimal System
UIAA=Union Internationale des Associations D'Alpinisme
FR=France/Sport
AUS=Australia
SAX=Saxony
CIS=Commonwealth of Independent States/Russia
SCA=Scandinavia
BRA=Brazil
UK=United Kingdom

Note: *All conversions are approximate. Search "International Grade Comparison Chart" at the AAJ website for further explanation of commitment grades and waterfall Ice/mixed grades.*

YDS	UIAA	FR	AUS	SAX	CIS	SCA	BRA	UK	UK
5.2	II	1	10	II	III	3			D
5.3	III	2	11	III	III+	3+			D
5.4	IV- IV	3	12		IV-	4			VD
5.5	IV+		13		IV	4+			S
5.6	V-	4	14		IV+	5-	4	4a	HS
5.7	V		15	VIIa		5	4		VS
5.8	V+	5a	16	VIIb	V-	5+	4+	4b	HVS
5.9	VI- VI	5b	17	VIIc		6-	5 5+	4c / 5a	E1
5.10a	VI+	5c	18	VIIIa	V	6	6a	5b	
5.10b		6a		VIIIa					E2
5.10c	VII-	6a+	19	VIIIb		6+	6b		E2
5.10d	VII	6b	20	VIIIc	V+	7-	6c		E3
5.11a	VII+	6b+		IXa			7a	5c	
5.11b		6c	21	IXb		7	7b		
5.11c	VIII-	6c+	22		VI-	7+			E4
5.11d	VIII	7a	23	IXc			7c	6a	
5.12a	VIII+	7a+	24	Xa			8a		E5
5.12b		7b	25		VI	8- 8	8b		
5.12c	IX-	7b+	26	Xb		8+	8c		
5.12d	IX	7c	27				9a	6b	E6
5.13a	IX+	7c+	28	Xc		9-	9b		
5.13b		8a	29				9c		
5.13c	X-	8a+	30		VI+	9	10a		E7
5.13d	X	8b	31	XIa			10b		
5.14a	X+	8b+	32	XIb			10c	7a	E8
5.14b		8c	33			9+	11a		
5.14c	XI- XI	8c+	34	XIc			11b	7b	E9
5.14d	XI+	9a	35				11c		E10
5.15a	XII-	9a+	36	XIIa		10	12a		
5.15b	XII	9b	37		VII		12b		E11
5.15c		9b+	38	XIIb			12c		
5.15d	XII+	9c	39						